Samuel Stehman Haldeman, Alexander John Ellis

Pennsylvania Dutch

A dialect of South German with an infusion of English

Samuel Stehman Haldeman, Alexander John Ellis

Pennsylvania Dutch
A dialect of South German with an infusion of English

ISBN/EAN: 9783337310776

Printed in Europe, USA, Canada, Australia, Japan

Cover: Foto ©Andreas Hilbeck / pixelio.de

More available books at **www.hansebooks.com**

PENNSYLVANIA DUTCH:

A DIALECT OF SOUTH GERMAN WITH AN

INFUSION OF ENGLISH.

BY

S. S. HALDEMAN, A.M.

PROFESSOR OF COMPARATIVE PHILOLOGY IN THE UNIVERSITY OF PENNSYLVANIA,
PHILADELPHIA.

LONDON:
TRÜBNER & CO., 8 AND 60, PATERNOSTER ROW.
1872.

NOTICE.

WHILE I was engaged with the third part of my *Early English Pronunciation*, Prof. Haldeman sent me a reprint of some humorous letters by Rauch, entitled *Pennsylvanish Deitsh. De Campain Breefa fum Pit Schwefflebrenner un de Bevvy, si alty, gepublished olly woch in "Father Abraham."* Perceiving at once the analogy between this debased German with English intermixture, and Chaucer's debased Anglo-saxon with Norman intermixture, I requested and obtained such further information as enabled me to give an account of this singular modern reproduction of the manner in which our English language itself was built up, and insert it in the introduction to my chapter on Chaucer's pronunciation, *Early English Pronunciation*, pp. 652-663. But I felt it would be a loss to Philology if this curious living example of a mixture of languages were dismissed with such a cursory notice, and I therefore requested Prof. Haldeman, who by birth and residence, philological and phonetic knowledge, was so well fitted for the task, to draw up a more extended notice, as a paper to be read before the Philological Society of London. Hence arose the following little treatise, of which I, for my own part, can only regret the brevity. But the Philological Society, having recently exhausted most of its resources by undertaking the publication of several extra volumes, was unable to issue another of such length, and hence the present Essay appears independently. Owing to his absence from England and my own connexion with the paper, which I communicated and read to the Philological Society, on 3 June, 1870, Prof.

Haldeman requested me to superintend the printing of his essay, and add anything that might occur to me. This will account for a few footnotes signed with my name. The Professor was fortunately able to examine one revise himself, so, that though I am mainly responsible for the press work, I hope that the errors may be very slight

Sufficient importance does not seem to have been hitherto attached to watching the growth and change of living languages. We have devoted our philological energies to the study of dead tongues which we could not pronounce, and have therefore been compelled to compare by letters rather than by sounds, and which we know only in the form impressed upon them by scholars of various times. The form in which they were originally written is for ever concealed. The form in which they appear in the earliest manuscripts has practically never been published, but has to be painfully collected from a mass of various readings. The form we know is a critical, conjectural form, patched up by men distinguished for scholarship, but for the most part entirely ignorant of the laws which govern the changes of speech. The very orthography is medieval. We are thus enabled to see as little of the real genesis of language, in form, in sound, in grammatical and logical construction, in short in the real pith of philological investigation—the relation of thought to speech-sounds—as the study of a full-grown salmon would enable us to judge of the marvellous development of that beautiful fish. Such studies as the present will, I hope, serve among others to stimulate exertion in the new direction. We cannot learn life by studying fossils alone.

ALEX. J. ELLIS.

KENSINGTON,
   23 APRIL, 1872.

CONTENTS.

PENNSYLVANISCH DEITSCH.

CHAPTER I.

PEOPLE—HISTORY—LOCATION—CONDITION.

The reciprocal influence of languages affords an interesting subject of investigation, and it is the object of this essay to present an outline of a dialect which has been formed within a century, and which continues to be spoken, subject to the influences which developed it. Of such languages, English, Wallachian, and Hindûstânî, are familiar examples.

Like other languages, the dialect of German known as Pennsylvania Dutch presents variations due to the limited intercourse of a widely-scattered agricultural population, and to the several dialects brought from abroad, chiefly from the region of the Upper Rhine, and the Neckar, the latter furnishing the Suabian or Rhenish Bavarian element. The language is therefore South German, as brought in by emigrants from Rhenish Bavaria, Baden, Alsace (Alsatia), Würtemberg, German Swisserland, and Darmstadt. There were also natives from other regions, with certain French Neutrals deported from Nova Scotia to various parts of the United States, including the county (Lancaster) where the materials for this essay have been collected. These, and probably some families with French names from Alsace, are indicated by a few proper names, like *Roberdeau, Lebo, Deshong* and *Shunk* (both for *Dejean*), and an occasional word like *júschtaménnt* (in German spelling), the French *justement*, but which a native might take for a condensation of *just-an-dem-ende.*

1

Welsh names like *Jenkins, Evans, Owen, Foulke, Griffith, Morgan,* and *Jones* occur, with the township names of *Breck-nock, Caernarvon, Lampeter, Leacock* ('Lea' as *lay*), and in the next county of Chester—*Gwinedd* and *Tredyffrin;* but there seems to have been no fusion between Welsh and German, probably because the Welsh may have spoken English. Local names like *Hanöver, Heidelberg* and *Manheim,* indicate whence some of the early residents came.

The French-American *ville* appears in German Pennsylvania, in *Bechtelville, Engelsville, Greshville, Lederachsville, Scherksville, Schwenksville, Silberlingsville, Wernersville, Zieglerville;* paralleled by the English *town* in *Kutztown, Mertztown, Schäfferstown, Straustown; burg* in *Ickesburg, Landisburg, Rehrersburg;* and the German *dorf* has a representative in *Womelsdorf.*

Pennsylvania German does not occur in the counties along the northern border of the state, but it has extended into Maryland, Western Virginia, Ohio, and farther west; and it has some representatives in western New York, and even in Canada. In many of the cities of the United States, such as Pittsburg, Chicago, Cincinnati, and Saint Louis, recent large accessions from Germany have brought in true German, and to such an extent that the German population of the city of New York is said to exceed that of every European city except Berlin and Vienna. The newer teutonic population differs from the older in living to a great extent in the towns, where they are consumers of beer and tobacco—luxuries to which the older stock and their descendants were and are but little addicted. The numerous allusions to the 'Fatherland' to be met with, belong to the foreign Germans—the natives caring no more for Germany than for other parts of Europe, for they are completely naturalised, notwithstanding their language.

Several thousand Germans had entered Pennsylvania before the year 1689, when a steady stream of emigration set in, and it is stated that their number was 100,000 in 1742, and 280,000 in 1763. They occupied a region which has located the Pennsylvania dialect chiefly to the south-east of the Alleghenies, excluding several counties near Philadelphia. Germantown, six miles from Philadelphia, although settled by Germans, seems to have lost its German character. The language under the name of 'Pennsylvania Dutch' is used by a large part of the country population, and may be constantly heard in the county towns of Easton on the Delaware, Reading (i.e. red-ing) on the Schuylkill, Allentown on the Lehigh, Harrisburg (the State capital) on the Susquehánna, Lebanon, Lancaster, and York.

A fair proportion of the emigrants, including the clergy, were educated, and education has never been neglected among them. The excellent female boarding schools of the Moravians were well supported, not only by the people of the interior, but also by the English-speaking population of the large cities, and of the Southern States—a support which prevented the German accent of some of the teachers from being imitated by the native teutonic pupils—for the education was in English, although German and French were taught. Booksellers find it to their advantage to advertise the current German and English literature in the numerous German journals of the interior, and there is a *Deutsch-Amerikanisches Conversations Lexicon* in course of publication, which gives the following statistics of one of the German counties.

"The German element is strongly and properly represented in Allentown, and in Lehigh county generally, where the German language has retained its greatest purity, and so strong is this element, that in the city itself there are but few persons who speak English exclusively. An evidence of this is found in the fact that in seventy of the eighty Christian congregations in the county, some of which are over one hundred years old, Divine service is conducted in the German language. Allentown has seven German churches: (two Lutheran, one Reformed, two Methodist, one United Brethren, and one Catholic); and nine German journals, of which are published weekly—*Der Unabhängige* [1] *Republikaner* (fifty-nine years old), *Der Friedensbote* (fifty-seven years old), *Der Lecha County Patriot* (forty-three years old), *Der Weltbote* (fifteen years old, with 12,000 subscribers), and *Die Lutherische Zeitschrift*. The *Stadt- und Land-Bote* is a daily, the *Jugendfreund* semi-monthly, with twenty thousand subscribers; and Pastor Brobst's *Theologischen Monatshefte* is monthly. Since the beginning of the year 1869, the German language has been taught in the public schools." [2] The Reading *Adler* is in its seventy-fourth, and the Lancaster *Volksfreund* in its sixty-second year.—Dec. 1869.

[1] Un-ab-häng-ig, un-off-hang-ing, in-de-pend-ent, Polish nie-za-wis-ty.
[2] Allentown has just completed one of the finest public school buildings in Eastern Pennsylvania.—*Newspaper, February*, 1870.

The convenient quarto German almanacs (with a printed page of about five and a half by seven and a half inches in size), were preferred to the duodecimo English almanacs, even among the non-Germans, until the appearance of English almanacs in the German format about the year 1825.

The early settlers were extensive purchasers and occupiers of land, and being thus widely scattered, and having but few good roads, the uniformity of the language is greater than might have been supposed possible. These people seldom became merchants and lawyers, and in the list of attorneys admitted in Lancaster County, commencing with the year 1729, the names are English until 1769, when *Hubley* and *Weitzel* appear. From 1793 to 1804, of fifty-two names, three are German ; from 1825 to 1835, twenty-four names give *Reigart* and *Long* (the latter anglicised). After 1860 the proportion is greater, for among the nine attorneys admitted in 1866, we find the German names of *Urich, Loop, Kauffman, Reinœhl, Seltzer,* and *Miller.* At the first school I attended as a child, there were but three English family names, and in the playground, English and German games were practised, such as ' blumsak ' (G. plumpsack), ' Prisoner's base,' and ' Hink'l-wai [1] was graabscht du do ? ' which was never played with the colloquy translated.

Pennsylvania Dutch (so called because Germans call themselves *Deutsch* [2]) is known as a dialect which has been corrupted or enriched by English words and idioms under a pure or modified pronunciation, and spoken by natives, some of them knowing no other language, but most of them speaking or understanding English. Many speak both languages vernacularly, with the pure sounds of each, as in distinguishing German *töd*

---

[1] As if ' hühn-kel weibe ' *chicken hawk*, ' wai ' rhyming with *boy*.

[2] In an article on (the) " Pennsylvania Dutch " in the ' Atlantic Monthly' (Boston, Mass., Oct., 1869, p. 473), it is asserted that " the tongue which these people speak is not German, nor do they expect you to call it so." On the contrary, the language is strictly a German dialect, as these pages prove. The mistake has arisen from the popular confusion between the terms *Dutch* and *German,* which are synonymous with many. In Albany (New York) they speak of the *Double Dutch Church,* which seems to have been formed by the fusion of a ' German Reformed' with a ' Dutch Reformed ' congregation. These are different denominations, now greatly anglicised. In 1867 the Rev. J. C. Dutcher was a Dutch Reformed pastor in New York.

(death) from English *toad;* or English *winter* from German *winter*, with a different *w*, a lengthened *n*, a flat *t*, and a trilled *r*—four distinctions which are natural to my own speech. Children, even when very young, may speak English entirely with their parents, and German with their grandparents, and of two house-painters (father and son) the father always speaks German and the son English, whether speaking together, or with others. The males of a family being more abroad than the females, learn English more readily, and while the father, mother, daughters, and servants may speak German, father and son may speak English together naturally, and not with a view to have two languages, as in Russia. Foreign Germans who go into the interior usually fall into the local dialect in about a year, and one remarked that he did so that he might not be misunderstood. Some of these, after a residence of fifteen or twenty years, speak scarcely a sentence of English, and an itinerant piano-tuner, whose business has during many years taken him over the country, says that he has not found a knowledge of English necessary.

The English who preceded the Germans in Pennsylvania brought their names of objects with them, calling a thrush with a red breast a *robin;* naming a bird not akin to any thrush a *blackbird;* and assigning to a yellow bird the name of *goldfinch*, but adopting a few aboriginal names like *racoon, hackee* and *possum*. The Germans did this to some extent, for *blackbird* saying 'schtaar' (G. *staar*,[1] starling,) for the *goldfinch* (oriole) 'goldamschl,' for the *thrush* (G. *drossel*) 'druschl,' for a *woodpecker* 'specht' (the German name), and for a crow 'krap.'

The *ground-squirrel* is named 'fensemeissli' (fence-mouse-lin, *fence* being English) ; a large grey squirrel is called ' eech-haas' (for *eich-hase*, oak-hare) ; and in Austria a squirrel is akatzel and achkatzel (oak-kitten). The burrowing marmot (Arctomys monax), known as ground-hog, is called 'gruu'daks' (from a fancied analogy with the German *dachs* or badger) and

---

[1] Words in single quotations are Pennsylvania German. The system of spelling is described in the next chapter. High German words are commonly in italics, or marked G.

in York County 'grundsau,' a translation of the English name.
The English *patridge* (partridge, Dutch patrijs) is Germanised
into 'pattereesəli' — also called 'feld-hinkli' (little field-
chicken),—hinkl being universally used for *chicken* or *chickens*.

The usual perversions by otōsis occur, as in the city of Baltimore, where foreign Germans say 'Ablass' for *Annapolis*
and 'Kälber Strasze' (Street of Calves) for Calvert Street—but
the citizens themselves have replaced the vowel of *what* with
that of *fat*, in the first syllable of this name; and the people of
New York now pronounce 'Beekman Street' with the syllable *beak* instead of *bake* according to the earlier practice.

A German botanist gave 'Gandoge' as the locality of an
American plant; a package sent by express to 'Sevaber' (an
English name), and a letter posted to the town of 'Scur E
Quss, Nu Yourck,' arrived safely; and I have seen a hand-
board directing the traveller to the English-named town of
'Bintgrof.' As these present no special difficulty, they are
not explained.

English *rickets* for 'rachîtis' is a familiar example of otōsis,
and it appears in the following names of drugs furnished by a
native druggist who speaks both languages, and who was able
to determine the whole from the original prescriptions.

Allaways, Barrickgorrick, Sider in de ment, Essig of Iseck,
Hirim Packer, Cinment, Cienpepper, Sension, Saintcun, Opien,
High cyrap, Seno and mano misct, Sking, Coroces suple-
ment, Red presopeite, Ammeline, Lockwouth, Absom's salts,
Mick nisey, Corgel, Chebubs, By crematarter potash, Balder-
yon, Lower beans, Cots Shyneel.

7

CHAPTER II.

Phonology of Pennsylvania Dutch.

§ 1. *Use of the Alphabet.*

In his "Key into the Languages of America," London, 1643, Roger Williams says that "the life of all language is pronunciation"—and in the comparison of dialects it deserves especial attention. To enable the reader the more readily to understand these pages, and to compare the words with literary German, the principles of German orthography will be used as far as they are consistent, but every letter or combination is in every case to be pronounced according to the power here indicated—except in literal quotations, where the originals are followed. A single vowel letter is always to be read short, and when doubled it must have the same sound, but lengthened—but as a single vowel letter is often read long in German, and as short vowels are often indicated by doubling a consonant letter, this absurd mode is sometimes used to prevent mispronunciation through carelessness.[1] The ' s ' is also sometimes doubled to prevent it from becoming English ' z ' with readers who, in careless moods, might rhyme ' as ' (as) with *has* instead of *fosse*. In a PG. poem of Rachel Bahn, commencing with—

> "Wie soothing vocal music is !
> Wie herrlich un wie schoe !"

[1] For example, as the vowel of German *schaf* is long, the PG. word 'schafleit,' which occurs in a quoted passage farther on, would be likely to be read 'schaafleit' (sheep-people or shepherds) instead of 'schaffleit' (work-people), although it is stated that in the spelling used, a vowel *must not be made long* unless its letter is doubled. "This tendency, and a trick of reading words like nisbut, *relation*, qismut, *fortune*, as if written *nisbut, qismut*, should be carefully guarded against. . . . Even is, as, rusm, will, in spite of the caveat, . . . become again in his mouth iz, az, ruzm, rather than the iss, auss, russm, intended."—*Gilchrist,* 1806.

most English readers would be likely to rhyme ' is ' with *phiz* instead of *hiss*, which will be prevented by writing ' iss,' etc.

Although I have visited various counties of the State at distant intervals, the facts given here pertain chiefly to a single locality, so that if it is stated, for example, that ' s ' with its English sound in ' misery ' does not occur, or that ' kəp ' (head) is used to the exclusion of *haupt*, it is not intended to assert that such a sound as *z*, or such a word as *haupt*, have not a local existence. In fact, although they are not recorded here, English *z*, *w*, and *v*, may be common enough. A German confounds *met* and *mat*, *cheer* and *jeer*, and when he becomes able to pronounce them all, he not unfrequently creates a new difficulty, and for *cherry* says *järry* (rhyming *carry*), and after he has acquired sounds like English *z*, *w*, and *v*, they might readily slip into his German speech.

The letter *b* and its spirant (German *w*) both occur, and the latter often replaces *b*, in one region ' ich haw ' (I have) replaces ' ich hab,' German *ich habe*, and ' nit ' replaces ' net ' (not), German *nicht*. The vowels of *up* and *ope* interchange, as in ' kəch ' or ' koch ' (cook) ' nəch ' or ' noch ' (yet) ; and it is difficult to determine whether the prefixes *ge-* and *be-* have the vowel of *bet* or *but*. Lastly, the nasal vowels are by some speakers pronounced pure. Should discrepancies be found upon these points, they are to be attributed rather to the dialect than to the writer—or to the two conjointly.

§ 2. *The Vowels.*

E. indicates *English;* G. *German;* SG. *South German;* PG. *Pennsylvania German* (or ' Dutch') ; .a preceding dot indicates what would be a capital letter in common print. It is used where capital forms have not been selected, as for æ.

a in wh*a*t, n*o*t; PG. kat (G. gehabt) *had ;* kats *eat.*

aa (ah [1]) in f*a*ll, *o*rb; PG. haas *hare* ; paar *pair* ; haan (G. hahn) *cook* ; tsaam (G. zaum) *bridle.*

a in *ai*sle, h*eigh*t, *ou*t. In a few cases it is written *å*. See under the dipthongs.

---

[1] High German *letters* which represent PG. *sounds* are in parentheses.

æ (ä, e¹) in fæt; hær (G. Herr) *Sir*; dær (and d'r, G. der) *the*; hærn (G. hirn) *brain*; schtærn, pl. schtærnə (G. stern) *star*; mær (G. mähre) *mare*; ærscht (G. erst) *first*; wærts-haus (G. wirtshaus) *inn*.

ææ (ä, äh) in baa, the preceding vowel lengthened.¹ PG. bæær (G. bär) *bear*; kæær E. *ear*.

e (ä, ö) in bet; PG. bet *bed*; net (G. nicht) *not*; apnémə (G. abnahme *decline*) PG. a wasting disease; het (G. hätte *had*), which, with some other words, will sometimes be written with ä (hätt) to aid the reader. In a few cases it is lengthened (as in thêre), when it is written ê, as in French.

ee (ä, äh, eh, ö) in ale; PG. meel (G. mehl) *meal*; eel (G. öl) *oil*.

ə (e, o, a) in *but*, mention;² PG. kəp (G. kopf) *head*; los (G. lass) *let*, hawə (a short, G. haben) *to have*.

i (ü, ie, ö) in finny; niks (G. nichts) *nothing*; tərik (G. zurück) *back*; miglich (G. möglich) *possible*; lit'rlich (G. liederlich) *riotous*.

ii (ih, ie, ü) in feel; fiil (G. viel) *much*; dii (G. die) *the*; riiwə (G. rübe) *turnip*; wiischt (G. wüst, ü long) *nasty*. It is the French î, which is sometimes used in these pages.

o in o-mit; los *loose*; hofnung *hope*. English *o* pronounced quickly.

oo in door, home; wool (G. wohl) *well*; groo (G. grau) *grey*.

u in full, foot; mus (G. musz) *must*; fun (G. von) *of*.

uu (uh) in fool; kuu (G. kuh) *cow*; guut (G. gut) *good*.

The true 'a' of *arm* does not occur, except approximately in the initial of au and ei. The proper sounds of ä, ö, ü are absent, and if these letters are used in a few cases to enable the reader to recognise words, the two former will be restricted to syllables having the vowel sound in *met*, and 'ü' to such as have that in *fit*.

§ 3.   *The Dipthongs.*

ei (eu) in height, aisle, German ei, with the initial '*a*' (italic) of Mr. Ellis (in his *Early English Pronunciation*), 'eu' has the same power in PG.

ai in boy, oil; somewhat rare, but present in the names Boyer, Moyer (from Meyer), ai (G ei) *egg*; ajər (aajər, aijər) *eggs*; hai (G. heu) *hay*; bai (sounding like E. boy, and from E.) *pie*; wai (G. weihe) *hawk*. Literary German has it in 'bäume' *trees*, and 'eu' (which is properly ei) is usually confounded with it in German.

əi, which Mr. Ellis (*ibid.*) gives as the power of English 'ai' (aisle) in London, occurs in the PG. exclamation 'həi,' used in driving cows, and naturalised in the vicinal English. Slavonic has (in German spelling) huj, and Hungarian hü, used in driving swine. Compare Schmidt, Westerwäld. Idiot., p. 276.

---

¹ The long vowel used by native speakers in Bath, Somersetshire, England.
² These two powers are not quite the same.

au in *house*; G. haus, PG. haus. English 'ou' is thus pronounced in adopted words like 'County,' or 'Caunty,' 'Township' or 'Taunschip.'

Care must be taken not to confound the initial of these pairs, for G. and PG. 'eis' (ice) and 'aus' (out) have the same initial vowel, while 'aister' would spell *oyster*.

§ 4. *Nasal Vowels and Dipthongs.*

PG. is not a harsh dialect, like Swiss. It has, however, the Suabian feature of nasal vowels,[1] but to a less extent. They will be indicated with (ˌ) a modification of the Polish mode. This nasality replaces a lost *n* (but not a lost *m*), and it does not pervert the vowel or dipthong, as in the French *un*, *vin*, as compared with *une*, *vinaigre*. Nor does it affect all vowels which have been followed by *n*, for most of them remain pure. Nasal 'ee' (in *they*, French *é*) is very common, but does not occur in French, and French *un* does not occur in PG. Being unaware of the existence of this feature, the writers of the dialect neglect it in the printed examples, which makes it difficult for a foreigner to comprehend them, because a word like 'aa' (the English syllable *awe*) would stand for G. *auch* (also), and when nasal (aaˌ) for G. *an* (on); and 'schtee' would represent both the German *stehe* and *stein*, as in saying 'I stand on the stone'—

G. Ich stehe auf dem stein.—PG. ich schtee uf m schteeˌ.

The following words afford examples :—

aaˌ-fang-ə (G. anfangen) *to begin*; aléeˌ (G. allein) *alone*; scheeˌ (G. schön) *handsome*; bee, (G. bein, pl. beine) *leg*, *legs*; keeˌ (G. kein) *none*; grii, (G. grün) *green*; duuˌ (G. thun) *to do*. Was het ᵉr geduuˌ? (G. Was hat er gethan?) *what has he done?* meiˌ (G. mein, meine) *my*; deiˌ (G. dein) *thy*; neiˌ (G. hinein) *within*; ei, being the only nasal dipthong.

The obscurity arising from a neglect of the nasal vowels appears in the following lines—

> " Die amshel singt so huebsch un' feih,
> Die lereh sie duht ihr lied sh neih;" . . .
> " Awhaemle duht mich eppes noh."—*Rachel Bahn.*

Final *n* is not always rejected, but remains in many words, among which are—'in' *in*; 'bin' *am*; 'un' *and*; 'iin' (him)

---

[1] Indicated in 1860 in my Analytic Orthography, §§ 661-3, and in my note to A. J. Ellis's *Early English Pronunciation*, 1869, p. 655, note 2, col. 2. "The lost final *n* is commonly recalled by a nasal vowel."

G. *ihn* (but hii, for G. *hin* thither); 'fun' (from) G. *von*;
'wan' (when); 'hen' (have) G. *haben*; 'kan' (can); 'schun'
(already) G. *schon*.

German infinitives in -en end in -ə in PG., a vowel not subject to nasality, so that when G. *gehen* (to go) remains a dis-
syllable it is 'gee'ə,' but when monosyllabised it becomes 'gee,'
—this vowel being nasalisable.   Similarly, G. *zu stehen* (to
stand) becomes 'tsu schteeə' and 'tsu schtee,;' G. *zu thun*
(to do) may be 'tsu tnu,'—'tsu tnuə,' or (with *n* preserved)
'tsu tuunə,' and G. *gehen* (to go) may have the same phases.

§ 5. *The Consonants.*

The Germanism of confusing b, p; t, d; k, g, is present in
PG. and they are pronounced *flat*, that is, with more of the
surface of the organs in contact than in English—a characteristic which distinguishes German from languages of the Dutch
and Low-Saxon (Plattdeutsch) type.[1] This must be remem-
bered in reading the examples, in which the ordinary usage
of these letters will be nearly followed.

The consonants are b, ch, d, f, g (in *get*, *give*), gh, h, j
(English *y*), k, l, m, n, ng, p, r (trilled), s (in *seal*, not as in
miser), sch (in *ship*), t, w (a kind of *v* made with the lips alone).
'ch' has the two usual variations as in *recht* and *buch*, and its
sonant equivalent 'gh' (written with 'g' in German) presents
the same two phases, as in G. *regen* and *bogen*. ' ng ' before a

---

[1] The real physiological generation of these *flat* consonants is very difficult for
an Englishman to understand. Dr. C. L. Merkel, of Leipzig, a middle-German,
confesses that for a long time he did not understand the pure b, d, not having
heard them in his neighbourhood. He distinguishes (*Physiologie der Mensch-
lichen Sprache*, Leipzig, 1866, pp. 146–156), 1. The "soft shut sounds" or
mediæ, characterized by an attempt to utter voice before the closure is released,
2. "the half-hard shut sounds" or *tenues implosivæ*, characterized by a sound
produced by compressing the air in the mouth by the elevation of the larynx, the
glottis being closed, which "therefore acts like a piston," followed by the sudden
opening of the mouth and glottis, allowing the vowel to pass, (this is his description of the *flat* sounds, which he says Brücke, a Low-Saxon, reckons among his
mediæ), 3. "the hard explosive shut sounds," characterized by a shut mouth
and open glottis through which the unvocalised breath is forced against the
closing barrier more strongly than in the last case, but without pressure from the
diaphragm; 4. "the aspirated or sharpened explosive sound," in which the last
pressure occurs with a jerk. The compound English distinction, p, b; t, d; k, g,
seem almost impossible for a middle and south-German to understand.—A. J. E.

vowel as in *singer*, hence 'finger' is *fing-er* and not *fing-ger*.
'n' before 'k' is like 'ng,' as in G. *links* (on the left), which
is pronounced like an English syllable. Vowels to be repeated
are indicated by a hyphen, as in ge-ennərt (altered), nei-ichkeit (novelty).

Should letters be wanted for English j, z, v, w, the first
may have *dzh*, and the others italic *z*, *v*, *w*, with ks for x.

As the reader of English who speaks PG. can learn the
German alphabetic powers in half an hour, PG. should be
written on a German basis, and not according to the vagaries
of English spelling, with its uncertainty and reckless sacrifice
of analogy. In print, PG. should appear in the ordinary
roman type, in which so many German books are now published.[1]

§ 6. *Stein or Schtein ?*

The sequents *sp*, *st*, are perhaps universally converted into
'schp' and 'scht' in PG., as in 'geescht' for *gehest*, 'hascht'
for *hast*, 'Kaschp'r' for *Caspar*, 'schtce,' for *stein*, and 'schpeck'
for *speck*, all of which are genuine German, as distinguished
from Saxon, Anglosaxon, and Hollandish, because *S is incompatible before labials* (w, m, p) *and dentals* (l, n, t) *in High
German.* Hence, where Dutch has *zwijn*, *smidt*, and *speelen*,
German has *schwein*, *schmidt*, and *schpielen;* and for Dutch
forms like *slijm*, *snee*, and *steen*, German has *schleim*, *schnee*,
and *schtein;* but as the German uses the conventional spell-
ings 'spielen' and 'stein,' he is apt to fancy that a law of
speech is of less importance than the flourishes of a writing-
master, or the practice of a printing-office, even when his own
speech should teach him the law.

That German has this feature practically, is proved by the
fact that words apparently in sp-, st-, become schp-, scht-,
when adopted into Russian, although this language has initial
sp-, st-,—a transfer of *speech* rather than of *spelling*, which is
as old as the thirteenth century, when the Old High German

---

[1] On the inconsistencies of Rauch's Orthography on an English basis, see my
note 2, p. 655 of Ellis's *Early English Pronunciation.*

'spiliman' (an actor) went into Old Slavonic as (using German spelling) 'schpiljman,' where 'spiljman' would have been more in accordance with the genius of the language.

§ 7.   *Vowel Changes.*

Altho the pronunciation of many words is strictly as in High German, there are the following important variations. German *a* becomes normally the vowel of *what* and *fall*, but it has the Swiss characteristic of closing to 'o,' as in 'ool' (eel) G. *aal*; 'ee, mool' (once) G. *ein mal*; 'woor' (true) G. *wahr;* 'joor' (year) G. *jahr;* 'frooghə' (to ask) G. *fragen;* 'frook' (a question) G. *frage;* 'doo' (there) G. *da;* 'schloofə' (to sleep) G. *schlafen;* 'schtroos' (street) G. *strasze;* 'nooch' (towards) G. *nach;* 'hoor' (hair) G. *haar*, but 'paar' (pair) and others do not change.

The vowel of *fat* occurs in 'kschœr' (harness) G. *geschirr;* 'hœrpscht' (autumn) G. *herbst;* fœrtl (fourth) G. *viertel;* kœrl (fellow) G. *kerl.*

German 'o' becomes 'u,' as in 'kumə' (*u* short, see § 2) *to come*, Austrian kuma, G. *kommen;* 'schun' (already) G. *schon;* 'fun' (of) G. *von;* 'wuunə' (to reside) G. *wohnen;* 'wuu' (where) G. *wo;* 'sun' (sun) Austr. sunn, G. *sonne;* 'suu,' and 'suun' (son) G. *sohn;* 'númitaag' and 'nómidaak' (afternoon) G. *nachmittag;* 'dunərschtaag' (thursday) G. *donnerstag;* 'hunich' (honey) G. *honig.*

German 'ei' is often 'ee,' as in 'heem' (home) G. *heim;* 'deel' (part) G. *theil;* 'seef' (soap) G. *seife;* 'bleech' (pale) G. *bleich;* eens (one) G. *eins;* 'tswee' (two) G. *zwei.*

Irregular forms appear in 'maulwarf' (mole) G. *maulwurf;* 'blĕs' (pale, rhyming *lace*) G. *blass;* 'siffer' (tippler) G. *säufer;* 'schpoot' (late) G. *spät*, ä long; 'm'r wellə' (we will) G. *wir wollen;* 'dii úmeesə' (the ant) G. *die ameise;* 'ep,' 'eb' (whether) G. *ob;* 'dœrfə' (to dare) G. *dürfen;* 'fœrichtərlich' (frightful) G. *fürchterlich;* 'ich fœricht mich dat [or dart, G. *dort*] anə tsu gee,.' *I fear me to go yonder.*

'Dat anə' is for G. *dort hin*, 'anə' being a Swiss adverb

made of G. *an* (on, towards). 'dat' is not common in PG. and it may have been brought from abroad, as it occurs in Suabian—

"Aepfel hott ma dott gsia, wie d' Kirbiss bey üss;" (Radlof, 2, 10.)—(Man hat dort gesehen) *Apples have been seen there like* (G. Kürbisse, PG. kæropsə) *pumpkins with us.*

The foregoing 'anə' appears in Swiss "ume und anne" (thither and hither) where 'ume,' Austr. 'uma,' is from G. *um* (about). Stalder refers 'anne' to G. *an-hin*, and Swiss 'abe' to *ab-hin*. Schmid (Schwäb. Wb., p. 23) has ane, dortane, dettano. Schmeller (Bayer. Wb. 1869, p. 91) cites Graff (1, 499), for Ohg. *ostana* (from the East), and Grimm (3, 205).

While PG. 'alt' and 'kalt' (old, cold, *a* in what) have the comparatives 'eltər' 'keltər,' the influence of *r* in 'karts' (short), G. *kurz*, and 'hart' (hard), produces 'kærtsər' and 'hærtər,' instead of G. *kürzer* and *härter*. Long *a* becomes long *u* in G. *samen* (seed), PG. 'suumə.'

§ 8. *Dipthong Changes.*

German 'au' sometimes becomes 'aa' (in call), as in PG. 'laafə' (to walk) G. *laufen;* 'glaabə' (to believe) G. *glauben;* 'kaafə' (to buy) G. *kaufen;* 'tsaam' (bridle) G. *zaum;* 'traam' (dream) G. *traum;* 'fraa' (wife, woman) G. *frau*, PG. pl. 'weiwər,' because, as the German plural of *frauen* could not well make 'fraaɔ,' the plural of *weib* was preferred.

German 'au' remains in PG. 'plaum' (plum) G. *pflaume;* 'daum' (thumb); 'haufə' (heap); 'saufə' (to sup); 'haus' (house); 'taub' (dove) G. *taube;* 'aus' (out); 'fauscht' (fist).

German 'au' becomes 'oo' (Eng. floor) in PG. 'groo' (grey) an earlier form of G. *grau;* 'bloo' (blue) G. *blau;* and the name 'Stauffer' is sometimes pronounced 'stoof'r.'

In the plural, 'au' becomes 'ei,' as in PG. 'haus,' pl. 'heiser;' 'maus' pl. 'meis;' 'laus' pl. 'leis;' 'maul' (mouth) pl. 'meiler' G. pl. *mäuler;* 'gaul,' pl. 'geil,' G. pl. *gäule* (horses); 'sau' (sow, hog), pl. 'sei,' G. pl. *säue, sauen.*

When 'au' has become 'aa' the German plural *äu* becomes 'ee,' as in 'beem' (trees) G. *bäume;* 'tseem' (bridles) G. *zäume.*

'Floo,' G. *floh* (flea) pl. 'floe' for G. *flöhe*, is due to the fact that German long ö is replaced by ee.

German *au* is *u* in the earlier PG. 'uf' (up) G. *auf*, found in Swisserland and other localities; but 'haus' is not *hûs*, and 'maul' is not *mül* as in Swiss.

§ 9. *Words lengthened.*

Some monosyllables are dissyllabised under the influence of trilled *r*, and of *l* (which is akin to *r*), as in 'Jar'ik' (York); 'Jœr'ik,' German *Georg* (George), perhaps the only example of the Berlin change of G to (German) J.

PG.	G.	E.	PG.	G.	E.
schtar'ik	stark	*strong*	dar'ich	durch	*through*
mar'ikt	markt	*market*	kar'op	korb	*basket*
er'əwət	arbeit	*work*	bər'ik	berg	*hill*
kær'ich	kirche	*church*	mil'ich	milch	*milk*
karrich	karren	*cart*	kal'ich	kalk	*lime*
geenə	gehen	*to go*	genunk	genug	*enough*
reeghərə	regnen	*to rain*	wammes	wamms	*jacket*

PG. g'seenə (seen) G. *gesehen*, occurs in South German, as in the following (Radlof 2, 100), which closely resembles PG.

. . . . vun der Zit an het me niks me vun em g'sehne un g'hört. *From that time on*, ('mē' G. man) *one* (hat) *has seen and heard nothing* ('mē' G. mehr) *more of him.*

G. Es fängt an zu regnen und zu schneien. PG. es fangt (not fängt) an, tsu reeghərə un tsu schneeə. *It begins to rain and to snow.*

§ 10. *Words shortened.*

Condensation is effected by absorption, as of *d* by *n* in 'wunər' (wonder) G. *wunder;* and of *f* by *p* in 'kəp' (head) G. *kopf;*—by the elision of consonants (an Austrian feature) as in 'wet' (would) G. *wollte;* 'net' (not) G. *nicht.*

By elision of vowels (particularly final *e*) as in 'schuul' (school) G. *schule*, 'tsammə' (together) G. *zusammen;* and by shortening vowels, as in 'siw'ə' (seven) G. *sieben;* 'gew'ə' (to give) G. *gēben;* G. *heurathen* (to marry), Suab. heuren, PG. 'heiərə'; G. *gleich* (like) PG. 'glei'; 'tsimlich' (tolerable) G. *ziemlich.*

PG.	G.	E.	PG.	G.	E.
niks	nichts	*nothing*	mr sin	wir sind	*we are*
wet	wollte	*would*	géseht'r	gestern	*yesterday*
set	sollte	*should*	nemmə	nehmen	*to take*
knəp	knopf	*button*	nam'itag	nachmittag	*afternoon*
knep	knöpfe	*buttons*	gebliwə	geblieben	*remained*
kich	küche	*kitchen*	jets [1]	jetzt	*now*
kuuchə	küchen	*cake*	parr'ə	pfarrer	*preacher*
wəch	woche	*week*	oowət	abend	*evening*
wəchə	wochen	*weeks*	weipsleit	weibsleute	*women*
kiw'l	kübel	*bucket*	rei,	herein	*herein*
blos	blase	*bladder*	nei,	hinein	*hither-in*
mcim	meinem	*to my*	draa,	daran	*thereon*
anər	ander	*other*	eltscht	älteste	*oldest*
nənər	einander	*each other*	tswiwlə	zwiebeln	*onions*
unor	unter	*under*	hend	hände	*hands*
drunə	darunter	*ther' under*	plets	plätze	*places*
nunər	hinunter	*down there*	nummə [1]	nun mehr	*only*
dro'wə	daroben	*above*	nimmə [1]	nimmer	*never*
driw'o	darüber	*ther' over*	mee [1]	mehr	*more*
drin	darin	*ther' in*	noo	darnach	*ther' after*
ruff	darauf	*there up*	pluuk	pflüg	*plow*
nuff	hinauf	*up there*	plüghə	pflüge	*plows*
sind	sünde	*sin*	kalénər	kalénder	*calendar*

As G. ' ū ' becomes ' i ' in PG., G. *lügen* (to tell a lie) and *liegen* (to lie down—both having the first vowel long) might be confused, but the latter is shortened in PG., as in ' œr likt ' (he lies down) ' ær liikt ' (he tells a lie).

    PG. Was wi' t ?   *What wilst thou?* G. Was willst du ?

      Woo't weepe ? Woo't fight ? Woo't teare thy selfe ? [2]

Ich wil fischa gee,.   *I will go to fish.*

Ich hab kschriwwə.   *I have* (geschrieben) *written.*

Sin mr net keiart ?   *Are we not married ?* G. Sind wir nicht geheirathet?
(or verheirathet.)

    Infinitive -n is rejected, as in the Swiss and Suabian dialects. In an Austrian dialect it is rejected when *m, n,* or *ng* precedes, as in singa, rena, nchma, for *singen, rennen, nehmen.*—*Castelli,* Wörterbuch, 1847, p. 31.

    The length of some vowels is doubtful, as in ' rot ' or ' root ' (red, like English *rŏte* or *rōde*), ' so ' or ' soo,' ' nochbər ' or ' noochbər,' ' əmol ' or ' əmool,' ' ja ' or ' jaa,' ' sii ' or ' sī ' (she, they, I in deceit, not in *sit*). Compare English ' Sĕe ! ' and ' Sĕe thêre ! '

    Accent in PG. agrees with that of High German. When indicated, as in danóot or danoot' (for the ' oo ' represent a single vowel, as in Eng. *floor*), it is to afford aid to the reader not familiar with German accent.

   [1] Swiss forms.

   [2] *Hamlet,* act 5, sc. 1, speech 106 ; folio 1623, tragedies, p. 278, col. 2.

CHAPTER III.

VOCABULARY.

The vocabulary of PG. has but few synonyms, a single word being used where High German has several, as 'plats' (place) for G. *platz* and *ort*. Of the German words for *horse* (pferd, ross, gaul, etc.), 'gaul' is universal in speech, *ross* seems not to be known, and *pferd* is almost restricted to print.[1] A colt is not called *füllen* as in German, but 'hutsch,' with a diminutival 'hutschli' (in Suabian *hutschel, hutschele*, Westerwald *husz*, Lusatian *husszche*.)

A pig is not *ferkel* (Lat. porc-ell-us, Welsh porch-ell) but 'seili' (from *sau*), and children call it 'wuts' (Suab. butzel) a repetition of this being used (as well in vicinal English) in calling these animals. 'Kalb' (calf, pl. 'kelwer') is named by children 'hameli'[2] when a suckling. Cows are called with 'kum see ! see ! see hameli ! see !' and when close at hand with 'suk suk suk' (as in for*sook*)—used also in the English of the locality.[3]

Of G. *knabe* (boy) and *bube*, pl. *buben*, PG. takes the latter as 'buu,' pl. 'buuwə;' and of the G. *haupt* and *kopf* (head) it prefers the latter as 'kəp.' Of the verbs *schmeissen* and *werfen* (to throw), *kriegen* and *bekommen* (to obtain), *hocken* and *sitzen* (to sit), *schwetzen* and *sprechen* (to talk), *erzählen* and *sagen* (to tell), PG. uses 'schmeissə,' 'kriighə,' 'həkə,' 'schwetsə' and 'saaghə' almost exclusively.

The suffix -lein, condensed to -li and -l, is the universal diminutival, as in Swisserland and South Germany—a small

---

[1] Of words not occurring in print, the Swiss, Bavarian, and Suabian form bruntsen replaces harnen and its synonyms.
[2] Seemingly akin to Swiss *ammeli, mammeli* (a child's sucking-glass), whence *mämmelen* (to like to drink). G. amme (a wet-nurse), in Bavaria, also a mother.
[3] PG. des kalb sukt (this calf sucks,) G. *saugt.*

house being called 'heissli' and not *häus-chen*, and a girl 'meedl'
and not *mädchen*. It is, however, very often associated with
the adjective klee, (little) G. *klein*, as in PG. 'e klee, bichli'
(a little book).

German *kartofeln* (potatoes) is rejected for G. *grundbirnen* [1]
under the form of 'krumpiiro,' where 'krum' is accepted by
some as *krumm* (crooked), while some regard the latter part
as meaning *pears*, and others as *berries*.

F'rleicht, Fileicht (perhaps, G. vielleicht) are in use, but the former seems the more common.

Sauerampl, G. sauerampfer (sorrel, Rumex).

Rewwer, Krik, Krikli (Eng. *river, creek*) have thrust aside G. *fluss*
and *bach*.

Laafe (to walk ; G. *laufen* to run, and to walk).

Schpring-e (to run, a Swiss usage. G. *springen*, to leap, spring, gush).

Petse (to pinch), Alsace pfetse, Swiss pfätzen, Suab. pfetzen.

Tref (Suab., a knock, blow). PG. 'ich tref dich' (I strike thee).

Schmuts (a hearty kiss). Swiss, Suab., in G. *schmatz*.

Un'ich (under), G. unter, occurs in provincial German as unn-ig and
unt-ig ; hinnig occurs also, PG. 'hinnich,' as in 'hinnich d'r diir'
behind the door.

> Wii m'r donaus gloffe sin, bin ich hinnich ün nooch gloffe. *As we walked out,
> I walked behind him.*

For 'hinnich,' Alsatian has hing-e, as in 'M'r geen hing-e
[nach den] noo de goorte noo'— *We go along behind the garden.*

Uumet, oomet, Austr. omad, Swiss amet, G. das grummet (after-
math). Suab. ämt, emt, ömd, aumad ; Bavar. âmad.

Arik, arrig (much, very), Swiss arig, G. arg (bad, cunning).

> PG. Ich hab net gwist [Suab. gwest] dass es so arrik reeghert. *I did not
> suppose it to be raining so hard.*

Artlich (tolerably) is the Swiss *artlich* and *artig*.

Ewwe, G. adv. ēben (really, even, just), but it is PG. 'eewe' when
it is the adj. *even.*

> Ich hab ewwe net gwist for sure eb er e fraa het eder net. (*Rauch.*) *I did not
> even know 'for sure' if he has a wife or not.*

amanat, *adv.* metathesised and adapted from G. *an einem Orte* (at a
place), a dative for an accusative *an einen Ort* (in a place) as

---

[1] This name seems to have been originally applied to the crooked tubers of the
Jerusalem artichoke, and *humming-bird* was probably applied to moths of the
genus *Sphinx* (named from the form of the larva) before the bird bearing this
name was known in Europe.

used here. In the example, 'ana' is G. *an* inflected, and *xŭ* of
xu schicken is omitted, as sometimes done in PG.

> ... wan als a brüf kummt f'r âmanat ana schika ... (*Rauch.*) *When
> ever a letter comes for to send on*—to be sent on.

Henkweide (weeping willow). G. Hängebirke, is hanging birch.

Tappar (quickly), as in Schpring tappar *run quick! be in a hurry*—
thus used in Westerwald, and as *very* in Silesia. G. tapfer (brave,
bravely), E. dapper.

Meenar (more), **Meenscht** (most), for G. *mehr, meist*, are réferable
to *mancher* and a hypothetic *mannigste.* 'Mee' and 'mee,'
(more), Swiss—"Was wett i meh?" *What would I more.*
"Nimme meh," *never more.* PG. 'Was wet ich mee? Nimmi
mee.' (See *Ellis*, Early English Pronunciation, p. 663, note 39.)

Schtrublich, schtruwlich. G. *struppig* (bristly, rough), Swiss *strub-
lig*, PG. 'schtruwlich' (disordered, uncombed, as hair). English
of the locality *stroobly.*

Neewich; SG. *nebensich*, Wetterau (upper Hessia) *nébig*, G. *neben*
(beside).

> "Naevrich der mommy ruht er now [Eng. *now*]
>   In sellem Gottes-acker ¹ dort,
>   Shraegs ² fun der Kreutz Creek Kerrich nuf, [hinauf.]
>   Uft denk ich doch an seller ort!"—*Rachel Bahn.*

Hensching, G. *handschue* (gloves, Sw. händschen) becomes a new
word with 'hen' for *hände* (hands), the ä umlaut being used to
pluralise, but the word is singular also, and, to particularise,
a glove proper is 'fing-er hensching' and a mitten 'fauscht-
hensching.' This termination is given to 'pœrsching' a peach.

Sidder (since), Swiss *sider, sitter*; Suabian and Silesian *sider*;
Scotch, etc., *sithens.*

Schpel (a pin), SG. *die spelle* (a better word than G. stecknadel);
Dutch *speld* (with *d* educed from *l*); Lat. SPIcuLa.

Botsar (masc. a tail-less hen), Holstein, *buttars.* Provincial G.
butsig (stumpy).

Mallikap (i.e. thick-headed, a tadpole). Swiss *mollig, molli* (stout,
blunt); Suabian *mollig* (fleshy). Alsatian muurkrontl (tadpole)
from muur, G. moder, Eng. *mud.* The PG. of western New
York has taken the New England word *polliwog.*

Blech (tin, a tin cup); dim. 'blechli.' Blechiche Bool (a tin *bowl*,
i.e. a *dipper*, a convenient word which seems not to have been
introduced). In Pennsylvanian English, a tin cup is *a tin.*

¹ Scarcely legitimate, the PG. word for a grave-yard being kærich-hof.
² Diagonally.

In old English, 'than' represented *than* and *then*, and PG. has
'dann' for both G. *dann* (then) and *denn* (for) ; and also 'wann' for
wann (when) and *wenn* (if), as in Rachel Bahn's lines—

"Doch guckt 's ah recht huebsch un' nice	Doch gukt 's aa recht hipsch un 'neis'
Wann all die Baehm sin so foll ice—"	Wan al dii beem sin so fal eis—

Yet it looks (auch) *also right fair and* 'nice' WHEN *all the trees are so full of ice.*

" Forn bild der reinheit is 's doh,	F'r 'n bild der reinheit [1] iss es doo,
In fact, mer kenne schne noh,	'in faekt,' m'r kenna seena noo,
Dass unser Hertz' [2] so rein muss seih,	dass unser haerts so rein [1] muss sei,,
Wann in des Reich mer welle neih."	wann in des reich m'r welle nei,.

For a picture of purity is it (da) *here,* '*in fact*' (wir können schen darnach) *we
can perceive therefrom, that our heart must be as pure,* (wenn in das reich wir
wollen hinein) IF *we would enter into the kingdom.*

Baschte (to husk maize), from 'bascht,' G. *bast* (soft inner bark,
E. bast), applied in PG. to the husk of Indian corn.—Rachel
Bahn (1869) thus uses it—

" Die leut sie hocke's welshcorn ab,	Dii leit sii hacke 's welschkarn ap,
'S is 'n rechte guhte crop,	's iss 'n rechte guute ' crap,' (fem.)
Un' wann's daer genunk werd sei,	un wan 's daerr genunk waert sei,,
Noh bashte sies un' fahres eih."	noo baschta sii 's un faare 's ei,.

The people they (ab-hacken) *chop off* ('s, das) *the maize,* (es ist) *it is a right
good* '*crop,*' *and when* (es) *it becomes* (dürr genug) *dry enough, they* (darnach)
afterwards husk it and (fahren) *haul it in.*

Greisslich (to be disagreeably affected). SG. grüselig, G. gräszlich
(horrible), E. grisly.

Noo, danoo', danoot', nord, G. darnach (then, subsequently).

Bendl (a string), schuubendl (shoe-string). Swiss bändel.

Schteiper, n. (Lat. stipes), a prop, as of timber. G. nautical term
steiper, a stanchion. **Schteipere**, v.t. to prop; to set a prop.

Ferhúttele, v. intrans. 'Ich bin f'r-huttlt,' (I am confused, per-
plexed.) ' Ich denk dii bissness iss 'n bissli f'r-huttlt.' (I think
the 'business' is a bit mixed up.) G. verhüdeln (to spoil, bungle.)

Paanhaas, as if, G. *pfanne-hase* (pan-hare). Maize flour boiled in
the metsel-soup, afterwards fried and seasoned like a *hare*. (Compare Welsh *rabbit*.) The word is used in English, conjointly
with *scrapple*.

Loos (a sow), as in Swiss and Suabian.

Laad, fem. (coffin), toodlaad, toodaland, as in Alsace. G. die lade
(chest, box, case). PG. bettlaad, Suab. bettlade, for G. bettge-
stell (bedstead).

---

[1] By analogy these words should be rei, and rei,heit, but as they are scarcely
PG. they are given as High German.
[2] This word is correct without the elisive mark, which perverts the syntax.

Schtreel, m. (a comb), Swiss, Alsatian, Suab. der strähl. But G.
striegel, PG. striegel, PG. strigl, is a currycomb.

Aarsch, the butt end of an egg, as in Suabian.

Falsch (angry), as in Swiss, Bavarian, and Austrian. PG. Sel hat
mich falsch g'macht. *That made me angry.*

Hoochtsich, Alsat. hoochtsitt, G. hochzeit (a wedding).

Heemeln, Swiss heimeln (to cause a longing, to cause home feelings).

" Wie hämelt mich do alles a' !"	Wii heemlt mich doo alles aa, !
Ich steh, un denk, un guck ;	ich schtee, un denk, un gukk ;
Un was ich schier vergessa hab,	un was ich schiir f'rgessa hab,
Kummt wider z'rück, wie aus seim Grab,	kummt widd'r tsrik, wii aus seim graab,
Un steht do wie e' Spook !" *Harb.*	un schteet doo wii a schpukk !

(G. Wie alles da anheimelt mich) *How all here impresses me with home, I
stand, and think, and look ; and what I had almost forgotten, comes back again
as out of its grave, and stands here like a ghost.*

Drop, pl. **drep** (simpleton, poor soul). "O du armer Tropff!"
(Suabian). *Radlof*, 2, 10. "Die arma Drep!"—*Harbaugh.*

Schwalme (Swiss, for G. schwalbe, a swallow).

Jaa (O. Eng. yes), is used in answer to affirmative questions.

Joo (O. Eng. yea), is used in answer to negative questions. See
Ch. viii. § 1, ¶ 12, and § 3, ¶ 2.

"Sin dii sacha dei, ? *Jaa*, sii sin." (Are the things thine ? *Yes*, they are.)
"Sin dii sacha *net* dei, ? *Joo*, sii sin" (Are the things *not* thine. *Yea*, they
are.) "Bischt du *net* g'sund ? *Joo*, ich bin."[1] (Are you *not* well? *Yea, I am well.*)

saagt, G. *sagt* (he says): **secht**, as if G. sägt, for sagte (he said), as
if it were a strong verb.

Gleich, to like, be fond of, Eng. to *like*, but perhaps not Eng.
See Ch. viii., ¶ 3. PG. ær gleicht s geld—*he loves money.*

Glei, adv. (soon).—ær kummt glei—*he comes* (will be here) *directly.*
Swiss *gly* and *gleich* have the same meaning.

Abartich, bartich, Ch. viii., § 3, ¶ 6 (adj. unusual, strange) ; (adv.
especially). G. *abartig* degenerate.

" Der dockter sogt eara complaint wær . . . conclommereashen im kup, so
dos se so unfergleichlich schwitsa mus in der nacht, abbordich wan se tsu
gedeckt is mit em fedder bet."—*Rauch*, Feb. 1, 1870. *The doctor asserts her
'complaint' to be . . . 'conglomeration' in the head, so that she must sweat un-
commonly in the night, PARTICULARLY when she is covered [tsu is accented] in
with the feather bed.*

Biibi, piipi, biibeli ; Swiss bibi, bibeli, bidli (a young chicken).
Used also to call fowls—the second form in the vicinal English,
in which a male fowl is often called a hé-biddy.

[1] The Rev. D. Ziegler.

The Swiss use in PG. of the genitive form *des* of the article, instead of the neuter nominative *das*, causes little or no confusion, because this genitive is not required, and its new use prevents confusion between *das* and *dass*. Where German uses *des*, as in *Der Gaul des* (or *meines*) *Nachbars* (the horse of the, or my, neighbor), PG. uses a dative form—

. . . dem (or meim for meinem) nochbor sei, gaul (the neighbor his horse). See the quotation (p. 28) from Schöpf.

PG. inflects most of its verbs regularly, as in 'gedenkt' for G. *gedacht*, from *denken* (to think). In the following list, the German infinitive, as *backen* (to bake), is followed by the third person of the present indicative (er) *bäckt*, PG. (ær) 'bakt' (he bakes). The PG. infinitive of *blasen, braten, fragen, rathen, dürfen, verderben*, is 'bloose, broote, frooghe, roote, dœrfe, f'rdœrwe.' 'bloose' (to blow) and 'nemme' (to take) occur below, in the extract from Miss Bahn.

G.	G.	PG.	G.	G.	PG.
blasen *blow*,	bläst	blooat	lesen *read*,	liest	leest
braten *bake*,	brät	broot	lassen *let*,	läszt	leest
brechen, *break*,	bricht	brecht	messen *measure*,	miszt	meast
dreschen *thrash*,	drischt	drescht	nehmen *take*,	nimmt	nemmt
dürfen *dare*,	darf	dœrf	rathen *advise*,	räth	root
fahren *drive*,	fährt	faart	saufen *tipple*,	säuft	sauft
fallen *fall*,	fällt	fallt	schelten *scold*,	schilt	schelt
fragen *ask*,	frägt	frookt	schlafen *sleep*,	schläft	schlooft
essen *eat*,	iszt	east	schwellen *swell*,	schwillt	schwellt
fressen *devour*,	friszt	fresst	sehen *see*,	sieht	seet
geben *give*,	giebt	gept	stehlen, *steal*,	stiehlt	schtealt
graben *dig*,	gräbt	graapt	tragen *carry*,	trägt	traagt
helfen *help*,	hilft	helft	verderben *spoil*,	verdirbt	f'rdœrpt
laufen *run*,	läuft	laaft	vergessen *forget*,	vergiszt	f'rgeast

"Der wind, horch yusht, wie er drum bloss'd, . . .

Gar nix for ihm fersichert is,

  Er nemmt sei aegner waek

Dorch ennich rissly geht er neih,

  Un geht ah nuf die staek."

D'r wint, harich juscht wii ær drum blooat, . . .

Gaar niks f'r iim f'raichart iss,

  ær nemmt sei, eegnar week,

darich ennich riaali geet ær nei,

  un geet aa 'nuf dii schteek.

The wind, just listen how it therefore (an expletive) *blows, . . . quite nothing is secure for* (on account of) *him, he takes his* (eigener weg) *own way; through* (einig, einiges) *any crack he goes* (hinein) *in, and goes also* (hinauf) *up the* (stiege) *stair.*

The reader of PG. may be puzzled with 'ma' as used in "ous so ma subject . . . mit ma neia Rail Road" (*Rauch*); 'fun ma' or 'fun əma,' Ger. dative *von einem*, Old High German 'vone einemo;' G. *dem*, Ohg. 'demo;' G. *meinem*, Gothic

'meinamma,' which accounts for the final PG. vowel. Miss
Bahn writes it ' mah '—

''S is noch so 'n anre glaener drup,	's iss noch so n anre gleenər drəp,
Mit so mah grosse dicke kup,	mit soo mə grossə dikkə kəp,
Der doh uf English screech-owl haest,	dær doo uf eng-lisch ' skriitsch-aul ' heest,
Der midde drin hut ah sci nesht.'	dær middə drin hat aa sei nescht.

*There is yet such another little fellow, with such a large thick head, this here
in English is called ' screech-owl,' the middle therein [of the tree] has also its nest.*

Remarking on "grosse dicke kup" in the second line, my
reverend friend Ziegler sends me the following declensions of
the united article and adjective. The dative is used for the
genitive, as will appear in the chapter on Syntax.

Nom., Accus.   en ('n) grosser dicker kopp,   ·
Dat., Gen.   emə ('mə) grossə dickə kopp.

Singular.

Nom.	der root wei, ... iss guut. *The red wine is good.*
Gen.	dem rootə wei, . . . sei, farb is schee,.
Dat.	„ „ „ . . . . hab ich 's tən fərdankə.
Acc.	dii rootə wei, ... hat ær gedrunkə.

Plural.

Nom.	dii rootə wei, ... sin guut. *The red wines are good.*
Gen.	dennə rootə wei, . . . iir farb etc. (G. der rothen Weine Farbe ist schön.)
Dat.	„ „ „ . . . hab ich 's etc. (G. den rothen Weinen.)
Acc.	dii rootə wei, ... hat ær, etc.

CHAPTER IV.

GENDER.

§ 1. *Gender of English Words in Pennsylvania German.*

German gender and declension might be said to be in a state of barbarism, were it not that some of the languages of savages have refinements which are wanting in the tongues of civilised people. German gender being in a high degree arbitrary and irrational, there seem but few principles applicable to introduced words, and yet, the linguistic instinct produces a measure of uniformity. The clear distinction in modern English between a spring and a well, does not exist between the German *der quell* (and *die quelle*, PG. 'dii qkel') and *der brunnen*, but German has *der spring* also, which may be used alone, or compounded in *springquell* or *springquelle*. Influenced by English, PG. uses 'dii schpring' for a natural spring of water, keeping 'd'r brunne' for a well, 'tsig-brunne' for a draw-well with a windlas and bucket—but also 'laafende brunne' for a spring.

As a German says 'dii' for the English article *the*, which he hears applied to everything singular and plural, and as this *die* is his own feminine and plural article, he will be likely to say 'dii fens' for *the fence*, 'dii set' (set, of tools, etc.), 'dii faundri' (foundry), 'dii bænk' (bank of a stream), 'dii færm' (farm), 'dii plantaasche' (plantation), 'dii témeti' (timothy hay), 'dii portsch,' 'dii schtæmp ('stämp' in print, for G. *der stempel*), 'dii watsch' (timepiece), 'dii *bel* hat *geringt*' (the 'bell' has 'rung'), " Stohrstube . . . mit einer offenen Front," (Store-room with an open front), "die *Fronte*[1] des Hauses" (the 'front' of the house), "Die Sanitäts *Board*," " Eine *Lot* Stroh," " Eine *Lotte* Grund," etc. All of these are feminine

[1] Such italics for English words are no part of the original.

in PG., together with the English nouns *alley*, *road*, *borough*, *square* (of a town) *fair*, *forge*, *creek* (a stream), *climate*, *bowl*, *vendue*, *court* (at law), *law*, *lawsuit*, *jury*, *yard* (of a house),—

Als Herr Yost . . . einen groszen Neufundländer Hund in seiner **Yard**[1] anders anbinden wollte, fiel ihn das Thier an . . . der Hund wieder an ihn sprang, und ihn gegen die **Fenz**[1] drängte, . . . *Der Pennsylvanier*, Lebanon, Pa. Sept. 1, 1869.

Of the masculine gender are *river* (PG. 'rewer'), *bargain*, *crop*, *beef* (but 'gedörtes beef' makes it neuter), *carpet*, *turnpike* (or *pike*), *store*, *gravel*, *shop*, *smith-shop*, *shed*, and of course words like *squire*, *lawyer*, and "*assignie*."

Of the neuter gender are "*das främ*" (frame), "*das flaur*" (flour, influenced by G. *das mehl*), das *screen*, das *photograph*, das *piano*, das *supper*, das *buggy*.

Wishing to know the gender of the preceding English words in another county, the list was sent to the Rev. Daniel Ziegler, of York, Pa., who assigns the same genders to them, adding der *settee*, die *umbréll*, die *parasol*, die *bréssant* (prison), das *lampblack*, das *picter* (picture), das *candy*, das *cash*, das *lumber* (building timber), das *scantling*, das *pavement*, das *township*.[2]

German *die butter* (butter) is masculine in PG. as in South Germany and Austria; and *die forelle* (the trout) is PG. 'dœr fərél.' G. *die tunke* (gravy) is neuter under the form 'tunkes' in PG., which makes the *yard* measure feminine, although in Germany (and in print here), it has been adopted as masculine.

Variations in grammatic gender are to be expected under the degenderising influence of English, but at present the

[1] This mode of indicating words is used to avoid corrupting the text with italics.

[2] As this essay is passing through the press, I add the following examples, which are all in print.

Der charter, deed (legal), humbug, lunch or lunsch, ein delikater Saurkraut-Lunch. Revenuetarif, crowd, fight, molasses, Select-Council, crop (fem. with Miss Bahn). Im Juli—schreit der Whipper-will.

Die jail, legislatur, Grandjury or grand Jury, ward (of a city), lane, toll, gate, pike or peik, bill (legislative), Cornetband or Cornet Band, eine grosze Box (of medicine), gefängniszbox, platform, manufactory, shelfing, counter.

Das County, committee or comite, picnic, screen (coal-screen), law (also fem.), trial, verdikt, basin (reservoir), Groszes Raffle für Turkeys und Gänse, ... ausgeraffelt werden.

German genders usually remain, as in *der stuhl* (chair), *der pflug* (plough, PG. 'pluuk'), *der trichter* (funnel, PG. 'trechtər'), *der kork* (cork, PG. karik), *der indigo, der schwamm* (spunge), *die egge* (harrow, PG. ' eek,' sometimes ' êk'), *die bank* (bench), *die wiese* (meadow, PG. ' wiss'), *die kiste* (chest or chist, PG. kist), *das tūch* (cloth), *das messing* (brass, PG. ' měs,' like Eng. *mace*), *das füllsel* (stuffing, PG. 'filtsl').

§ 2. *The German Genders.*

In various aboriginal languages of America there are two genders, the animate and the inanimate—with a vital instead of a sexual polarity; and while German can and does associate gender and sex, its departure from this system is marked by objects conspicuously sexual, which may be of the neuter gender, and by sexless objects of the three genders.

It is easy to see why *das kind* (the child) is neuter, but under the ordinary view of the rise of grammatic gender, it is not easy to see why, in modern German, *der leib* (body) should be masculine, and *das weib* (woman, wife) of the same gender as the child—why *die liebe* (love) should be feminine, and *der friede* (peace) masculine. In German, the genders are incongruous, in English they are congruous, the masculine and feminine being correlatives, with correlative relations to the neuter also, and by dropping the false nomenclature of the German genders, we may be able to get a more philosophic view of them as they now exist, independently of the Old High German system of gender and declension, which accounts for their later condition.

If we adopt *strong* for the German masculine gender, there would be nothing gained if the feminine were called weak, but with the first as *strong*, the second as *soft*, and the third as *dull*, we would have three terms which do not suggest correlation or sex, and we might see nothing irrational in the fact that *man* might be of the strong, and *woman* of the dull gender ; and that *peace* might be strong, and *love* soft.

Of the *strong* gender are mann, dieb, freund, mord, mund, hase (of energetic action), aal, salm, fisch, tisch (*δίσκος*), käse (CASEUS), schnee, klei, stock, fink (a strong-billed bird), apfel (naturally harsh), stahl, stiefel, schuh, strumpf, fusz, keil, bart, baum, daum, dorn,[1] punkt, stich, beginn, rubin, diamant, klump, kummer, verstand, name, tag, halm (a rough material), floh, krebs, skorpion, hummer, hals, fels, saft, bau, rath, werth, zoll, flusz, Rhein, raub, acker, bogen.

Of the *soft* gender are birne, hand, historie (Lat. -IA), liebe, hoffnung, wohnung, stadt, burg (implying also jurisdiction), sonne, gluth, milch, rahm, amsel, drossel, butter, feder, gans, maus, ratte, luft, frucht, nacht, macht (as if personified), armuth, kraft, furcht, kunst, haut, frau, wurst, schnur, bahn, marsch, welt.

Of the *dull* gender are weib, grab, brod,[2] blei, eisen, gold, silber, zinn, (but der zink,) geld, feld, land, vieh, pferd (the type being agricultural), rind, joch, pech, haar, auge, bein, dorf, ding, mensch, mädchen, volk, hirn, leben, wort, buch, gesetz, herz, gemach, loth, glück, werk, beil, messer, schwert, glas, fenster, feuer, licht, wetter, wasser, bier, malz, kraut, lamm, ei, haupt, kalb, loch.

---

[1] From a Gothic masculine in -us,—*das horn* being from a Gothic neuter in -n.
[2] Primitive bread was probably rather heavy than light—if a mnemonic view may be taken.

CHAPTER V.

§ 1. The English Infusion.

Pennsylvania German has long been recognised as a dialect
with certain English words, which are sometimes inflected in
the German manner. Sportive examples were quoted in the
last century, and one is occasionally cited as characteristic,
which occurs in Joh. Dav. Schöpf's Travels (1783-4) published at Erlangen, in 1788, and thus quoted by Radlof,[1] but
in German characters :—

"Mein Stallion ist über die Fehnsz getscheumpt, und hat dem Nachbor sein
whiet abscheulich gedämatscht." (My *stallion jumped* over the *fence* and horribly
damaged my neighbor's *wheat.*)

This example is probably spurious and a joke, because PG.
'hengscht' and 'weetse' (instead of *stallion* and *wheat*) are in
common use—for the Pennsylvania farmer uses German terms
for introduced European objects, and if he calls *rye* 'karn'
(G. korn), instead of *roggen*, this itself is a German name for
what is in some localities regarded as corn by excellence.
Another example of Schöpf has 'geklaret land' (cleared land),
and 'barghen' (bargain), which are correct.

The German brings with him a vocabulary which is not
quite adapted to the objects around him, and he improves his
language by dropping such of his words as have an indefinite
meaning, replacing them with terms which have an exact and
scientific value, where High German is weak and indefinite—
having failed to Latinise its vocabulary at the revival of learning. The Pennsylvanian uses 'fenss' or 'fents' (not "fehnsz")
for the English *fence*, because the German *zaun* is equally a
hedge; he uses 'flaur' (or 'flauer' Eng. flour) as well as the
German *mehl*, because the latter is equivalent to English meal ;
he seizes upon *bargain* as better than anything in his vernacu-

[1] Mustersaal aller teutschen Mund-arten, . . . Bonn, 1822, vol. 2, p. 361.
By a type error, *m* of getscheumpt was omitted. See also Dr. Mombert's History
of Lancaster County, Pennsylvania, 1869, p. 373.

lar; and he restricts G. *wagen* (with the sound of 'waghə') to *wagon*, adopting a variation like "bändwagen" for a vehicle used by a musical band, using 'kerritsch' (" carriagemacher") for the English *carriage*, altho 'kutsch' (G. kutsche) is also in use. He adopts English expressions for clearing land and speaks of a *clearing* (which he makes feminine) because the destruction of forests by chopping and burning is not a European practice. Railroads were probably built in America before they were in use in Germany, and in Pennsylvania, our English name was imitated in 'reelroot' ('Plankenroad' is in print) or, as in many other cases, the word was translated into "riegelweg." At a later date the foreign name "eisen-bahn" was brought in by later immigrants—and "riegel-bahn" is in use.

§ 2. *Newspapers.*

The Pennsylvania German appreciates humor, and to avoid the humorous and often illegitimate use of English words, the first examples in these pages will be selected from the adver-tisements of about a dozen different newspapers, all printed in the barbarous German character, and published at distant points in Pennsylvania. In such compositions, the attention of the public is called to common objects in a vocabulary which can be accepted without hesitation, and in a style somewhat above the colloquial, in which a horse is called 'gaul' and not *pferd* ('pfært') as usual in print. The spelling is some-times English and sometimes more or less Germanised, without much affecting the pronunciation, as in "store" (a re-tail shop[1]) or "stohr" (buchstore, storehalter, stohrhaus), which are equally 'schtoor'; "frame," (främe, früm, frähm), are equally the English *frame;* "schap" (shap, schop, schopp, shop, pl. schöp); "township" (townschip, taunschip); "county" and "caunty"; "turnpike" and "turnpeik"; "cash" and " casch."

In some localities, English names of streets like *King, Queen, High, Water, Chesnut Street,* are used in German speech and print, and in others, *Königstrasze, Quienstrasze, Highstrasze, Wasserstrasze* and *Chesnutstrasze,* are preferred.

[1] See note 1 on next page.

As parenthetic words like (Dry Goods) occur in the originals, explanations will be [in brackets], and attention will be called to strictly English words by putting them in *italics*.

The " Pennsylvanische Staats-Zeitung " (published at Harrisburg, the State Capital) claims a larger circulation than any English journal of that city, and the number for Nov. 25, 1869, will be quoted here in the original spelling. Here, where English introduced words might be expected throughout, certain French words are adopted from the German dictionaries, such as *reparaturen, delikatessen,* lagerbier *salon* (also *saloon*)[1] *etablissement, engagiren, quotiren, instruiren, autorisiren, ordonnanz.* Others are rather English than French, as *pavements, arrangements, publikationspreisen, textbücher, jury, city, controle* (. . . so wie dasz die City alleinige Controle über denselben Committee . . . .), *connektion, construktion, order, governör, provisionen, groceries.*

Beste Familien-Mehl, in Fässern [in another journal—Roggen*flauer per bärrel—preim flaur*] *superfine per Bärrel; Prime* weitzen *;* Roggen [rye] *per Buschel.* Korn [maize or indian corn, properly called Welschkorn in the same column under the quoted Lancaster prices, where " Korn" means rye.] Hafer; *Middlings; Shorts.*

In the Price-current we find—

Fische . . . *Rock* [Labrax lineatus]; *Pike* [for Hecht, pl. Hechte, a known term]; *Halibut; Haddock; Sturgeon; Trout; White Perch* [Labrax albus, vel mucronatus]; Weisze Fische [Coregonus albus]; Härringe; *Catfische* [Pimelodus, more commonly called ' katsofisch'].

Fleische . . . *Roast Beef per* Pfund; *Rump Steaks; Surloin;* Hammelfleisch; Schweinfleisch; Gedörrtes *Beef* [Getrocknetes Rindsfleisch is quoted from Pittsburg]; *Beef* Schinken; . . . *Mess Pork;* . . . Schmalz in *kegs; Lard*-Oel; Butter (roll . . . print) [with 'roll' and ' ' print' in Roman type]; Molasses [commonly called malássioh]; Süszkartoffeln [a translation of sweet-potatoes, instead of bataten]; *Schellbarks* [nuts of the shell-bark hickory]; Aepfelbutter (Latwerg) [G. Latwerge, PG. látwærik, translated from E. apple-butter].

In the humorous department we find—

Ein ähnliches Räthsel wie sell eine, war scho [schon] früher im *Päper*; . . . Sie sind *gemuvt ?*[2] *Very well,* . . . Sell isch e guat's[3] Plätzel . . . sellem Joseph am Eck[4] lasse mer nix [lassen wir nichts] zu leids thun; . . .

[1] Any place where liquor is retailed is called a saloon, and in a certain town a cabin with a single room is labeled DON JUAN WALLING'S SIGN EMPORIUM.
[2] ' You have *removed* ' (your residence), but the third person plural is not thus used in PG.　　　　[3] G. ein gutes, but the Austrian extension *güät* is not PG.
[4] Neuter for feminine, as in Bavarian and Austrian.

The next examples are condensed from journals of various localities, all printed in the German character. The spelling and use of italics as before.

Der Grosze Wohlfeile *Dry Goods Store.* Jetzt eröffnet: Direkt von New York; *Bärgens* in Weiszgütern und Ellenwaaren (Dry Goods), Gemischte *Mohairs;* Schöne *Dress Ginghams; Long Cloth* [another has Langes Tuch].

Country Orders werden mit *promptheit* ausgeführt . . . Groszhandels oder *Wholesals* Preisen zu *Retailen* oder einzelnen [others have "im groszen und kleinen," " Groz und Klein-Verkauf"] . . . *Ingrain* oder Blumiger *Kärpet;* . . . *Entry* und Treppen [stair] *Carpets; Cottage-Carpets; Floor* Oel-Tücher [another has Boden-Oeltücher]; Marseilles und *Honeycomb Quilts; Matting,* weisz und bunt.

Allgemeine *Stohr*güter; Tücher für *Ladies Cloaks* [another has Damen *Cloakstoffe.*] . . . *Ladies Dress-Goods* [others have *Dresz*güter, *Dresz-*Anzüge, *Dreszwaaren*]; *Fäncy-*Waaren; Ueberdecken; *Quilts* und Tisch-*Diapers; Napkins; Ticking* beim Stück; *Carriage Trimmings;* Extra grosze *gequilte comfortables; Blänkets; Counter Paints* [counterpanes]; *Dry Goods* für Frühjahr und Sommer. Kein *Humbug.*

Millinery Waaren; *Ladies-, Misses-,* und Kinder Stroh und *Fäncy Bonnets* und *Flats;* Corsetten; *Hoops* [others have *Hoops*röcke, and *Hoopskirts* in neuer *Shapes*]; Haar Zöpfen; Rollen; *Braids; Puffs; Dress-Trimmings.* Unsere "*Fits*" sind vollkommen. *Yankee-Notions* [another has *Notionen*]. *Shelfing* und *Counter* für einen *Stohr.*

Pelzwaaren jeder Art, . . . Zobel; *Chinchilla; Ermin;* Siberien-*Squirrel; Fitch;* Wasser-*Mink.*

Wholesale und *Retail* Händler in Aechten *Rye Whiskeys* von verschiedenen *Bränden,* Ausländischen und Einheimischen *Brändies,* Weinen, *Gin* [G. Wachholderbranntwein], feiner Claret, *Scotch Ale, Fancy Liquors, Pine* Apfel Syrup, *Cherry* Wein und Kirschen *Brandy, Demijohns* und *Bottels* von allen Gröszen.

Neue *Scale* Pianoes, mit eisernen Gestellen, *overstrung Bass* und Agraffe *Bridge.* Ein schönes *Second Hand* Piano. Instrumenten zu groszen *Bärgen* . . . *Rotary Valve* [1] und *Side Action* [1] Instrumente [wind instruments].

Eisen-*Store* [Eisen-*Stohr,* Hartewaaren, Hardwaaren, Eisenwaaren] Küchen *Ränges;* Extra *Grätes; Furnäces; Bar-Room-*Oefen; *Air-Tight* und alle Sorten *Parlor* Oefen; *Heating-*Oefen [also Heiz-Oefen]; *Brilliant Gas Burner;* tragbare *Heaters,* und Gasbrenner; Feuer-*bricks;* Springs; *geforged* und gerolltes eisen; *Schäfting; Safes;* Meisel [properly meiszeln] in *Setts; Razor Straps* und *Hones; pullys; Carvingmesser, Butschermesser; Varnisch* [for Firniss]; Neues Kohlen*sereen; Boiler* von allen Sorten; *Brasz*arbeit; Kaffeemühlen . . . verschiedene Haushaltgeräthschaften . . . . welche *Retail* oder *Wholesale* zu den billigsten Preisen verkauft werden . . . Sie garantiren völlige Satisfaction.

Porzellan-Waaren *Stohr : Queens*waaren; *Dinner Sets; Toilet Sets; Toy Thee Sets; Chamber Sets;* Schüszeln mit Deckel; *Bowlen* (Bowls) aller Arten; *Pitchers* aller Arten; Suppen *Tureens* . . . all die letzten *Styles* [Styl is also in use]. Ein groszer Vorrath *Waiters* und Thee-*Trays* . . . Haus-*Furnisching* Waaren . . . Vasen . . . *Chimney Tops.*

---

[1] These four words are printed in Roman type.

Schuh*store*: *India-Rubber*, *Lasting* und *Button* Schuhe ; hoch *polisch Gaiters* für frauen . . . *Kid* Schuhe . . . *Schlippers.*

Juwellen, *Watschen* und Uhren auf Hand [also 'an Hand' for vorräthig]; *Watschen* in goldenen und silbernen *Cäsen* [another has *Repeating*-Taschenuhr, for Repetiruhr] ; *Watschen*-ketten ; Damen goldene *Brācelet Setts ; Studs ; Sleeve*knöpfe ; Messern [for Messer].

Möbel-Waarenlager: Auswahl aller Arten Möbel . . . *Bureaus* [also Burös, Buros, Büros] ; *Sideboards* [*Seidbord, Desk*] ; *Dining*-Tische ; *Lounges ; Settees ;* [also *Setties*] ; *Wardrobes* [also Garderobe-Artikel, and Kleiderschrank, the proper term]. *Cänesitz* Stühle ; Fenster-blenden [and *Blinds*] ; *What-Nots ;* Spiegel mit Gold-*Främs ; Spring*betten . . . . *Parlor, Chamber*, und Küchen Möbeln . . . und alle andern Artikel welche in Möbel-*Stohrs* zu finden sind.

Bauholzhof [others have *Lumber-yard* and Bretterhof] . . . Alle Sorten von Bauholz wohl *geseasonet* [also vollkommen ausgetrocknet];' *Wetterboarding ;* *Weiszpein* [for Fichte] und *Hemlock* [for Tanne] *Joists* und *Scäntling* [another has *Hardwood Skäntling*] jeder Gröeze; *Bill-Stuffs ; Fenst*offen [for pl. stoffe, others have *Fensing* and *Fens*pfosten] ; *Flooring* [also Flurbretter] ; *Panel Lumber ; Poplarboards* [also Pappel] ; *Pickets* [also *Pälings*, both for Pfähle] von allen längen.

Buchdruckerei . . . *Job* Schriften ; Programme; Circulars; *Tickets ;* Karten ; *Blänks ; Handbills ;* Pamphlete ; *Billheads ;* . . . an seinem alten Ständ.

Oeffentliche *Vendu* [and Vendue—" *Vendue Creier* und Auktionär."] . . . Eine Bauerie [also *Farm*, and *Plantasche*] zu verkaufen . . . 110 Acker, 70 *geklart* [and *geklärt*] gelegen in *Londonderry Taunschip, Lebanon* [often Libanon] *County*, an der Strasze führend vom Palmyra *Landing*-Platze nach der *Jonestaun Road*, grenzend an den *Lebanon Valley* Riegelweg [and Rigelweg—a verbal translation of Railway. Others have—"*Es* grenzt an die Libanon Valley *Rail Road*," and "Libanon Thal Eisenbahn."] 2 meilen vom *Stockyard* [location for cattle]. Die Verbesserungen sind ein groszes *weddergebordetes* [Eng. weather-boarded ; another has " *Främ* Haus wettergebordet"] *Främhaus* [*Frähmscheuer, Bankscheuer, Frame*-Arbeitshop] neu tapezirt [papered] . . . mit fünf Stuben auf dem zweiten *Floor ; Garret* [others have Dachstube, and Dachzimmer] Küche und Keller. Eine Cisterne [also *Cistern*] mit 33 *Hogsheads ;* Kohlenbin unter dem *pävement* . . . Eine Bau*lotte* [building lot of ground] 50 Fusz *front* [also— die *Fronte*, and *front*irend.] Schmied*schap* [*Wagenschoppen*] ; *Wagensched* [zwei Wagen*schäde*] mit *Cribs* [and Krippen, Welschkorn*krieb*, Korn*kribbe*, Korn*kribb*] ; *Log*scheuer [also Block-Wohnhaus, Logfräm*haus*, blöckernes Haus] ; mit Stein *Basement* [another has " Stallhoch Steinmauer"—the height of the stables of stone].

Das Land ist vom besten *Gravel* [also *Gravel*-Land, *Flint*, Kalkstein, Kalchstein, Feuerstein], und unter guten *Fenzen* [and *Fensen*, alles unter *Fenz*, gut einge*fenzt*].—Laufendes-Wasser geht durch den Scheuerhof [also Scheucry*ard*]. Es ist bequem zu Post*offices*, Kirchen, Schulen, Mühlen, *Stohres*, und Handwerkern.

Ein 6-jähriger brauner Gaul; . . . ein junges *Baypferd;* ein *Sorrel*pferd ; ein *Fallingtop-Buggy;* ein *Rockaway;* ein *Spring*wagen [*huckster*wagen]; ein *Stohr*wagen mit drei *Springs;* eine *Sweep Power* Dreschmaschine ; eine *Set Stäge*geschirr; *Yankie*geschirr; *Front*geschirre [for horses in front]. Welschkorn*scheller* [also Welschkornschäler, Welschkorn*scräper*, Welschkornausmacher, hand*scheller*]; Schneid*box*; Wagen*box* [and Wagen*body*]; *Molasses-Faktry;* Mückengeschirre [Fliegen-Geschirre, Fliegennetze]; 1 *Lot Hausen's* [housings for horses]; Windmühle, [translation of windmill, for Kornschwinge]; 1 *Sink* [kitchen sink - bench]; *Martingales;* *Check*leinen; Cirkel-Säge [another has *Circular*säge] mit *Främ* und *Sträp.*

Einige Pflanzgrundbeeren von *Prince Alberts* Sorte.

CHAPTER VI.

SYNTAX.

The confusion of forms in the declension of German articles, pronouns, and adjectives, as given in print, is avoided in dialects, and on the upper Rhine all classes use the masculine nominative *der* for the accusative *den*, thus making a step towards rational grammar—the feminine *die* and the neuter *das* being equally nominative and accusative. According to Radlof, from Swisserland to Holland, on both sides of the Rhine, there is scarcely a locality where the nominative is distinguished from the accusative and the dative, and he cites as examples—"ich trinke rother Wein" (for *rothen*); "ich habe der Esel gesehen" (for *den Esel*); "ich sitze auf der Baum" (for *dem Baum*).[1] In PG. this *rother* for *rothen* is sometimes cut down to 'root,' the common PG. neuter form, particularly with the *definite* article, as in—

Ich trink d'r root wei,.   *I drink the red wine.*
Was f'r wei, wit [willst du] trinke?   *What kind of wine willst drink ?*
Ich trink tschenerli rooter wei,.[1]   *I 'generally' drink red wine.*

[1] . . . "Von der Schweiz an zu beiden seiten des Rheines hinab bis an Hollands grünzen, giebt es kaum einige Gegenden, wo man den Koch vom Kellner, den Herrn vom Knechte, den Hammer vom Ambofze, d.i. den Werfall (*Nominativ*) vom Wenfalle (*Accusativ*) und dem Wemfalle (*Dativ*) richtig zu unterscheiden vermöchte. Bald hört man nehmlich : "ich trinke rother Wein" bald : "ich habe der Esel gesehen" bald : "ich sitze auf der Baum." s.f."—*Dr. Joh. Gottl. Radlof*, Mustersaal aller teutschen Mund-arten, . . . Bonn, 1822 ; 2, 90.
Stalder (Schweiz. Idiotikon, 1812) gives the accusatives of *der* and *ein* as agreeing with the nominative, and under *ein* (1, 37) he has,—Acc. wie der Nom., welches überhaupt zu bemerken ist.
[When I read extracts from this Treatise before the Philological Society on 3 June, 1870, Prof. Goldstücker and Dr. E. Mall, the latter an Alsatian, both considered that this presumed substitution of the nominative for the accusative or dative case must be a misapprehension. Dr. Mall declared himself totally unaware of it. Both considered that it must have resulted from the disappearance of the inflectional -*m*, -*n* (the latter of which is the rule certainly in the Rhine region), and the degradation of the preceding *e* vowel into *o*. This would account for "ich trinke rother Wein," considering *rother* to mean 'roota,' but would not account for "ich habe der Esel gesehen," in which the *r* must be taken as trilled, unless we consider that first *den* was made into 'do,' and then the 'r' *evolved* as in the Cockney's 'idea-r of things.' Hence the original passages on which the assertions in the text are founded, have been added.—*Alex. J. Ellis.*]

G. Wir geben guten Lohn. PG. M'r gewwə guutər loo,. *We give good wages.*

.ən guutər freind (n guuti fraa, n guut haus) is n guut ding. *A good friend* (masc.), *wife* (fem.), *house* (neut.) *is a good thing* (neut.).

Sellər mann hət mei, huut alles ufgebrəchə. *That man has broken* (meinen) *my hat* (alles auf) *all up.*

Ich bin naus in dər hoof un bin unsərər kats uf dər schwants gətrettə, selli hət mich gekratst. (*Nep.*) *I went* (hinaus) *out, in* (G. den Hof, m.) *the yard, and trod on* (G. den Schwanz) *the tail of our cat, she scratched me.*

. . . weil ich mich geschämmt hab, bin ich uf dər schpeichər geschniikt oone ən wərt tsu saaghə. (*Nep.*) *While I shamed myself, I 'sneaked' up to* (den) *the loft without a word to say.*

G. Das Wetter ist den ganzen Tag schön gewesen. PG. s wetter iss d'r gants (or gans) daak schee, gwest. *The weather has been fine the entire day.*

G. Ich gehe in den Keller. PG. Ich gee in dər kellər. *I am going into the cellar.*

In the next, *Stuhl* being masculine, the nominative *der* is used for the dative *dem*, but the accusative *ihn* ('n) is preserved—

ər hət uf d'r schtuul k'həkt, un hət n f'rbrəchə. *He sat on the chair and has broken it.*

G. Liebe deinen Nächsten, als dich selbst. *Love thy neighbor as thyself.* PG. Liib dei, nochbər ass wii dich sclwer.

G. Lĕgĕ das Buch auf dēn Tisch. *Lay the book on the table.* PG. Lceg s buch uf d'r tisch.

Here, if 'den tisch' were used in PG. it would rather mean *this* table,' because there is a tendency to use articles as demonstratives, saying ' dœr ' for G. *dieser*, and ' sellər ' (G. *selbiger*) for G. *jener,*—' sel ' (G. selbiges) being its neuter, and ' selli ' (G. selbige) its feminine and plural. This ' sel' is found in Swisserland, and other parts of the Rhine region. Its Alsatian form *tsel*, with initial *t*, shows that it is akin to G. *dasselbe*. Notwithstanding its resemblance in form and function to Provensal *sel* or *cel*, French *celui, celle*, they are without etymologic relation. See Ch. VII., § 2. p. 43, and § 4, p. 45 ; and *Ellis*, Early English Pronunciation, p. 662, note 15.

' Das ' (the) and ' es ' (it) have a tendency to confusion under the short form 's used for both. ' Dass ' (that) remains, and

---

[1] " Dii Jarik Kaunti leit, wann sii fum roota wei, schwätzə, saaghə g'weenlich —"Ich trink rootər wei,." Wann sii awər kee rootər hen, dann trinkə sii weisser wann sii n kriighə kennə." *The Rev. D. Ziegler,* letter of Jan. 15, 1870 (literatim).

the neuter nominative article is changed from G. *das* to PG.
' des,' as in ' des buch' (the book)—but as ' des buch ' may
mean *this book*, the function of the article is performed by
reducing this ' des ' to 's, as in—

.s buch iss mei, *the book is mine*—des buch iss mei, THIS *book is mine*.

" Donn hab ich gedenkt [not *gedacht*], d e s is doch now ordlich plain
deitsch," . . . (*Rauch.*[1])   *Then I thought*, THIS *is at-any-rate ' now ' tolerably
' plain' Dutch.*

Dœr mann iss krankər (not *kränker*) wie d'r annər.   THIS *man is sicker than
the other.*   (G. als der andere.)

G. Ein Mann und eine Frau waren hier diesen Morgen.   *A man and a woman
were here this morning.*   PG. Es war ən mann un ən fraa hiir des mårighe.
There was a man and a woman here this morning.

G. Ich wünsche dass er komme.   *I wish that he come.*   PG. Ich wott (or
wott, for *wollte*) dass ær deet [G. thät] kummə.   *I would that he would come.*
Swiss—I wett, asz er chäm.   *Stalder*, 1, 112.

Swiss *asz* for *dass* is often used in PG., as in—

Wann ich geglaabt hätt 'ass er mich net betsaalt (or betsaalə deet), so hätt
ich 'm gar net gebárikt (or gebaricht).   *If I had believed that he would not pay
me, I would* (gar nicht) *not at all have* (geborgt) *trusted him.*

Wann ich gedenkt [not G. *gedacht*] hätt 'ass es net woor wæær, dann hätt ich
's net geglaabt.   *If I had not supposed it to be true, I would not have* (geglaubt)
believed it.

G. Wäre er reich, er würde nicht betteln.   *Were he rich he would not beg.*
G. Wenn er reich wäre, so würde er nicht betteln.   PG. Wann ær reich wæær,
deet ær net bettəln.   *If he were rich, he would not beg.*

PG., like Swiss,[2] dislikes the imperfect tense, and prefers
G. *Ich habe gedacht* (I have thought), to G. *Ich dachte* (I
thought), which gives forms like—

Wii ich n gesee, hab, hab ich gedenkt ær wært k'sund.   *As I saw him* (having
seen him) *I thought he would get well.*

Ich bin gangə *I have gone ;* not G. Ich gieng *I went*, not gegangen *ygone*.

Whan myn houfbond is fro the world i-gon,—*Chaucer*, (*Wright's ed.*) 1. 5629.
With menftralcy and noyfe that was (y-)maked, l. 2526.
Bet is to be (y-)weddid than to brynne. l. 5634.

PG. has also ' kummə ' (has come) for G. gekommen, showing a tendency to follow a law which caused ge- (y-, i-) to be
dropped in English.   The practice seems to have started with

---

[1] In a spelling based upon English, and not fully phonetic.   See *Ellis*, Early
English Pronunciation, pp. 654–661.
[2] *Stalder* (1, 46) says that the imperfects war, hatte, sagte, kam, rufte, kaufte,
would be scarcely understood in Swisserland.

gekommen and *gegangen*, because they are much used, and their initial guttural absorbs the guttural *g-* or *k-* of the prefix. In an Austrian dialect,[1] *ge-* disappears before *b, p, d, t, z,* as in " Ih bin kumma" (I have come), PG. Ich bin kumma.

PG. Ich hab s [G. gekauft] kaaft im schtoor.   *I bought it at the 'store.'*
Haecht mei̯, briif krikt ? *Hast* (G. gekriegt) *received my letter ?* Ich schreib n briif. *I write a letter.*

" Der Charle hat jung geheiert un   D'r ' Tscherli ' hot jung k'eiort un
hat e fleiszige Fra krickt," *Wollen-*   hot e fleissighe fraa krikt.
weber, p. 78.
' *Charley' married young and got an industrious wife.*
G. Es regne. *It may rain.*   PG. s maak (G. mag) reeghere.
G. Es regnete. *It might rain.*   PG. s kennt (G. könnt) reeghere.
G. Es habe geregnet. *It may have rained.*   PG. s konnt reeghe hawwe.

PG. has the Swiss *als* (hitherto, formerly, always), a form in which it is not shortened into *a's,* as in—

ær hot als ksaat ær wor (or wæror) miir niks schuldich. (*Ziegler*).   *He has hitherto said he is to-me nothing indebted.*

Mr. Rauch, in his partly English spelling, has—

" Er hut aw behawpt das mer set   .ær hot an behaapt dass mor set
sich net rula lussa bi seiner fraw,   sich net ' ruule' losso bei seinor fraa,
un das de weiver nix wissa fun   un dass dii weiwor niks wisso fun
denna sacha, un das es kens fun eara   denne sache, un dass es kens fun eere
bisness is we an monn vote odder   ' bissness' iss wii en mann ' woot,' odor
we oft er a l s drinkt."   wii oft ær als drinkt.

He (has) maintained that one should not (lassen) *let* (sich) *one's-self be ' ruled' by one's wife, and that the* (weiber nichts wissen) *women know nothing of such things, and that it is* (keines von ihre) *none of their ' business' how a man ' votes,' or how oft he* (als) ALWAYS *drinks.*

In the following Suabian example (Radlof 2, 17) *als* is a form of G. alles (all), and *schmieren* is used as in PG. for *to pay off, to trick.*

Kurz! i will ella eba macha   In short, I will make all so even
Dafz oim 's Herz im Leib mu'fz lacha; that the heart in one's body must laugh;
I will an de Tuifel fchmiera,   I will also trick [den] the devil
Dafz er Niemd kan verführa,   that he none can lead astray—
Hack' ihm boyde Hörner o,   chop for him both his horns off
Dafs er nimme ftecha ka-.   that he cannot thrust again.

PG. ' dass' for *als* (with the sense of *as*), and ' dass wan ' G. *als wenn* (South German of Breisgau *as wenn*) for *as if,* seems peculiar.   The German adverbial particles admit of a wide range of meaning, and in Low Austrian certain inversions occur, as *aussa* (aus-her) for G. *heraus; aussi* (aus-hin), also in old Bavarian, for G. *hinaus*, which would allow PG. 'dass' to be referred to *als dass* or da(r)als.[1] But independently of this surmise, the cutting down of the pronouns *des* (G. das) and *es* to '*s*, and *als* to *ass*, makes it as easy to accept *dass* for *als*, as 'd of English 'I 'd rather,' for *had* instead of *would*. Farther, as *da* has *als* for one of its meanings, this *dass* may be *da* with the adverbial suffix -*s*.[2]

"·des land is aw frei for mich so goot das for dich."—*Rauch*, p. 32.	. . . des land is aa frei f'r mich soo guut dass f'r dich.

This (not *the*) *country is* (auch) *also free for me as well* AS *for thee.*

"net wennicher dos sivva hunnert for dich un mich" . . .—*Rauch*, 1869.	. . . net wennichər dass siwə hunərt f'r dich un mich.

Not less THAN *seven hundred for thee and me.*

"Er will hawa dos ich bei eam aw roof in Filldelfy, un dat dos wanns tsu meiner advantage wær wann ich kumm."—*Rauch*, Aug. 16, '69.	.ær will hawə dass ich bei iim aa‚ruuf in Fildelfi, un duut dass wann s tsu meinər 'atfæntitsch' wær wann ich kumm.

He will have that I (bei) *at-the-house-of him* [G. anrufen, perverted to an English idiom] *call-on in Phildelphi* [the common pronunciation] *and* (he) *does* AS IF *it* (were) *would be to my 'advantage' if I come.*[3]

"Selly froke hut mich awer sheer gorly schwitza macha, un ich hob g'feeld yusht grawd das wann ich mich full heaser hulder tæ g'suffa het un g'mixd mit tansy, katzakraut un bebbermint."—*Rauch*, Aug. 9, 1869.	Selli frook hət mich schïr gaarli schwitsə machə, und ich hab kfiilt juscht graad dass waan ich mich fol heesər huldər tee ksəffə het un 'gmikst' mit 'tænsi' [s not as ɩ] katsəkraut un 'bebbərmint.'

[Dieselbe Frage] *That question however almost* [G. gar] *quite made me sweat, and I felt just exactly* AS IF *I had* (G. gesoffen) *drunk myself full of hot* (G. Holder) *elder tea, and 'mixed' with 'tansy' catnip and 'peppermint.'*

"'s scheint m'r wærklich as wann du im sinn bätscht in deine alte daaghə noch a Dichtər tsu gewe (tsu wærrə). Awer ich færricht 's iss tsu schpot; du hätscht ə paar joer friiər aa‚fange sollə, dann wær viileicht ebbəs draus [G. worden] warrə."[4] *It appears to me really* AS IF *you intended in your old days yet to become a poet. But I fear it is too late; you should have commenced a few years earlier, then perhaps something might have come of it.*

[1] Suabian condenses *da unten* to *dunda*. The Rev. D. Ziegler suggests that this 'dass' may have arisen from a *d*, as of 'grad' (G. gerade) before 'as' of *als*, as in—ær schwätzt grad *as* wann [G. wenn] ær reich wær. (He speaks just as if he were rich.)   [2] See *Hald.* Affixes. p. 213.
[3] The present tense ('wann ich kumm') is used here for the G. subjunctive *wenn ich käme*.
[4] The Rev. D. Ziegler, transliterated by himself.

The next is from the description of a willow-tree with the 'nesht' (pl. of G. *nast*[1]) branches broken by ice.[2]

"Er guckt net gans so stattlich meh,	.ær gukt net gans soo achtattlich mee
Er guckt net gans so gross un' schoe	ær gukt net gans soo gross un schee,
D a s wie er hut die anner woch	dass wii ær het dii anər woch
Wu'r all sei nesht hut katte noch."	wuu 'r all sei, nescht het kattə noch.

It (nicht mehr) *no more looks quite so stately, it looks not* (ganz) *quite so large and fine,* AS THAT *it did the* (andere) *other week,* (wo er *where he*) *when it* (hat gehabt) *has had all its boughs.*

At present PG. is exhibiting a tendency to drop G. *zu* (to), the sign of the so-called infinitive, altho in the following examples perhaps most speakers would use it.

Wann fangscht aa, [tsu] schaffə ? *When do you begin* [to] *work ?*
Ich hab aa fangə schaffə. *I have begun* (to) *work.*
. . . fiil annəri hen hart prowiirt sich farne naus schaffə. (*Rauch*.)
Many others (have) *tried hard* (to) *work themselves* (G. vorn) *forward.*

---

[1] The usual German is *ast*, pl. *äste*. Schmeller (*Mundarten Bayerns*, art. 610) notices the following examples of this initial *n* in Bavarian dialects; his phonetical spelling is given in italics, and interpreted into the present in brackets : der *Nä'n* [Noon] 'A'then : *Ndst* [nost] Ast; die *Näf'n* [noozn] 'A'sen ; *Naff·l* [nassl] Assel ; *Ndrb* [narb] Arb ; *Neichté* [neichte] Eichte ; *Nuərs'* [Nuərə] Urhab ; *Nuefch* [Nuesch] Uesch. In art. 545 he also gives the form *s Luefsch*, and in art. 636, the form *s⁻Rdufⁿ*, for Uesch, a gutter, and 'A'sen, a beam or joist. *Ndrb* is the staple on the door, which carries the padlock ; *Eicht* is a little while. The following are examples of omitted initial *n*, (ib. art. 611) ; *dər* '*Apoleon* Napoleon ; '*idə*' nider, '*Ankinet* Nanquinet ; '*Impfs⁻'burg* Nymphenburg ; ganz '*atürli*' natürlich ; '*eben*, '*isbm* neben ; '*achər*, '*achə*' nachher ; '*E'st*, '*isft* Nest. St. Antwein und St. Nantwein, Aventin Chron. Edit. v. 1566, fol. 470.—Compare the English added initial *n* in *niokname* (nekename for ekename, see Pr. Parv.), *niggot*, *nugget* for ingot ; *newt* for eft, ewt ; *nawl* for awl ; *nunkle* for uncle ; *Nan*, *Ned*, *Noll*, for Anne, Edward, Oliver :—and the omitted initial *n* in *adder* (old edres and neddres), *apron* for napron, *eyas* for nias.—A. J. Ellis.

[2] Poems. By Rachel Bahn. York, Pa. 1869. Containing twenty pages of "Poems in Pennsylvania Dutch." Noticed by me in Trübner's *American and Oriental Literary Record*, Jan. 24, 1870, p. 634. The following may be consulted also :
Gemälde aus dem Pennsylvanichen Volksleben . . . . von L. A. Wollenweber. Philadelphia und Leipzig. Schäfer und Koradi, 1869.
Harbaugh's Harfe. Gedichte in Pennsylvanisch-Deutscher Mundart. Philadelphia, Reformed Church Publication Board, 1870.
On the German Vernacular of Pennsylvania. By S. S. Haldeman. Trans. Am. Philological Association, 1869-70.
Lancaster Pa. WEEKLY ENTERPRISE (newspaper), with a weekly article by Mr. Rauch.
Der Waffenlose Wächter (monthly newspaper). Gap P.O., Lancaster Co. Pa.
Early English Pronunciation, . . . by Alexander J. Ellis, F.R.S., F.S.A. London, 1871. Twelve pages (652-65) are devoted to Pennsylvania German.
P'älzische G'schichte' . . . von Franz von Kobell. München, 1863. In the main, this little volume of 'Palatinate Stories' comes nearer to Pennsylvania German than any other I have seen.

"De mæd . . . hen kea so kleany bonnets g'hat di nix sin for hitz odder kelt ; es wara rechtshaffene bonnets, das mer aw sea hut kenne ohna de brill uf du."—*Nep.*

Dii meed hen kee, soo klee ni 'bannets' katt dii niks sin f'r hits ed'r kelt ; ee waars rechtschaffeno 'bannets,' dass m'r aa seea het kenno, oone dii brill uf [tsu] duu,.

The girls (haben gehabt) *had no such small 'bonnets'* (die) *which are nothing for heat or* (kälte) *cold ; there were honest 'bonnets' that* (mir) *one* (such) *also could see without putting the spectacles on.*

PG. Sometimes distinguishes between the present tense and the aorist, as in Swiss—" er thuot choh " (he does come)—

Sellər hund knarrt.   *That dog growls* (has a habit of growling).
Sellər hund tuut (G. thut) knarrə.   *That dog is now growling.*
D'r mann tuut essə—ər iss am essə.   *The man is eating—he is at eating.*

PG. does not use equivalents to *neither* and *nor.*

G. Er ist *weder* reich *noch* arm.   *He is neither rich nor poor.*   PG. ər iss net reich un net aarm.
E. He is *either* sick *or* lazy.   PG. ər iss krank odər faul.   (Or, adopting *either* and its idiom) ər iss 'iitər' krank ədər faul.

In a case like the last, no matter how well the speaker knows English, he must *not* pronounce a word like 'either' in the English mode, because it would be an offense against the natural rhetoric of the dialect.

CHAPTER VII.

COMPARISONS WITH OTHER DIALECTS.

§ 1.   PG. *not Swiss.*

PG. is not Swiss, altho it has a number of Swiss characteristics, and the line (Radlof, 2, 68)—

> " Was isch säll für e sufere kärli ?"

is very near its PG. form—

> Was isch sel f'r e saubor kærli ?   *What sort of cleanly fellow is that ?*

PG. has both 'ær iss' and 'ær isch' (he is) according to the locality, of which the latter may be less common. The Rev. D. Ziegler (a native, like myself) refers the 'isch' variety to the Mennonite and Dunker population, and as there were many Dunkers (or Tunkers) where my early years were passed, I heard more of this than of the other.

The indicative mood present tense of *haben* and *sein* are, with some variations, as follows (Stalder, 1, 47–50)—

Swiss.	PG.	Swiss.	PG.
i hab ;	ich hab, hap, *I have.*	i bi ;	ich bin, *I am.*
de hest ;	du hescht, *thou hast.*	de bisch, bist ;	du bischt, *thou art.*
er hed, hett ;	ær hot, *he has.*	er isch, ist ;	ær iss, isch, *he is.*
mer hend ;	m'r hen, *we have.*	mer sind ;	m'r sin, *we are.*
der bend ;	d'r hent, *you have.*	der sind ;	d'r sint, *you are.*
sj hend ;	sii hen, *they have.*	sj sind ;	sii sin, *they are.*

Here the dative singular *mir* (to me) is used in the nominative plural instead of *wir* (we), and also in impersonal expressions ; and the dative singular *dir* (to thee) is similarly used for *Ihr* (you), as in 'd'r sint' for G. *Ihr seid* (you are). G. *Ihr habet* (you have) has forced its *t* upon the first and third persons plural of the Swiss forms ; and in PG. the second person is sometimes forced upon the third, as in the following, from the Wollenweber's Gemälde (in the German character), 1869, p. 124,—

For äbout 32 Johr z'rick, do h e n t unsre ... Schaffleut ... im Stenbruch geschafft, un sten gebrochs, for do grosze Damm zu fixe.

'Fr ebaut' tswce-un-dreissich joor tsrik, do hent unsre . . . schaffleit . . . im schtee,bruch geschafft, un schtee, gebrocho f'r di grosse 'damm' tsu fixə.

'*For about*' *thirty-two years back, here have our laborers worked in the quarry, and quarried stone to* '*fix*' *the big* '*dam.*' (Here the English *fix* and *dam* are used, instead of G. *fixiren*, and *der damm*.)

Here the first *for* may be regarded as English, but the second occurs in the Palatinate—"for den Herr Ring sehr ungünschtig" (Kobell), *for Mr. Ring very unfavorable*—"for sei Lügerei,"—*for his truthlessness.*

The next is extracted from a poem by Tobias Witmer, dated from the State of New York, June 1, 1869, printed in the 'Father Abraham' English newspaper, in roman type, and reprinted Feb. 18, 1870. The original spelling is that of Mr. Rauch, and is not reproduced. Dialectic words are s p a c e d, and English words are here put in *italics*. The translation is rather free.

Geburts-Daak—An mei, Alti.

Oo wass is schennər uf dər welt
d a s s blimlin, root un weiss ?
un bloo un g e e l,[1] im ærblə[2] felt
wass sin sii doch so *neis* !
Ich wees noch guut, in s e l l e r tseit
hab ich niks liiwərs duu,[3]
d a s s in dii wissə—lang un breit
so blimlin ksuucht wii duu.
Doch iss əs schun ə lang-i tseit
sid'r ich dart in dem felt,
dii blimlin ksuucht, uf lang un breit,
un uf dei, *busəm* k s c h p e l l t.
D' r h e n t emool ə gærtl kat—
mei, schwestərli un duu ;   [schpaat
ich hab ə *pripeerd* mit hak un
dii blummə nei, tsu duu,;
un wuu ich hab im grossi s c h w e e l,
dii kii dart h i n n ə ksuucht,

Birthday—To my Wife.

Oh what is finer in the world
than flowrets red and white ?
and blue and yellow in the field
how beautiful and bright.
I know yet well that in that time,
nought would I rather do,
than in the meadows long and wide
such flowrets seek as you.
Yet it is quite a lengthened time,
since I in yonder field,
sought out the flowers far and wide,
and on thy bosom pinned.
You also had a garden bed—
you and my sister fair,
which I prepared with hoe and spade
to set the flowers there ;
and where I in the ample vale[4]
the cattle there had sought,

[1] G. gelb, Ohg. gelo, Swiss, etc., *gäl yellow.*
[2] Not PG. ærpsə, G. erbsen (peas), but a form of *erdbeers* (strawberry).
[3] G. Ich habe nichts lieber gethan. (G. adj. and adv. *lieber*, adverbialised with -s.) *Nothing would I rather have done.*
[4] The word is "schwœhl" in the original—probably borrowed from the local English word *swale.* Wuu, G. wo, *where.* The author was born in 1816, at Niagara, in a small colony which had emigrated from Lancaster county, Pennsylvania—his father in 1811. The colony received additions about the year 1830.

dii *lædi-schlipporss*, weiss un g e e l,
hab ich mit, heem gebracht,
un hab sii in s e l gærtl plaxtst
bei nacht, in muundəs licht :　[*wantst* [1]
d'r h e n t s net gwist, bis juscht *æt*
h e n t dür s *gegest* s war mich.

the lady-slippers, gold, and pale,
with me I homeward brought,
and in that garden bed at night
I set them when the moon was light.
You did not know who it could be,
but all at once you thought of me.

§ 2.　PG. *not Bavarian.*

PG., Bavarian, Austrian and Suabian have the vowel of
fall, and nasal vowels. In Pangkofer's *Gedichte in Altbayer-
ischer Mundart*, are the PG. words 'aa' *also;* 'bissel' *a little;*
'ebbas,' G. etwas *something;* 'do is' *there is;* 'glei' (also
Austrian) *soon;* 'sunst,' G. sonst *besides;* 'frumın,' G. fromm
kind; 'kloo' *claw;* 'kumma,' G. gekommen *come;* Ohg.
'coman' and 'cuman' *to come;* 'mir' *we,* for G. wir; 'sel,' G.
dasselbe *that-same;* but PG. has not 'mi' *me;* 'di' *thee;*
'hoarn' *horn;* 'hout' *has;* 'thuan' *to do;* 'g'spoasz,' *sport;*
'oamal' *once;* 'zwoa' *two,* G. zwei, PG. 'tswee'; wei, PG.
'weip' *wife;* zon, PG. 'tṣum' *to the.*

The following example of upper Bavarian is given by Klein,[2]
beside which a PG. version is placed for comparison.

"Schau, nachbe', wàs mei' freud' is,—
In suntàe', in der frûe,
Gern lûs' i' in mei'n gâârt'l
'n kircheläut'n zue.

Sii nochbər wass moi, freet iss !
Am sundaak marrgbə frii,
Gærn həær [3] ich in mei̱m gærtli
Dii kærchə-*bellə* hii̱.[4]

"Dà is 's so still und hâcmli',
Kâe' lärm, kâe g'schrâe kimmt 'nei':
In'n himmi kà's nit schöner
W' as in mei'n gâârt'l sei'."

Do 's iss so schtill un heemlich,
Kco, jacht, kee, kschrei kummt nei̱.;
Im himml kann s not scbce,nər
Wii s in mei̱m gærtl sei.

See neighbor, what my joy is, on Sunday in the morn ; I listen in my garden,
to the church-bell ring. Here it is so still and calm, no turmoil, no strife comes
within ; in heaven (kann es nicht) *it cannot be fairer than* (es) *it is in my little*
garden.

---

[1] = *at once.* Dr. Jones, 1701, gives 'wæns, wænst' as the English pronunciation in Shropshire and some parts of Wales. Buchanan, 1766, gives 'wæns'
as correct English.—*A. J. Ellis.*
[2] Die Sprache der Luxemburger. Luxemburg, 1855.
[3] This word varies to heer, and horch may be used.
[4] Here *hii̱*, is given for the rhyme, the proper word being G. *da*, PG. 'doo.'
On this account the Rev. D. Ziegler makes the following variation on my
version—　　　Sii noochbər was mei, frect iss,
　　　　　　　Wann ich im gærtli schtee,
　　　　　　　Gærn heer ich frii am sundaak
　　　　　　　Dii kærchəbellə geh.

§ 3. PG. *not Suabian.*

The Pennsylvania Germans have traditional stories against the Suabians, although their population is in part derived from the upper (Pfalz) Palatinate; and some Suabians settled in Northumberland County, Pa., the evidence of which remains in the name of a stream, *Schwaben* (or *Swope*) Creek.

PG. resembles Suabian in using 'e, ee' for ö, and 'ii' for ü—in the loss of infinitive -*n*,—in turning final -*n* into a nasal vowel (as in sei͜, for *seyn*), and in saying 'du bischt,' 'du kannscht,' etc. (for G. *du bist*), 'du witt' for *du willst;* 'nimme' for *nicht mehr;* 'glei' for *gleich* in the sense of *soon* —but the adjective 'gleich' (similar) remains. PG. does not turn *o* into *au*, as in Suabian '*braut*,' '*hauch*,' for *brot, hoch;* nor cut down G. *ich habe* to '*i ha*'; it does not add elements, as in '*bois*' for G. *bös*, PG. '*bees*,' '*bluat*' for G. *blut*, '*reacht*' for *recht*, '*kuine*' for *keine*, and '*stuinige fealder*' for *steinige felder*, a peculiarity of Suabian, Alsatian, Swiss, Bavarian and its kin Austrian. PG. has archaic '*hees*' (hot) for G. *heisz*, but nothing like Bavarian *haas*.

Difference of pronunciation causes confusion of speech between speakers of different dialects, as shown by Dr. Rapp in his Physiologie der Sprache, 4, 131. In the 'Fliegende Blätter' (13, 158) there is a dialogue called 'Ein Deutsch-Böhme' (a German Bohemian), between a *Bauer* and a *Städter*—but a Swiss speaker is now added, with the rejoinder to his remark.

Bauer. Wie is de Suppe so häsz!
Städter. Man sagt ja nicht häsz, sondern heisz. Has [G. hase, PG. haas *hare*] nennt man das Thier. . . .
Bauer. Dös häszt bei uns Hös!
Städter. Das ist wieder falsch. Hös bedeutet jenes Kleidungsstück, womit Eure langen Beine bedeckt sind.
Bauer. Dös häszt Hus!
Schweitzer. Aber mer sind jetz im Huus.
Bauer. Dös iss 'n *Haus*!

Diminutives in PG. and Suabian are made with -li; both use 'des' for *das*, 'uffm' for *auf dem*, 'biira' for *birnen*, 'g'hat' or 'kat' for *gehabt*, 'suu,' for *sohn*, 'schoof' for *schâf*, 'Schwop' for *Schwâbe*, 'als' for *alles*, and 'as' for *als*.

§ 4.　PG. *not Alsatian.*

In the very German county of Berks there is an Elsass township, which indicates an Alsatian influence. As a German province of France,[1] two languages are in use, and are taught in the schools, but the French is Germanised in pronunciation, as may be verified among the Alsatian and German servants of Paris. Being akin to Swiss and Suabian, PG. has some points in common with this dialect, without being influenced by French.

Alsatian differs from PG. in having *i haa* for 'ich hab,' *tsel* for 'sel' (G. *derselbe*), *bluət* for 'bluut,' *üss* for 'aus,' *hüs* for 'haus,' *tsiit* for 'tseit,' *bisch* for 'bischt,' *biim* for 'bei'm,' *morje* for 'marrghə.'

PG. and Alsatian turn some *b*-s to *w*, they have the vowels of *fall, what, up,* and have 'prowiirə' for *probiren,* 'ass' for *als,* 'do' for *da,* 'joo' for *ja,* 'joor' for *jahr,* 'hoor' for *haar,* 'fun' for *von,* 'isch' for *ist,* 'jets' for *jetzt,* 'uff' for *auf,* 'druff' for *dorauf,* 'uff'm' for *auf dem,* 'raus' for *daraus,* 'draan' for *daran,* 'iwwər' for *über,* 'dno' for *darnach;* PG. 'əffə,' Alsat. 'offə,' G. *ofen;* 'bal' for *bald,* 'm'r' for *wir,* 'm'r muss' for *man musz,* 'mee' for *mehr,* 'welli' for *welche;* 'was batt s' (what boots it).

The following lines (Radlof, 2, 110) are extracted from a piece of Alsatian which well illustrates the concurrent use of two languages. The French should be read in the German mode. Other French words occur in Radlof's examples, such as allong *allons,* tur *tour,* schalu *jaloux,* anterpoo *entrepôt,* bangenet *baïonnette.* The original of the following is in German (gothic) and French (roman) print according to the lan-

---

[1] This was written before the Franco-German war which re-annexed Alsatia to Germany. When I read out the first example in Chapter VIII. (*Wüdər aa geschmiirt*), to the Philological Society, on communicating this paper, 3 June, 1870, Dr. E. Mall, an Alsatian, who was present, remarked that it reminded him throughout of his native dialect, of which he thoroughly recognized the pronunciation. I may remark that I have never heard PG. pronounced, although I have heard Austrian, Saxon, Rhenish, Bavarian, and Swiss dialects, and read solely by the phonetic orthography here given.—*A. J. Ellis.*

guage, here imitated by roman and italic types.   The speaker
is telling a friend how she was addressed by a stranger :

> So kummt ä Wälscher her, und macht mit Kumblemente,
> Und redt mich gradzu an.—Mach er kein Spargemente,[1]
> Hab i glich zu ihm g'sait. Loss Er, was ich 'ne bitt,
> Mich mine Waih fortgehn ; ich kenn de Herre nit.
> *„Sans avoir, front er mich, l'honneur de vous connaître,*
> *„Vous êtes seule ici, voulez-vous me permettre*
> *„De vous offrir mon bras pour vous accompagner ?*
> *Allez, Mousié, sa ich, allez-vous promener,*
> Und spar Er sich die müh ; Er musz sich nit trumpire,
> Ich bin von dene nit die mer am Arm kann führe.[2]
> *„Vous êtes bien cruelle, arrêtez un moment,*
> Sait er, und kummt soglich mit sine Santimang. . . .
> Zu diene, hab i g'sait ; losz Er mich aber gehn,
> Min Ehr erlaubt mir nit noch länger do zu stehn.
> *„Je n'insisterai pas, mais veuillez bien m'apprendre,*
> *„Si demain en ces lieux vous daignerez vous rendre.*
> Behüt mich Gott davor ! i gib kein *rendez-vus.*
> *Adié, mousié, adié, je ne vus* [sic] *verrai plus.*

Translation.—Thus comes a Frenchman up and proceeds with compliments,
and (an-redet) accosts me (gerade zu) directly. Make no formalities,[1] I said
to him at once. Let me, what I beg ('ne, G. ihn) him, continue (meinen weg)
my way—I know not the (herren) gentlemen. " *Without having,*" he (frägt)
asked me, " *the honor of knowing you, you are alone here, will you permit me to
offer you my arm to accompany you ?*" Go, sir, (sagte) said I, *Proceed with your
walk*—and spare himself the trouble ; he must not deceive himself, I am not of
those who can be conducted on the arm.[2] " *You are very cruel, stay a moment,*"
says he—and comes at once with his sentiment. . . . At your service, I said,
he should let me go, my honor would not allow me to stand there longer. " *I
do not insist, but will you kindly inform me, if to-morrow in these places you will
deign to return.*" Preserve me heaven from it ! I give no *rendez-vous ; adieu,
sir, adieu, I will not see you more.*

§ 5.   PG. *is akin to several South German Dialects.*

Like *Suabia*, the name of *Pfalz* has disappeared from the
map of Europe, and what was once the Lower Palatinate, is
now to be looked for chiefly in Baden, Bavaria, and Darmstadt.

[1] F. E. Petri (Handbuch der Fremdwörter, 1845) explains *Spargimént* or
Spargemént as "ein ausgestroutes Gerücht, Ausgesprenge, Geträtsch oder Gerede ;
Aussprengsel," in short, *gossip* or *idle talk*, evidently from Latin *spargere.*—
A. J. Ellis.
[2] Compare Goethe's *Faust* —
  Faust.   Mein schönes Fräulein, darf ich wagen,
         Meinen Arm und Geleit Ihr anzutragen ?
  Margarete.   Bin weder Fräulein, weder schön,
         Kann ungeleitet nach Hause gehn.—*A. J. E.*

It was partly bounded by Alsatia, Baden, and Würtemberg, and Manheim was the chief city. A few examples, condensed from Kobel, will show the nearness of its dialect to PG.

So nehmt er dann desz Album desz uff 'm Tisch gelego is. *So takes he then the album that is laid on the table.* So is 'm glei' ei'gfalle'. *So it soon happened to him.* Guck emol, do is er, mer kennt 'n. *Look once, here he is, one knows him.* Wei is er dann do drzu kumme? *How then has he come?* Desz will ich Ihne sage. *That I will tell you.* Mer hot nix mehr vun 'm g'hört. *Nothing more has been heard of him.* Mir babe [PG. mr hen] alls minanner 'gesse. *We ate all together.* Juscht am selle Tag is e' Gascht a'kummo. *Precisely on that day a guest arrived.* Mit emo finschtre' Gesicht. *With a dark face.* Sacha macha for die Leut. *To make things for people.* Bsunnors *especially;* ghat *had;* drbei *thereby;* schun *already;* sunscht nix *besides nothing;* drvun *thereof;* eens *one;* zweo *two;* keens *none;* unner *under;* druff *on;* johr *year;* wohr *true;* kummt rei [PG. rei] *come in;* ne *no;* jetz' *now;* gedenkt *supposed;* fraa *woman;* kopp *head;* weesz *knows;* meeschter *master;* e' gut' kind *a good child.*

The South German dialect of Breisgau has G. *er hilft* (he helps, PG. ær helft), *g'seit* (as in Alsatia) for *gesagt*, PG. 'ksaat,' *us* for G. and PG. 'aus,' *i* for *ich*, *herrli* for *herrlich*, (PG. hærrlich), *wön* for *wollen*, *zit* (as in Alsatia) for *seit*, *aue* for *augen* (eyes, PG. aughə, Alsat. auə), *de* for *du*, *gen* for *gegeben* (given, PG. gewwə, sometimes suppressing *ge-*, to which attention has been called). Besides *gen*, the following Allemanic example (Radlof, 2, 99) contains *wore* for *geworden*, and *uskratzt* for *ausgekratzt*—

"Se han kurzwilt un Narrethei triebe, un am End isch der Hirt keck wore, un het em Mümmele e Schmützle gen, un se het em seldrum d'Aue nit uskratzt."

They trifled and fooled, and finally the shepherd (ist keck geworden) *became bold, and* (hat gegeben) *gave* (dem) *to the water nymph a kiss, and she did not* (dasselbe darum) *on-that-account* ('em' for *ihm*) *scratch out his eyes.*

In the following examples, the Breisgauish and PG. are probably more nearly allied than might be supposed from a comparison of the spelling. The Alsatian and PG. are in the same alphabet.

German.	Breisgau.	Alsace.	PG.	English.
regenbogen,	regeboge,	râjobâu-o,	reeghabooghə,	*rainbow.*
wo, von,	wu, vun,	wuu, fun,	wuu, fun,	*where, of.*
da, mal,	do, mol,	doo, mool,	doo, mool,	*here, times.*
schaf,	schof,	schoof,	schoof,	*sheep.*
schlafen,	schlofe,	schloofe,	schloofə,	*to sleep.*
und, gelt,	un, gel,	un, gel,	un, gel,	*and, truly!*
wohnen,	wuhne,	woonə,	wuunə,	*to reside.*
kommen,	kumme,	kummə,	kummə,	*to come.*
gesehen,	g'schne,	g'sên,	kseenə,	*seen.*
jahr, auch,	johr, au,	joor, au,	joor, aa,	*year, also.*
nachbar,	nochber,	nochbər,	nochbər,	*neighbor.*
nicht, nichts,	nit, nix,	net, niks,	net, niks,	*not, nothing.*
selbiger,	seller,	tsellər,	sellər,	*that one.*

German.	Breisgau.	Alsace.	PG.	English.
es ist jotzt,	's isch jetz,	es isch jets,	s isch jets,	it is now.
etwas,	ebbes,	eppəs,	ebbəs, eppəs,	something.
nunmehr,	nummce,	(nimmə),	nummi,	now.
darunter,	runter,	(nuntər),	runtər,	under.
als, einem,	as, eme,	as, əmə,	as, mə,	as, to a.
man kann,	mer kann,	m'r kann,	mər kann,	one can.
sie haben,	sie hen, han,	sii haan,	sii hen,	they have.
wir sind,	mer sin,	m'r sin,	m'r sin,	we are.
weiszt,	wescht,	weischt,	weescht,	knowest.
das, hat,	des, het,	des, hot,	des, hət,	the, has.

In the next three lines of Breisgauish (Radlof, 2, 95) words which agree more or less with PG. are in italic—

"*Do isch au kei Plätzle meh,*   Here is also no spot more,
Wu i könnt *mi* Haupt [1] *hinlege,*   where I might my head repose,
Wenn i *vun der Arbet geh.*"   when I from my work depart.

The following (Radlof, 2, 92) is also in the Breisgau dialect:

Siehsch de, Kind, de Regeboge, . . .   Seest thou child the rainbow, . . .
Gel, das isch e Pracht vun Farbe, . . .   truly it is a glory of color, . . .
Nqeh het jetz mit de Sine   Noah has now with (the) his [people]
E Johannisfirle g'macht,   made a (midsummer) Johannes-fire [2]
Un in Herrlikeit un Pracht   and in splendor and glory
Isch der Herr debi erschine,   the Lord (dabei) thereat appeared,
Un zum Noch het er g'sproche :   and to Noah has he spoken :
Guck, e Zeiche setz i fest,   Behold, a sign I firmly set   [me,
Wil de Fride mit mer hest,   whilst thou (hast) keepst peace with
's Wort des hab i niemol broche   the word—that have I never broken
Un de Herr het's Wort au g'halte,   and the Lord has the word also kept,
Den der Regeboge steht,   for the rainbow stands
Wenn Gott au im Wetter geht,   whenever God goes in the tempest,
Un er loazt de Zorn nit walte.   and he (lässt) allows not (den) the
      [anger to rule.

[1] Scarcely PG., ' kəp ' (G. kopf) being used.
[2] See Pulleyn's Etym. Compendium, 1853, at BONE-FIRES. [See also, Jacob Grimm, *Deutsche Mythologie*, pp. 567-597, for fires generally, and pp. 583-593, for these Midsummer fires in particular.—*A. J. Ellis.*]

CHAPTER VIII.

EXAMPLES.

§ 1. *Wiidər aa,geschmiirt.*

¶ 1. Dass dii meed ən wunnərbaarər schtəff sin, wen [wann?] sii f'r mennə ausgrukə, wærd iir aa schun ausgefunnə hawə. Sii sin so schlippərich wii ən flsch, un wan m'r meent m'r hätt cens fescht, dan knabbərt 's schun an nər annərə ang'l.

TRICKED AGAIN.—*That the maidens are a wondrous matter if they* (ausgucken) *look out for husbands* (werdet Ihr) *will you* (auch) *also have* (schon) *already discovered. They are as slippery as a fish, and when one supposes* (subjunctive er hätte) *he might have one fast,* (it nibbles) *there is already nibbling at* (einer andern) *another hook.*

¶ 2. Ich hab eich do schun foor 'səm' tscit tərik f'rtseelt, wii ich mit d'r 'Hænnə' ei,kummə bin, un was f'r 'kælkəleesch'nss' dass ich gemacht hab f'r n 'schtoor' úftsusétsə an dem alti Schnüpikl seinər kreits-schtross.

I have recounted (euch) *to you here 'some' time ago, how I paid attentions to 'Hannah,' and the 'calculations' that I made to set up* [an English idiom] *a 'store' at old Schniepickel's Crossroads.*

¶ 3. 'Well,' selli tscit hab ich mich bei d'r 'Hænnə' wiischt aa,geschmiirt gefunnə (kfunnə), f'r ich hab gemeent, dass sii niimand sunscht 'gleichə,' un liiwər drei moonat lang gebrootənə rattə fressə deet, wii an eenighər annərər kærl tsu denkə—

'Well,' that time I found myself badly[1] tricked with 'Hannah,' for I believed that she 'liked' nobody else, and (thät lieber fressen) *would rather devour fried rats three months long, than to think on any other fellow ;*

¶ 4. un dii 'seem' tseit hat sii dem 'Sœm' Hinnərbee, 'kumpanii' gewwə, un tsu annəri ksaat, sii wətt sich liiwər ufhenkə un

---

[1] A Swiss use of the G. wüst (waste, confused, wild).

4

d'r hals mit d'r həls-sceg apschneidə, as so on alt 'griinharn' wii
mich heiərə.

*and the ' same' time she gave ' Sam ' Hinterbein 'company,' and said
to others, she would rather hang herself and cut off the neck with the
wood-saw* (als) *than to marry such an old greenhorn as me.*

¶ 5. Du kannscht dür denkə, dass mich sel f'rtscrnt hot un dass
ich mei, 'plœns' weeghə schtoorhaltə an dem kreitsweek pletalich
ge-ennərt hab.

You can imagine to yourself that that (verzürnt) *angered me, and
that* (plötzlich) *suddenly I* (habe geändert) *changed my plans about
storekeeping at the Crossway.*

¶ 6. Ich hab mich dann ən bissl rúmgegúkt un gefúnnə dass
drəwə an d'r 'Passəm krik' ən 'ncisi opning' f'r n tíchtighər
'schmœrtər' kœrl wii ich eenər bin, wœr.

I then looked me (ein bisschen herum) *a little round and* (gefunden)
found that (droben) *up on ' Possum creek' was a ' nice opening ' for a*
(tüchtig *tight*) *capable ' smart' fellow, as I am one.*

¶ 7. Dart am ek wuunt d'r alt ' Ecb' Windbeissər uf m groosi
schtik land ; dem sei, 'Mceri' hət m'r 'əbaut' aa,kschtannə, un
alləs sunscht dart rum hət m'r recht guut gefállə (kfallə), juscht
hət dii 'Mceri' so gaar eewich füil schweschtər un briidər, dass als
kee, plats f'r uns tsweeo im haus waar, un in dii scheir geeə mussto,
wann m'r mit ən-annər schwetsə wəttə.

There on the corner lives old 'Abe' Windbeisser on a large piece (of)
land ; whose ' Mary about' pleased me, and all (sonst dort herum)
besides there-about pleased me right well, only Mary had (gar ewig so
viel) *quite ever so many sisters and brothers, that* (there) *was always
no place for us two in the house, and* (we) *must go in the barn when
we would speak with oneanother.*

¶ 8. Sell hət m'r 'əf-koors' net so árik aa,kschtannə, awər
(aawər) dii Mceri hət gemeent des wœr niks, m'r misst sich ewwo
tsu helfə wissə.

*That 'of-course' was not so very agreeable to me, but Mary con-
sidered that to be nothing ; one must know* (eben) *exactly how to help
one's self.*

¶ 9. En tseit lang iss 'nau' alləs guut gangə, meini 'kœlkə-
leeschənss' waarə wiidər 'reddi' un dii Mceri hət mir tsu
f'rschteeə gewwə, dass ich eenichə tseit mit iirom daadi schwetsə
un dann d'r parrər [and parrə] beschtéllə kennt.

(*For*) *some time* '*now*' *all went well, my* '*calculations*' *were again* '*ready*,' *and Mary had given me to understand that any time I could speak with her* (Swiss dädi) *father, and then engage the minister.*

¶ 10. 'Well,' d'r neekscht sundaak, ich hab iim ksaat dass ich un sei‚ Meeri unsər meind ufgemacht hättɔ tsu heiərə, un froog iin ep ær eɔnich eppəs [or ebbəs] dageeghə hätt.   Nee‚, secht ær, ich hab niks dageeghə, aawər həscht du dann dii 'Mænda' heit kscene ?

'*Well*' *the next Sunday I told him that I and his Mary had* (English idiom) *made up our* '*mind*' *to marry, and asked him* (ob) *if he had* (einiges etwas) *any*(some)*thing there-against.   No,* (*sägt,* for G. sagte) *said he, I have nothing against it—but have you seen* '*Amanda*' *today ?*

¶ 11. "Iir hen mich lets f'rschtannə," saag ich, "ich will dii Meeri heiərə, net dii Mændə."   (Du muscht wissə, dii Mændə iss ¹əbaut' seks joor eltər wii dii Meeri un net neekscht soo guutgukich.)

"*You have understood me* [Swiss and SG. ʝetz] *wrongly,*" *say I,* "*I wish to marry* '*Mary*' *and not* '*Amanda*'."   (*You must know,* '*Amanda*' *is* '*about*' *six years older than* '*Mary*,' *and not* (next) *near so goodlooking.*)

¶ 12. "Joo, ich hab dich recht guut f'rschtannə, aawər du bischt noch net 'ufgepooscht.'   Geschtər marighə iss dii Mændɔ nooch 'Hen' Greifdaalərs 'schtoor' un hət sich eppəs kaaft—'Griischən' Bendər glaab ich heescht sii des ding.

"*Yes, I have understood you right well, but you are not yet* '*posted*' *up.   Yesterday morning* '*Amanda*' *went to* '*Hen.*' *Gripedollar's* '*store*' *and bought herself something—* '*Grecian*' *Bend* (pun on *bend* and *bänder,* ribbons,) *I believe she calls the thing.*

¶ 13. "Wii dii Meeri sel geseenɔ (or kseenə) hət, wærd sii gans (or gants) närrisch dofoor', un fangt aa‚ mit d'r Mændə tsu handlə, weil d'r 'schtoorkiipor' juscht dii céntsighə moschiin' katt hət.

When Mary saw it she becomes quite silly (dafür) *for it, and begins to bargain with Amanda, as the* '*storekeeper*' (hat gehabt) *had but the single machine.*

¶ 14. "Well, sii sin net eenich [geworden] warrɔ bis geeghə oowət, un dann hen sii 'egriid,' das dii Meeri dich tsu d'r Mændə ufgept, un dii Mceri dii Griischən Bendər kriikt !"

" *Well, they were not* (einig) *in accord till* (gegen abend) *towards evening, and then they 'agreed' that Mary would give you up to Amanda, and she should get the Grecian Bend.*"

¶ 15. F'rschwappt? Mich uf den 'Griischən' Bendər 'f'rschwappt,' oone mich ærscht tsu frooghə?!

'*Swapped*'! *Me* '*swapped*' *on the Grecian Bend*, (ohne mich erst zu fragen) *without first asking me?!*

¶ 16. "So schteet s 'nau,' dii Mændə is drunnə im kuuschtall, wann du f'lcicht ærscht mit iir dərweeghə schwetsə witt."

"*So stands it 'now,' Amanda is* (darunter) *down there at the stable, if you perhaps* (willst) *will first speak with her about it.*"

¶ 17. Ich? mit iir dərweeghə schwetsə? Iss gaar not nootwennich! Wann mich deini meed kaafə, f'rkaafə un f'rschwappə kennə, dann sollə sii aa scenə, dass sii mich kriighə. 'Guutbei.'

I? speak with her about it? (*It*) *is quite unnecessary. If your girls* (können kaufen) *can buy, sell, and 'swap' me, then* (sollen sie auch sehen) *shall they also see that they get me. 'Goodby.'*

¶ 18. Ich wees not was dii Windbeissər meed[1] mit un oone Griischən Bendor fun miir denkə, aawər was ich fun iinə denk wees ich, wærd diir s aawər 'ennihau' not saaghə.

I know not what the Windbeisser girls with and without Grecian Bend think of me, (aber ich weiss) *but I know what I think of them— but will 'anyhow' not tell it to you.*

¶ 19. 'Nau' hab ich im sinn noch eé mool[2] tsu prowiirə, sobál ich n 'tschænss' ausfinn, un wann m'r s aa dann net glikt, geb ich s uf un wærd ən altor 'bœtschələr.'[3]

I now have in mind (zu probïren) *to try yet* (einmal) *once, as soon as I find out a 'chance,' and if it also prospers not then with me, I will give it up and be an old 'bachelor.'*

§ 2.   *Wii kummt əs?*

¶ 1. Ich lees ciər tseitung 'reglər' alli woch, un weil ich alsfart so füil nei-ichkeit'n drin lees, do bin ich schun oft (əft) uf dii 'nosch'n' [gekommen] kummə iir [müsset] misst alləs wissə.

---

[1] This 'meed' is singular and plural, but the singular is more commonly meedl, SG. maidle, G. mädchen. It differs from maad (sing. and pl. G. magd), a female servant.

[2] Being emphasised, the accent is on the first syllable, while in 'əmool' (below § 2, ¶ 3) it is on the second.

[3] Condensed and transliterated from the (German) *Bucks County Express*, Doylestown, Pa. July 20, 1869.

How COMES IT? *I read* (eucr) *your journal 'regular' every week, and as I constantly read so many novelties in it,* (da then) *have I indeed often come to the 'notion' you must know everything.*

¶ 2. Wann epper sich ufhengt, ədər heiərt, ədər eppəs schteelt, ədər gærn ən guuti 'affis' hätt, ədər in dii 'tscheel' kummt, ədər sich n fing-er apschneidt, ədər sei, 'plats' f'rkaaft, ədər n hinkl schteelt, ədər 'guuf'rniir' wærrə will, ədər im 'gəttər' kfunne wært, ədər seini tseitung net betsaalt, dann kann m'r sich druf f'rlassən, dass əs in dii tseitung kummt.

If (Swiss *epper,* masc. of G. etwas,) *anyone hangs himself, or marries, or steals* (G. etwas) *anything, or would like to have a good 'office,' or gets into 'jail,' or cuts himself a finger off, or sells his 'place'* (or *farm*), *or steals a chicken, or wishes to become 'governor,' or is* [gefunden] *found in the 'gutter,' or does not pay for his journal, then one can depend upon it that it gets into the newspaper.*

¶ 3. Ich bin ən altər bauer un f'rschteo net fiil, un weil iir alles tsu wissə scheint, doo will ich eich əmoól ən paar sachə froogho, dii ich gærn wissə deet.

I am an old farmer and do not understand much, and as you seem to understand everything, I will here ask you once several things, which I would like to know.

¶ 4. Wii kummt əs, dass dii jung-i bauərəbuuwə graad brillən un schtək traaghə missə, wann sii in dii 'kallitsch' [geschickt werden] kschikt wœrrə? Ich hab als gemeent ich wollt mei, 'Sæm' aa in dii 'kallitsch' schiko, aawər wann dii leit graad schlechti aaghə kriighə un laam wœrrə, dann behalt ich mei, 'Sæm' liiwər dəhcem un lærn iin selwer als oowəts.

How comes it, that the young farmer-boys must immediately carry spectacles and (stöcke) *sticks when they are sent to 'college'? I have hitherto thought I would send my 'Sam.' to 'college,' but if people immediately get bad eyes and become lame, I will rather keep him at home and teach him myself of evenings.*

¶ 5. Wii kummt əs, dass deel weipsleit in eirəm .iistən (Easton) soo aarm [sein wollen] sei, wellə un doch soo lang-i frackschwents uf 'm 'peefmənt' noochschleefə? [Werden] wœrre[1] selli weipsleit betsaalt f'r s 'peefmənt' [sauber] sauwər tsu haltə, ədər wii [können] kenne sii 'affoordə' soo aa,tsugeeə?

How comes it, that (theil) *part* (of the) *women in your Easton* (sein wollen) *pretend to be so poor, and yet* (nach-schleifen) *drag along*

---

[1] G. *worden* becomes 'warrə.' See § 1, ¶ 14.

such long frock (schwänze) *tails on the 'pavement'? Will those women be paid for keeping the 'pavement' clean, else how can they 'afford' to proceed thus?*

¶ 6. Wii kummt es, dass dii jung-i buuwə selli meed, woo reichi, daadis [Swiss düdi] hen, liiwər noochschpringə als dii aarmi? Gukt sel net als wii wann sii meer uum s geld gewwə [thäten] deetə als wii uum dii meed? Wann ich ən meedl wœr un hätt so ən 'boo,' dann deet ich iin mit d'r feiərtsang furtschtéwərə.

How comes it, that the young men (lieber nachspringen) *sooner run after those girls who have rich* [the plural -s is English] *fathers, than the poor ones? Looks it not just as if they would give more for the money than for the maid? If I were a girl and had such a 'beau,'* (then) *I would* [stöbern, ö long] *drive him forth with the fire-tongs.*

¶ 7. Wii kummt es, dass n deel jung-i leit nimmi deitsch leesə un schwetsə kennə, wann sii mool 'jes' un 'noo' saaghə kennə? Meim [dative for genitive] nochbər, dem Maardi Halsbendl sei, eltəst'r [sohn] suu‚ dær so deitsch waar wii saurkraut des schun siwwə mool ufgwærmt iss, waar kœrtslich əmool in d'r schtatt, un wii œr wiid'r heem kummə iss, do waar ær so eng-lisch, dass ær schiir gaar nimmi mit seim daadi un mammi schwetsə kann. Sii sin 'nau' arik im 'truwl' un sei‚ daadi meent, sii misst'n iin naus nooch Kniphaus'n schikkə, f'r iin wiid'r (widr) deitsch tsu machə.

How comes it that some young people are no longer able to read and speak German if they only know how to say 'yes' and 'no'? The eldest son of my neighbor Martin Neckband, who was as Dutch as sourcrout which has been warmed up seven times, was once recently a week in town, and when he had returned home again, there was he so English that he could scarcely speak anymore with his father and mother. They are 'now' greatly in 'trouble,' and his father thinks they must send him out to Kniphausen to make him German again.

¶ 8. Wie kummt es, dass dii aarmi leit weeenlich dii meerschtən hund un katsə hen? Do bei uns wuunt n famílje, dii als bettələ muss, un dii fiir groosə hund un siwwə katsə hot. Sii selwər saaghə, sii misst'n so fiil hund hawə f'r dii diib aptsuhaltə.[1]

How comes it, that poor people (gewöhnlich haben) *commonly have the most dogs and cats? Here near us lives a family which must always beg, and which has four large dogs and seven cats. They themselves say, they* (müszten haben) *were obliged to have so many dogs to keep away the thieves.*

[1] Condensed from the (German) *Correspondent & Demokrat*, Easton, Pa. Aug. 25, 1869.

§ 3.

Will widd'r Biiweli[1] *sei₁.*	*Will be a Boy again.*

¶ 1.

.əs reeghərt heit, mr kann net naus
un ə iss so 'loonsəm' doo im haus;
  mr wees net wii mr fiilt.
ich will mool duu, als wœœr ich klee,
un uf d'r éwərscht schpeicher gee,
  dart hab ich uftmools kschpiilt.

It rains to-day, one cannot out,
and t is so 'lonesome' in the house;
  one knows not how one feels,
I will once do as were I small
and in the highest garret go—
  there have I ofttimes played.

¶ 2.

.ən biiwli bin ich widdər jetz,
wu sin mei, k r u t s ə un mei, klets?
  nau wœrt n haus gebaut!
əs schpiilt sich doch net guut alée,—
ich bin joo doch kee, biiwli meo!
  was kluppt mei, hœrts so laut!

An urchin am I now again,
where are my corn-cobs and my blocks?
  'now' will a house be built!
one plays indeed not well alone—
I am in fact no urchin more!
  my heart how loud it beats!

¶ 3.

Harrich! was 'n wunnərbaarə sach!
d'r reeghə rapplt uf 'm dach
  gaar nimmi wii œr hat!
ich hab 's als kœœrt mit leichtəm hœrts,
nau gepts m'r arik hcemwee schmœrts,
  kennt heilə wan ich wet.

And hark! how wonderful it is!
the rain now rattles on the roof
  no more as it once did!
I heard it once with buoyant heart,
but now it gives a home-sick smart,
  I could weep if I would.

¶ 5.

Des schpiilə geet net, səl ich fart?
was iss uf selli balkə dart?
  'nau' bin ich widdər buu!
dart ben m'r keschtə ausgeschtreit,
tsu dœrrə uf dii Krischdaak tseit—
  deet 's gleichə widdər duu!

The play succeeds not, shall I forth?
what is upon that timber there?
  'now' I 'm a boy again!
there did we spread the chesnuts out
to have them dry for Christmas time—
  would 'like' to do t again!

¶ 6.

.ən biiwli sei,—sell iss d'r wœrt—
dii keschtə 'rooschtə' uf d'r hœrt—
  was het des als gekracht!
Sell iss forbei. Ich fiil 's im gmiid,[2]
es schpiilt 'n rechtəs heemwee liid,
  d'r reeghə uf 'm dach!

To be a boy—that is worth while—
to 'roast' the chesnuts on the harth—
  what crackling that produced!
t is gone—I feel that in my soul
it plays a real home-sick tune—
  the rain upon the roof!

¶ 7.

Dort schteet dii 'seem' alt walnus kischt,
ich wunner 'nau' was dart drin isoh?
  's muss eppəs 'bartich sei,.
Kallénər, tseitung, bicher—hoo!
dii alti sachə hen sii doo
  all sunnərscht-sewərscht[3] nei,.

There stands the 'same' old walnut chist
I wonder 'now' what may be in t,
  it must be something (abartig) rare.
Books—calendars—newspapers—oh
the olden objects have we here
  all upside down within.

[1] The spelling of the original is 'Buwelle,' without the *umlaut*, which others use. The original has 'owerscht' in the fifth line, but the *umlaut* is in use, and seems to be required, as in Bavarian. For notes [2] and [3] see next page.

¶ 8.

' Nau ' bin ich aawer recht en buu,	But ' now ' I truly am a boy
weil ich do widder scene duu	because I now again behold
des alt bekannte sach.	this old familiar thing.
Harrich! hæærscht d'r reeghe! 'Jes	Hark! Hearst the rain! 'Yes, yes
indiid '—	indeed,'
er schpiilt en rechtes heemwee liid	it plays a proper home-sick air
dart oowe uf 'm dach!	up there upon the roof!

¶ 13.

Sii henke net am balke mee	They hang not on the cross-beams more
dii bindle fun dem kreiter tee,	the bundles of botanic tea,
un allerlee gewœrts;	and every kind of root;
' nau ' will ich widder biiwli sei,—	'now' I will be a boy again
ich hool sii f'r dii mammi rei,—	and for my mother bring them in—
sell ' pliist ' mei, biiwli hœrts.'	that ' pleased ' my boyish heart.

— HARBAUGH.

² G. gemüth.
³ G. das *unterste zu oberst* (topsy-turvy). Compare PG. ' hinnorscht-feddarscht'
(wrong end foremost).
⁴ Transliterated extract from a longer poem in the *Father Abraham*, Lancaster,
Pa. Feb. 1869.

§ 4. *Anglicised German.*

The following factitious example, full of English words and idioms, is from a New York German newspaper, and purports to be written by a German resident in America. The spelling recalls the name HEYFLEYER over a stall in the stables of the King of Wurtemberg. The writer of the letter spells his name in three ways, instead of ' Schweineberger,' as given in the tale.

Landkäsder, Penfilvenia, North-Amerika, 32. Dezr. 52.

Dheire Mudder!—Du Würst es nit begreife kenne, alfz ich dort weck bin, hawen alle Leit gefacht, der Hannes werrd nit gud ausmache, das ich jetzt fo gut ab binn. Awer, well, jetzt g'hör' ich zu de Tfchentel-Leit in unfre Zitti unn eeniger Männ, wo in Iurop en werri fein Männ is, dhät laohche, bikahs er gleichte fo gut auszumache, als der John Swinebarker.

Obfchon, ich unterftehe des Büffeneff beffer as die andre Dotfchmänn, wo eweri Teim fo fchlecht edfchukädet bleibe, as fe in Iurop ware; Wer hier gleicht, gud auszumache, mufz fich zu de amerikanifche Tfchentel-Leit halte, wo eweri Männ Something lerne kann.

Du kannft auch zu mein dheires Eliänorche fage, das es kommen kann; fie kann der hohl Däy im Rockel-Schär fitze, ich fend hir included fixtig Dollars, mit das kann fie über Liwerpuhl und Nujork zu mich komme, und verbleibe Dein moft zänkvoll Son John Swincberger.

Bofchkrippt: Du muft die Monni for des Bordo auslege; ich will fend es Dir mit dem nächfte Letter. John Schweinebärker.

CHAPTER IX.

English Influenced by German.

§ 1. *German Words introduced.*

If the Germans of Pennsylvania adopted many words from English, the English speaking population applied the appellation of *German* or *Dutch* to unfamiliar varieties of objects, such as a *Dutch cheese*, a *German lock;* or they adopted the original names, as in calling a form of curds *smearcase* (G. schmierkäse) in the markets and prices current. German forms of food have furnished the vicinal English with *sourcrout, mush, shtreisslers, bretsels, fawstnachts,*[1] *tseegercase, knep* (G. Knöpfe, the *k* usually pronounced), *bower-knep, noodles;* and in some of the interior markets, endive must be asked for under the name of ' œntiifi,' even when speaking English. Dutch gives *crullers,* but *stoop* (of a house) is hardly known. In English conversation one may hear expressions like " He belongs to the *freindschaft* " (he is a kinsman or relation); " It makes me *greisslich* to see an animal killed " (makes me shudder and revolt with disgust—turns my stomach). A strong word without an English equivalent.

The German idiom of using *einmal* (once) as an expletive, is common, as in " Bring me a chair once," and when a person whose vernacular is English says, " I am through another " (I am confused), he is using a translation of the German *durch einander,* PG. 'dárich enánner.' Of such introduced words, the following deserve mention.

Metsel-soup, originally pudding broth, the butcher's perquisite, but subsequently applied to a gratuity from the animals he has slaughtered.

---

[1] Shrove-tide cakes—with the PG. pronunciation, except *st.*

Shinner, G. schinder (a knacker,[1]) an objurgatory epithet applied by butchers to farmers who compete with them in the market.

Speck, the flitch of salt bacon, particularly when boiled with sour-crout, hence, 'speck and sourcrout.'

Tsitterly, calf's-foot jelly.

Hartley, a hurdle for drying fruit.

Snits, a snit (G. schnitz, a cut), a longitudinal section of fruit, particularly apples, and when dried for the kitchen. The term is in use in districts where German is unknown.[2]

Hootsle, PG. hutsl, G. hotzel, a dried fruit; Bavar. and Suab. hutzel, a dried pear. In Pennsylvania, a peach dried without removing the stone.

Dumb (G. dumm) is much used for *stupid*.

Fockle (G. fackel), a fisherman's torch.

Mother (PG. from G. mutter-weh, not parturition, but) a hysterical rising in the throat. The word occurs in old and provincial English.[3]

Chipmunk, a ground-squirrel (Tamias); *chip* probably from its cry, and Swiss *munk*, a marmot.

Spook (G. Spuk), a spectre; and the verb, as—"It spooks there," "The grave-yard spooks."

Cristkintly (PG. Krischtkintli, G. Christ Kindlein), the Christ Child who is supposed to load the christmas trees and bring presents at christmas. Perverted in the Philadelphia newspapers to *Kriss Kringle*, *Kriss Kingle*, and *Kriss Kinkle*.

Christmas-tree, a well-known word for a well-known and much used object, but absent from the American dictionaries.

Bellsnickle, PG. beltsnikkl (G. *Pels* a pelt, skin with hair, as a bear-skin, here used as a disguise, and perhaps associated with *peltzen*, to pelt,) and *Nickel*, *Nix*, in the sense of a demon. (Suab. Pelzmärte, as if based on *Martin*). A masked and hideously disguised person, who goes from house to house on christmas eve, beating (or pretending to beat) the children and servants, and throwing down nuts and cakes before leaving. A noisy party

---

[1] G. Knochen (bones).

[2] A teacher asked a class—If I were to cut an apple in two, what would you call one of the pieces? "A *half*." And in four? "A *fourth*." And if I cut it in eight equal pieces, what would one of them be? "A *snit*!"

[3] Compare—O, how this mother swells up toward my heart!
        Hysterica passio, thou climbing sorrow,
        Thy element's below.—*King Lear*, act 2, sc. 4, speech 20, v. 54.
                                                                —*A. J. Ellis.*

accompanies him, often with a *bell*, which has influenced the English name.

These, I suppose, were Christmas mummers, though I heard them called "Bell-schnickel."—*Atlantic Monthly*, October, 1869, p. 484.

Gounsh, n. and v.i.   As *to seesaw* implies reciprocal motion, so *to gounsh* is to move up and down, as upon the free end of an elastic board.   PG. 'Kumm, mr wolla gaunscha.'   (Come, let us gounsh.)   Suab. gautschen; Eng. to *jounce*.[1] ·

Hoopsisaw (PG. húppsisaa, also provincial German).   A rustic or low dance, and a lively tune adapted to it.   Inferior lively music is sometimes called 'hoopsisaw music,' 'a hoopsisaw tune.'[2]

Hoove, v.i. a command to a horse to back, and used by extension as in "The men hooved (demurred) when required to do more work."   Used in both senses in the Swiss *hüfen*, imperative *hüf!* and Schmeller (*Bayr. Wörterb.* 2, 160) gives it as Bavarian.

Hussling-, or **Hustling-match,** PG. hossl-mœtsch (with English *match*), a raffle.   From the root of *hustle*, the game being conducted by shaking coins in a hat and counting the resulting heads.

Sock up, "to make a man sock up," pay a debt, produce his *sack* or pouch.   This is uncertain, because, were a PG. expression to occur like "Du muscht ufsakka" (you must sock up), it might be borrowed from English.

Boof, peach brandy.   In Westerwaldish, *buff* is water-cider,—cider made by wetting the pomace and pressing it a second time.

Sots, n. sing. G. satz, home-made 'yeast' as distinguished from 'brewer's-east.'

Sandman, "The sandman is coming,"—said when children get sleepy about bedtime and indicate it by rubbing the eyes.   Used thus in Westerwald and Suabia.[3]   Children are warned against touching dirt by the exclamation (bæætschi).

Snoot, for snout, a widespread teutonic form.

---

[1] The German word appears to be *gautschen* without the *n*. So Schmeller (Bayerisches Wörterbuch, 2, 87) "*gautschen, getschen*, schwanken, schaukeln." Adelung (Wörterbuch der hochdeutschen Mundart, 2, 439) explains it as a technical paper-maker's word for taking the sheets out of the mould and laying them upon the press-board, *Gautschbret*. He adds that a carrying chair was formerly called a *Gautsche*, and refers it to *Kutsche* and French *coucher*.—*A. J. E.*

[2] Compare Papageno's song in Mozart's *Zauberflöte*:
Der Vogelfänger bin ich ja
Stets lustig, heisa, hopsasa.—*A. J. Ellis.*

[3] Known probably throughout England. Known to me, a Londoner, from earliest childhood.—*A. J. Ellis.*

§ 2. *Family Names Modified.*

With several concurrent languages, the deterioration of names is an obvious process. Among the mixed population of Baltimore, the name 'Bradley' is to a Frenchman *Bras-de-long;* for 'Strawberry' (alley) and 'Havre-de-grâce' (in Maryland) the Germans say *Strubbel,* and *Hasel-im-gras;* and the Irish make the following changes—

Carron (French)	*Scarron*	Schöffeler	*Scofield*
Coquerelle	*Corcoran*	van Dendriessche	*Driscol*
de Vries	*Freezer*	van Emstede	*Hampsted*
Giessen	*Gleason*	Winsierski	*Winchester*
Grimm	*Grimes*	Fayette Street	*Faith St.*
Henning	*Hannon*	Alice Ann St.	*Alexander St.*
Rosier	*Rosetree*	Happy Alley	*Apple Alley*

A German with a name which could not be appreciated, was called *John Waterhouse* because he attended a railroad tank—a name which he adopted and placed upon his sign when he subsequently opened a small shop. A German family became ostensibly Irish by preferring the sonant phase of their initial —calling and writing themselves *Grady* instead of Krady; a name 'Leuter' became *Lander;* 'Amweg' was tried a while as *Amwake* and then resumed; and in a family record, the name 'George' is given as *Schorts.* A postoffice 'Chickis' (Chikiswalungo—place where crayfish burrow) received a letter directed to *Schickgets,* another *Schickens Laenghaester Caunte,* and 'Berks County' has been spelled *Burgix Caunte.*[1]

The following German and Anglicised forms may be compared,—

Albrecht	*Albright*	Frey (free)	*Fry*
Bachman	*Baughman*	Früauf	*Freeauf*
Becker	*Baker, Pecker*	Fuss (foot)	*Foose*
Dock	*Duck*	Geisz (goat)	*Gise*
Eberhardt	*Everhart*	Gerber	*Garber*
Eberle	*Everly*	Giebel	*Gibble*
Eckel	*Eagle*	Gräff	*Graff, -o, -ae*
Ege[2]	*Hagy ?*	Guth	*Good, Goot*
Ewald	*Evalt*	Haldeman	*Holderman*[3]
Fehr	*Fair*	Herberger	*Harberger*

---

[1] The geographical names at the close of Chapter I. p. 6, are Kentucky, Safe Harbor, Syracuse, and Pinegrove. The drugs are aloes (pronounced as in Latin!), paregoric, citrine ointment, acetic acid, hiera picra, cinnamon, Guiana pepper, gentian, cinchona, opium, hive syrup, senna and manna mixed, sulphate of zink, corrosive sublimata, red precipitate, aniline, logwood, Epsom salts, magnesia, cordial, cubebs, bichromate of potash, valerian (G. Báldrian), laurel berries, cochineal.   [2] Rhymes plaguey, even in English localities.

[3] As if from the plant *elder,* instead of Swiss halde, a *steep* or *declivity*—the name being Swiss.

Hinkel	*Hinkle*	Pfautz	*Fouts, Pouts*
Hofman	*Hoofman*	Pfeiffer	*Pyfer*
Huber	*Hoover*	Reif (ripe)	*Rife*
Kaufman	*Coffman*	Reisinger	*Riesinger*
Kaufroth	*Cuffroot*	Riehm	*Ream*
Kebler	*Kaylor*	Roth (red)	*Roath, Rote*
Kochenauer	*Goughnour*	Ruth	*Root*
Koick	*Cowhawk*	Schellenberger	*Shallyberger* [1]
Krauskopf	*Krosskop*	Schenk	*Shank*
Kreider	*Crider*	Scheuerman	*Shireman*
Kreybil	*Graypeel*	Schnebele	*Snavely*
Kühnlein	*Coonly, -ley*	Schneider	*Snyder, Snider*
Kutz	*Kutts*	Seip	*Sype, Sipe*
Leitner	*Lightner*	Seipel	*Seiple, Sible*
Leybach	*Libough*	Seitz	*Sides*
Mayer	*Moyer*	Senz	*Sense*
Meyer	*Mire*	Spraul	*Sprowl*
Mosser	*Musser*	Stambach	*Stambough*
Mosseman	*Musselman*	Strein	*Strine*
Neumeyer	*Narmire?*	Valentin	*Felty*
Noll	*Null*	WeltzhuBer	*Beltzhoo Ver* [2]
Nüssli	*Nicely, Nisely*	Wetter	*Fetter*
Oberholtzer	*Overholser*	Wild	*Wilt*

So 'Schleyermacher' passed thro *Slaremaker* to *Slaymaker*; and by a similar process, farther changes may take place, like Mutsch to *Much*, Bertsch to *Birch*, Brein to *Brine*, Schutt to *Shoot* or *Shut*, Rüppel to *Ripple*, Knade (gnade *grace*) to *Noddy* Buch to *Book*, Stahr to *Star*, Fing-er to *Fin-ger*, Melling-er to *Mellin-jer*, Stilling-er[3] to *Stillin-jer*, Cöver to *Cöver*, Fuhrman to *Foreman*, Rohring[4] to *Roaring*, Gehman to *Gayman*.

Names are sometimes translated, as in *Stoneroad* for 'Steinweg,' *Carpenter* for both 'Schreiner' and 'Zimmermann,' and both *Short* and *Little* for 'Kurz' or 'Curtius.'

Part of a name may be anglicised, as in Fink*bine*, Espen*shade*, Traut*woine*—where the first syllable has the German sound. Fentz*maker* is probably a condensation of Fenstermacher.

It is remarkable that speakers of German often use English forms of baptismal names, as *Mary* for Maria, *Henry* for

---

[1] And Shellabarger, American Minister to Portugal, 1869.
[2] The 'b' and 'v' of the two forms have changed place.
[3] These names, with Rauch, Bucher, the Scotch Cochran, etc., are still pronounced correctly in English speaking localities in Pennsylvania; and at Harrisburg, 'Salade' rhymes *holid'y*.
[4] The organists Thunder and Rohr gave a concert in Philadelphia some years ago. In New York I have seen the names 'Stone and Flint,' and 'Lay and Hatch,' where the proper name takes précedence.

Heinrich, and *John* (tschan, shorter than the medial English sound) for Johannes.[1]

Of curious family names without regard to language, the following may be recorded—premising that proper names are especially subject to be made spurious by the accidents of typography.[2]

Ahl, Awl, Ammon, Annĕ, Barndollar, Baud, Bezoar, Bigging, Blades, Bohrer, Boring, Book, Bracken, Bricker (bridger), Buckwalter, Burkholder and Burchhalter (burg-holder), Byler, Candle, Candour, Care, Case, Channell, Chronister, Condit, Cooher, Cumberbus (Smith's Voyage to Guinea, 1744), Curgus or Circus, Dehoof, Dialogue, Ditto, Dosh, Eave, Eldridge (in part for Hildreth), Erb, Eyde, Eyesore (at Lancaster, Pa.), Fassnacht (G. fastnacht *shrovetide*), Feather, Ferry (for the Walloon name Ferreo[3]); Friday, Fornaux, Furnace, Gans (*goose*, Gansert, Gensemer, Grossgensly), Gift (poison), Ginder, Gruel, Gutmann (good--man) Hag (hedge), Harmany, Hecter, Hepting, Herd, Heard, Hergelrat (rath *counsel*), Hinderer, Hock, Holzhauer and Holzhower (woodchopper), Honnafusz (G. hahn *a cock*), Kash, Kitch, Koffer, Landtart, Lawer, Leis, Letz, Licht, Line, Lipp, Lœb (lion), Lœwr (at St. Louis), Mackrel, Manusmith, Matt, Marrs, Mehl, Mortersteel, Mowrer (G. maur *a wall*), Napp, Neeper (Niebuhr?), Nohaker, Nophsker, Ochs, Over, Oxworth, Peelman, Penas (in Ohio), Pfund, Popp, Poutch, Quirk, Rathvon (Rodfong, Rautfaung), Road, Rottenstein (in Texas), Rutt, Sangmeister, Scheuerbrand, Schlegelmilch, Schlong (snake), Schœttel, Segar, Seldomridge, Senn, Service (in Indiana), Shaver, Shilling, Shinover, Shock, Shot, Showers, Skats (in Connecticut), Smout, Spoon, Springer, Steer (in Texas), Stern, Stetler, Stormfeltz, Strayer, Stretch, Stridle, Sumption, Surgeon, Swoop (a Suab-ian), Test, Tise, Tice (Theiss?), Tittles, Towstenberier, Tyzat (at St. Louis), Umble, Venus, Venerich, -rik, Vestal (in Texas), Vinegar('s Ferry, on the Susquehanna), Vogelsang, Wallower, Waltz, Wolfspanier, Wonder, Woolrick (for Wulfrich?), Work, Worst, Yaffe, Yecker, Yeisley, Yordea, Zeh, Zugschwerdt.

---

[1] In the following inscription on a building, 'bei' instead of 'von' shows an English influence. The author knew English well: was a member of the state legislature, had a good collection of English—but not of German books—and yet preferred a German inscription—

ERBAURT BEI JOHN & MARIA HALDEMAN 1790.

Inscriptions are commonly in the roman character, from the difficulty of cutting the others.

[2] As in 'Chladori' for *Chladni*, in the American edition of the Westminster Review for July, 1865. The name Slyvons stands on the title-page as the author of a book on Chess (Bruxelles, 1856), which M. Cretaine in a similar work (Paris, 1865) gives as Solvyns. Upon calling Mr. C.'s attention to this point, he produced a letter from the former, signed *Solvyns*.

[3] The forms of this name are Ferree, Ferrie, Fuehre, Ferie, Verre, Fiere, Firre, Ferry, Feire, Fire; and as 'Ferree' is now pronounced *Free*, this may be a form also. In the year 1861, when in Nassau, I observed that the English visitors pronounced the name of a building in four modes, one German and three not German—Bâdhaus, Bath-house, Bad-house, and Bawd-house.

Among the following curious, incompatible, or hȳbrid [1] names, titles (except that of ' General ') have been mistaken for proper names—Horatio Himmereich, Owen Reich, Caspar Reed, Dennis Loucks, Baltzer Stone, Addison Shelp, Paris Rudisill, Adam Schuh, Erasmus Buckenmeyer, Peter Pence, General Wellington H. Ent, General Don Carlos Buel, Don Alonzo Cushman, Sir Frank Howard, Always Wise (probably for Alöis Weiss).   In November, 1867, Gilbert Monsieur Marquis de Lafayette Sproul, asked the legislature of Tennessee to cut off all his names but the last two.

---

[1] Latin HIBRIDA.   I have marked the first English syllable short to dissociate it from the *high-breed* of gardeners and florists, which ' hȳbrid ' suggests.

CHAPTER X.

IMPERFECT ENGLISH.

§ 1. *Broken English.*

Specimens of English as badly spoken by Germans who have au imperfect knowledge of it, are common enough, but they seldom give a proper idea of its nature. The uncertainty between sonant and surd is well known, but like the Cockney with *h*, it is a common mistake to suppose that the misapplication is universal,[1] for were this the case, the simple rule of reversal would set the speakers right in each case.

It is true that the German confounds English *t* and *d*, but he puts *t* for *d* more frequently than *d* for *t*. In an advertisement cut from a newspaper at Schwalbach, Nassau, in 1862—

Ordres for complet Diners or simples portions is punctually attented to and send in town—

there seems to be a spoken reversal of *t* and *d*, but I take ' send' to be an error of grammar, the pronunciation of the speaker being probably *attentet*, and *sent*. "Excuse my bad riding" (writing) is a perversion in speech. A German writes ' dacke' *take*, 'de' *the*, 'be' *be*, 'deere' *deer*, ' contra' *country*, and says :—

I am œbple [able] to accommodeted with any quantity of dis kins of Ruts [kinds of roots]. Plics tirectad to . . . Sout Frond Stread . . . nort amorica.

Here there is an attempt at the German flat *p* (p. 11) in the *bp* of ' able'; the surd *th* of ' north' and ' south' becomes *t*, and the sonant *th* of ' this' becomes *d*—' with ' remaining under the old spelling. The *p* of ' please' remains, but *d* of ' direct' becomes *t*; and while final *t* of ' front' and ' street' becomes

---

[1] A boy in the street in Liverpool (1866) said to a companion—"'e told me to 'old up my 'ands an' I 'eld em up." He did not say *h*up, *h*an' *h*I, *h*em.

d, the first *t* in 'street,' and that in 'directed,' are kept pure
by surd *s* and *cay*.   The rule of surd to surd and sonant to
sonant is neglected in most of the factitious specimens of
broken English.

The next is an instructive and a genuine example, being
the record of a Justice of the Peace in Dauphin County (that
of Harrisburg, the State Capital).   It will be observed that
the complainant bought a house, and being refused possession,
makes a forcible entry and is resisted.   The spelling is irregular,
as in 'come' and 'com,' 'the' and 'de,' 'did' and 'dit,' 'then'
and 'den,' 'nothin and 'nosing,' 'house' and 'hause,' 'put'
and 'but,' 'open' and 'upen.'

The said . . . sait I dit By de hause and I went in de hause at de back winder
and den I dit upen de house and Dit take out his forniture and nobotty Dit
disstorbe me till I hat his forniture out; I did but it out in de streat Before the
house; and then he dit Com Wis a barl and dit nock at the dore that the Dore
dit fly open and the molding dit Brack louse[1] and then I dit Wornt him not to
come in the hause and not to put anneysing in the hause and he dit put in a barl
Into the hause and I did put it out and he dit put it in again and then he did put
In two Sisses[2] and arout the barl against Me; and then I dit nothin out annez-
more and further nosing more; Sworn & Subscript the Dey and yeare above
ritten before me . . . . J.P.—*Newspaper.*

The beginning and close follow a legal formula.   The PG.
idiom which drops the imperfect tense runs through this, in
expressions such as 'I did open,' 'I did put,' 'I did warned,'
etc.; but as might be expected, the English idiom is also
present, in 'I went' and 'he throwed.'   Making allowance
for reminiscences of English spelling, and the accidents of
type, this is an excellent specimen of the phases of English
from German organs.   · It shows that sonants and surds do not
always change place, as in *did, nobody, disturb, out, that, not,*

[1] Compare with a word in the following note sent to a druggist in Harrisburg,
Pa. " Plihs lebt meh haf Sohm koh kohs Peryhs ohr Sähmting darhts guht vohr
Ah lihttel Dahg Gaht lausse vor meh."   [*Louse* for *loose* is common in the north
of England.   Thus in Peacock's Lonsdale Glossary (published for the Philological
Society, 1869) we find: "**Louse,** *adj.* (1) loose.   O.N. *laus,* solutus.   (2) Im-
pure, disorderly.—*v.t.* to loose.   "To *lowse* 'em out on t' common " =To let
cattle go upon the common.—To be at a louse-end.   To be in an unsettled, dis-
sipated state.—Lous-ith'-heft, *n.* a disorderly person, a spendthrift."—*A.J.Ellis.*]
[2] The *two* shows that this is a plural.   When recognised, it will be observed
that the law of its formation is legitimate.

come, which are not necessarily turned into *tit, nopotly, tisdurp, oud, dad, nod, gum.*[1]

In the foregoing example, the final *t* of *went* (where some might have expected 'wend'), *dit* for 'did,' *hat* for 'had,' *streat, wornt* for 'warned,' *put, srout* for 'throwed,' and *subscript,*—is for Latin -AT-US, English -*ed*, and as this is *t* in German, it is retained by the language instinct, even when represented by 'd,' as in *gol-d.* Were there not something different from mere accident here, Grimm's Law would be a delusion. The *t* of *out, disturb,* and the first one in *street,* is due to the surd *s* beside it, or in the German *aus* and *strasse.*

In *the, de; then, den; wis; anneysing, nosing; srout,* the sonant *th* becomes *d* by glottōsis,[2] and the surd one *s* by otōsis, or *t* by glottosis also, and 'no*th*ing' is more likely to become no*ss*ing or no*tt*ing, than no*dd*ing—and English *z* is not known to many German dialects. On the other hand, *z* as the representative of sonant *th*, is legitimate in the broken English of a Frenchman.

The *p* of 'open' and the *g* of 'against' are influenced by the German forms *öffnen* and *gegen.*

In "I dit nothin out annexmore"—*any* is made plural, and 'did out' (for the previous 'put out') seems to be a reminiscence of the German *austhun.*

§ 2. *The Breitmann Ballads.*

In these ballads Mr. Leland has opened a new and an interesting field in literature which he has worked with great success, for previous writers wanted the definite, accurate knowledge which appears in every page of Hans Breitmann, and which distinguishes a fiction like the Lady of the Lake from a

---

[1] For the word 'twenty-five,' the speaking and singing machine of the German Faber said *tventy-fife,* in imitation of its fabricator, using *t* and *f* because they occur in the German word. Similarly, feif for *five* appears in the following joke from an American German newspaper :—

"Ein Pennsylvanisch - Deutscher hatte zwei Pferde verloren und schickte folgende Annonce : Ei loft mein tu Horfes! Der wonne ift a Sarrelhorn, langen Schwanzthäl, fchort abgekuthet, aber weederum ausgrown; der annerwonn is bläcker, aber mit four weiht Fisht an en weifzen Strich in his Fähs. Hu will bring mein tu Horfes bäck to mi, will rezief feif Thalers reward."

[2] *Hald.* Analytic Orthography, § 294.

figment like Hiawatha.   Here we have an attempt to re-present the speech of a large class of Europèan[1] Germans who have acquired English imperfectly, and who must not be confounded with the Pennsylvania German, altho the language of the two may have many points in common.

Apart from their proper function, and under their present spelling, the Breitmann ballads have but little philologic value.   Instead of being the representative of an average speech, they contain forms which can hardly occur, even when influenced by the perversity of intentional exaggeration, such as shbeed, shdare, shdory, ghosdt, exisdt, lefdt, quesdious, excepdion, and where the sonant *d* occurs beside the surd *sh*, *f*, and *t*, in the lines :—

' De dimes he cot oopsetted[1]	[1] oopsettet.
In shdeerin lefdt und righdt.[2]	[2] G. recht.
Vas ofdener[3] as de cleamin shdars[4]	[3] G. öfter. [4] shtarrs.
Dat shtud de shky[5] py[6] nighdt.'	[5] sky. [6] G. bei.

In these pages an *average* speech is assumed as the basis of comparison, and also the average German who does one thing or avoids another in language.   In such examples of bad English, surd and sonant (*p,b ; t,d ; k,gay*) must be confused, and German words like ' mit ' for *with*, and ' ding ' (rather than ' ting ' or ' sing ') for *thing*, may be introduced at dis-cretion, as in Mr. Leland's use of *ding, mit, blitzen, erstaun*ished (for *-isht*), *Himmel, shlog*, and others.

When German and English have the same phase, it should be preserved, *book* (G. *buch*) has a sonant initial and a surd final in both languages ; a German therefore, who brings his habits of speech into English, will not be likely to call a book a *boog, poog*, or *pook ;* and Mr. Leland's habits as a German

[1] This accent is not wanted for Englishmen of the present day.   Noah Webster (Dissertations on the English Language, Boston U.S. 1789, p. 118) says: "Our modern fashionable speakers accent *European* on the last syllable but one. This innovation has happened within a few years. . . . . Analogy requires *Euro'pean* and this is supported by as good authorities as the other."   He adds in a footnote.   "*Hymenean* and *hymeneal* are, by some writers, accented on the last syllable but one ; but erroneously.   Other authorities preserve the analogy." Milton has *hymenéan*, P. L. 4, 711.   Milton's line " Epicurean, and the Stoic severe," P. Reg. 4 280, is strange, however the word may be accented ; Shak-spere's " keep his brain fuming ; Epicūrean cooks," A. and C., act 2, sc. 1, sp. 9, v. 24, is distinct enough.   If the long diphthong or vowel in Latin were a proper guide, we should have to say *inimī'cal, doctrī'nal, ami'cable*.   These words are accented on the same plan as those taken from the French.   And this would give the common *Eurō'pean*, which is now strictly tabooed.—*A. J. Ellis.*

scholar have led him to write *book*, *beer* (and *bier*) *fear*, *free*, *drink*, *denn*, *trink*, *stately*, *plow*, *born*, *dokter*, *togeder*, *hart* (hard), *heart*, *tead* (dead), *fought*, *frolic*, *goot*, *four*, *hat* (had, hat,—but in the latter sense it should have been *het*), *toes*, *dough* (though), *tousand*, *pills*, etc.   Under this rule, his 'ploot' and 'blood' (G. blut) should have been *blut* :—

benny	*penny*	dwice	*trice*	pefore	*before*	prown	*brown*
blace	*place*	fifdy	*fifty*	pegin	*begin*	py	*by*
blaster	*plaster*	giss	*kiss*	pehind	*behind*	prow	*brow*
breest	*priest*	led	*let*	plue	*blue*	sed	*to set*
creen	*green*	mighdy	*mighty*	pone	*bone*	streed	*shtreet*
deers	*tears*	pack n.	*back*	prave	*brafe*	veet	*feet*
dell	*tell*	pall	*båll*	pranty	*brandy*	vifdeen	*fifteen*
den	*ten*	peard	*beart*	preak	*break*	vine	*fine*
dwelve	*tvelf*	pecause	*because*	prings	*bringss*	wide	*vite*

In cases where the two languages do not agree in phase, either phase may be taken, as in 'troo' or 'droo' for English *through* with a surd initial, beside German *durch* with a sonant; but as German cognate finals are more likely to be surd than sonant (as in lock*wouth* for logwoo*d* at the end of Ch. I. p. 6), *goot*, *hart* and *holt*, as breitmannish forms, are better than *good*, *hard*, and *hold*.   Mr. Leland practically admits this, as in 'barrick' (G. *berg*, a hill), which, however, many will take for a *barrack*.[1]   The following have a different phase in German and English—

day tay	door toor	-hood -hoot	red ret
ding ting	dream tream	hund- huntert	said set
dirsty tirsty	drop trop	middle mittle	saddle sattle
done tone	fader fater	pad path	drink trink

but *k*, and the pure final German *s* would turn *d* to *t* in 'bridges,' 'brackdise,' 'outsides,' 'holds,' 'shpirids;' it would turn *g* to *k* in 'rags,' and it makes 'craps' (crabs) correct. The power of English *s* can scarcely be said to belong to average German, or to the breitmannish dialect; it should therefore be *ss* in 'doozen,' 'preeze' (breeze), and 'phaze.' When it is present it occurs initial, and we have 'too zee' once, against numerous *s* initials like see, sea, say, so, soul, six.

The ballads have many irregularities in spelling like—as, ash; is, ish; one, von; two, dwo; dwelf, dwelve, twelve, zwölf (for tvelf); chor, gorus; distants, tisaster; dretful; tredful; eck (the correct form), egg; het, head, headt;

[1] The probable breitmannish form of scythes is given in these pages. Compare "Pargerswill, Box [Parkersville, Bucks] Kaundie Pennsilfäni."

groundt, cround, croundt ; land, lantlord, Marylandt; shpirid, shpirit, shbirit ; drumpet; trumpet ; foorst, foost, first, virst ; fein, vine; wont, vent ; old, olt, oldt ; teufel, tyfel, tuyfel.

English *J* is placed in soobjectixe, objectified, jail, jammed, juice, jump (shoomp, choomp) ; it is represented by *sh* in shoost, shiant, shinglin ; by *ch* (correctly) in choin, choy, choke, enchine; by *g*, *dg* in change, hedge ; and by *y* in Yane and soobjectifly—which is not objectionable. English *Ch* remains in catch, child, chaps (and shaps), fetch, sooch, mooch ; and it becomes *sh* in soosh (such), shase, sheek.

English *Sh* is proper in shmoke, shmile, shplit, shpill, shpoons, shtart, shtick, shtrike, shtop, shvear ; it is omitted in smack, stamp, slept ; and it is of doubtful propriety in ash (as), ashk, vash (was), elshe, shkorn, shkare, shky.

English *D* final is often written *dt* that the word may be recognised and the sound of *t* secured, as in laidt, roadt, shouldt, vouldt, findt, foundt, roundt (and round), vordt (and vord), obercoadt. English *ed* and its equivalents should bo *et* or *t* in broken English, as in loadet, reconet, pe-markt, riset, signet, rollet, soemet, slightet, declaret, paddlet, mate (made), kilt ; -*ed* being wrong, as in said, coomed, bassed, scared, trinked, smashed, rooshed, bleased.

English *F, V, W*, receive the worst treatment, and are judged by the eye rather than by speech. German *folgen* and English *follow* are turned into 'vollow'; German *weil* is 'vhile' and 'while.' Other examples are wind and vindow ; vhen, vhenefer (turning not only German *v*, but English *v* into *f*), fery for *very*,—but svitch, ve (we), veight, vink, are proper. The following example is from 'Schnitzerl's Philosopede '—

' Oh vot ish all [1] dis eartly pliss ?	[1] *ol* in *folly*.
Oh, vot ish [4] man's soocksoss ? [2]	[2] soocccss.
Oh, vot is various kinds [3] of dings ?	[3] *s* turns *d* into *t*.
Und vot is [4] hoppiness ?	[4] *iss* or *ish*, not both.
Ve find a pank node in de shtreedt,[5]	[5] shtreet.
Next[-sht] [6]dings [6] der pank ish [7] preak !	[6] dingss. [7] *d* requires *b*.
Ve folls [1] und knocks our outsides [8] in,	[8] G. *seit*, and final *s*,
Ven ve a ten-shtrike make.'	require *t*.

CHICKIS, near COLUMBIA, PENNSYLVANIA,
Feb. 16, 1870.

TRÜBNER & CO.'S PUBLICATIONS.

A DICTIONARY OF ENGLISH ETYMOLOGY.
By HENSLEIGH WEDGWOOD.

Second Edition, thoroughly revised and corrected by the Author, and extended to the Classical Roots of the Language. With an Introduction on the Formation of the Language. Imperial 8vo. pp. lxxii. and 744, double columns, cloth. 26s.

AMERICANISMS: THE ENGLISH OF THE NEW WORLD.
By M. SCHELE DE VERE, LLD.,
Professor of Modern Languages in the Univ. of Virginia. 8vo. pp. 685, cloth. 12s.

STUDIES IN ENGLISH:
OR, GLIMPSES OF THE INNER LIFE OF OUR LANGUAGE.
By M. SCHELE DE VERE, LL.D., Professor of Modern Languages in the University of Virginia. 8vo. cloth, pp. vi. and 365. 10s. 6d.

A DICTIONARY OF THE OLD ENGLISH LANGUAGE.
Compiled from Writings of the xii., xiii., xiv., and xv. Centuries. By FRANCIS HENRY STRATMANN. Second Edition. 4to. Part I. pp. 160. 10s. 6d. Part II. pp. 160. 10s. 6d.

THE WORKS OF WILLIAM SHAKESPEARE.
Edited according to the first printed copies, with the various readings, and Critical Notes, by F. H. STRATMANN. I. The Tragicall Historie of Hamlet, Prince of Denmarke. Demy 8vo., pp. vi. and 120, sewed. 3s. 6d.

AN OLD ENGLISH POEM OF THE OWL AND THE NIGHTINGALE.
Edited by F. H. STRATMANN. 8vo. cloth, pp. 60. 3s.

LANGUAGE AND THE STUDY OF LANGUAGE.
Twelve Lectures on the Principles of Linguistic Science. By WM. DWIGHT WHITNEY, Professor of Sanskrit, etc., in Yale College. Second Edition, augmented by an Analysis. Crown 8vo., cloth, pp. xii. and 504. 10s. 6d.

THE HOMES OF OTHER DAYS.
A History of Domestic Manners and Sentiments during the Middle Ages. By THOMAS WRIGHT, Esq., M.A., F.S.A. With illustrations from the Illuminations in Contemporary Manuscripts and other Sources. Drawn and engraved by F. W. Fairholt, Esq., F.S.A. One vol., medium 8vo., 350 Woodcuts, pp. xv. and 512, handsomely bound in cloth. 1l. 1s.

VOLUME OF VOCABULARIES,
Illustrating the Condition and Manners of our Forefathers, as well as the History of the forms of Elementary Education, and of the Languages Spoken in this Island, from the Tenth Century to the Fifteenth. Edited by THOMAS WRIGHT, Esq., M.A., F.S.A., etc., etc. [In the Press.]

THE CELT, THE ROMAN, AND THE SAXON.
A History of the Early Inhabitants of Britain down to the Conversion of the Anglo-Saxons to Christianity. Illustrated by the Ancient Remains brought to Light by Recent Research. By THOMAS WRIGHT, Esq., M.A., F.S.A., etc., etc. Third Corrected and Enlarged Edition. [In the Press.]

LONDON: TRÜBNER & Co., 8 AND 60, PATERNOSTER ROW.

LINGUISTIC PUBLICATIONS

OF

TRÜBNER & CO.,

8 AND 60, PATERNOSTER ROW, LONDON, E.C.

Ahlwardt.—THE DIVÁNS OF THE SIX ANCIENT ARABIC POETS, Ennábiga, 'Antara, Tarafa, Zuhair, 'Algama, and Imruolqais; chiefly according to the MSS. of Paris, Gotha, and Leyden, and the collection of their Fragments: with a complete list of the various readings of the Text. Edited by W. AHLWARDT, Professor of Oriental Languages at the University of Geifswald. 8vo. pp. xxx. 340, sewed. 1870. 12s.

Aitareya Brahmanam of the Rig Veda. 2 vols. See under HAUG.

Alabaster.—THE WHEEL OF THE LAW: Buddhism illustrated from Siamese Sources by the Modern Buddhist, a Life of Buddha, and an account of the Phra Bat. By HENRY ALABASTER, Esq., Interpreter of Her Majesty's Consulate-General in Siam; Member of the Royal Asiatic Society. Demy 8vo. pp. lviii. and 324. 1871. 14s.

Alcock.—A PRACTICAL GRAMMAR of the JAPANESE LANGUAGE. By Sir RUTHERFORD ALCOCK, Resident British Minister at Jeddo. 4to. pp. 61 sewed. 18s.

Alcock.—FAMILIAR DIALOGUES in JAPANESE, with English and French Translations, for the use of Students. By Sir RUTHERFORD ALCOCK. 8vo. pp. viii. and 40, sewed. Paris and London, 1863. 5s.

Alger.—THE POETRY OF THE ORIENT. By WILLIAM ROUNSEVILLE ALGER, 8vo. cloth, pp. xii. and 337. 9s.

Alif Lailat wa Lailat.—THE ARABIAN NIGHTS. 4 vols. 4to. pp. 495, 493, 442, 434. Cairo, A.H. 1279 (1862). £3 3s.
This celebrated Edition of the Arabian Nights is now, for the first time, offered at a price which makes it accessible to Scholars of limited means.

Andrews.—A DICTIONARY OF THE HAWAIIAN LANGUAGE, to which is appended an English-Hawaiian Vocabulary, and a Chronological Table of Remarkable Events. By LORRIN ANDREWS. 8vo. pp. 560, cloth. £1 11s. 6d.

Anthropological Institute of Great Britain and Ireland (The Journal of the). Sir JOHN LUBBOCK, Bart., M.P., F.R.S., President. Published Quarterly.

Vol I., No. 1. January–July, 1871. 8vo: pp. 120–clix, sewed. Illustrated with 11 full page Plates, and numerous Woodcuts; and accompanied by several folding plates of Tables, etc. 7s.

CONTENTS.—On the Development of Relationships. By Sir John Lubbock, Bart., M.P., F.R.S., President A.I.—On the Racial Aspect of the Franco-Prussian War. By J. W. Jackson, Esq., M.A.I.—On the Pre-historic and Proto-historic Relations of the Populations of Asia and Europe, in reference to Palæo-Asiatic, Caucaso-Tibetan, Palæo-Georgian, &c. By Hyde Clarke, Esq.—Report on the Results obtained by the Settle Cave Exploration Committee out of Victoria Cave in 1870 (with 2 plates).—The Builders of the Megalithic Monuments of Britain. By A. L. Lewis, Esq., M.A.I.—The Mental Characteristics of Primitive Man as exemplified by the Australian Aborigines. By C. L. Wake, Esq., Dir. A.I.—Notes on a Comparative Table of the Australian Languages. By the Rev. G. Taplin (with folding tables).—On the Position of the Australian Languages. By W. H. I. Bleek, Esq., Ph.D.

APPENDIX.—A Description of some Archaic Structures in Cornwall and Devon. By A. L. Lewis, Esq., F.A.S.L.—Some Objections to the Theory of Natural Selections as explained by Mr. A. R. Wallace. By Henry Muirhead, Esq., M.D.

500.

8.2.72.

Vol. I., No. 2. October, 1871. 8vo. pp. 121-264, sewed. 4s.

CONTENTS.—On the Stone Monuments of the Khâsi Hill Tribes, and on some of the peculiar Rites and Customs of the People. By Major H. H. Godwin-Austen, F.R.G.S.—Vocabulary of the Cornu Tribe of Australia. By Dr. W. A. Peehey.—Chinese Mohammedans. By J. Anderson, Esq., M.D., F.R.S.—On Divination and Analogous Phenomena among the Natives of Natal. By Rev. Canon H. Calloway, M.D.—A Description of the Quissama Tribe. By F. G. H. Price, Esq., F.R.G.S., M.A.I.—On the Races of Patagonia. By Lieut. Musters, R.N.—On Chinese Burials. By Dr. W. Eatwell.—On the Discovery of a Cairn at Khangaum. By J. J. Carey, Esq. (communicated by Dr. A. Campbell.)—On a Cist found in Argyllshire. By Dugald Sinclair, Esq. (communicated by Dr. A. Campbell.)—On a Kitchen Midden in Cork Harbour. By G. M. Atkinson, Esq.—Mode of Preparing the Dead among the Natives of the Upper Mary River, Queensland. By A. McDonald, Esq. (communicated by W. Boyd Dawkins, Esq., F.R.S.)—On some Forms of Ancient Interment in Co. Antrim. By J. Sinclair Holden, Esq., M D., F.G.S.—On the Analogies and Coincidences among Unconnected Nations. By H. W. Westropp, Esq.—The Westerly Drifting of Nomades from the Fifth to the Nineteenth Century. Part VI. The Kirghises or Bourouts, the Kazaks, Kalmucks, Euzbegs, and Nogays. By Henry H. Howorth, Esq.—Part VII. The Thukine or Turks Proper, and the Hoeitehe or Uzes.—Anthropological Miscellanea.

Arabic, Persian, and Turkish Books (A Catalogue of). Printed in

the East. Constantly for sale by Trübner and Co., 8 and 60, Paternoster Row, London. CONTENTS.—Arabic, Persian, and Turkish Books printed in Egypt.— Arabic Books printed in Oudh.—Persian Literature printed in Oudh.— Editions of the Koran printed in Oudh.—Arabic Books printed at Bombay.— Persian Books printed at Bombay.—Arabic Literature printed at Tunis.— Arabic Literature printed in Syria. 16mo. pp. 68, sewed. 1s.

Asher.—On the Study of Modern Languages in General, and of the

English Language in particular. An Essay. By David Asher, Ph.D. 12mo. pp. viii. and 80, cloth. 2s.

Asiatic Society.—Journal of the Royal Asiatic Society of Great

Britain and Ireland, from the Commencement to 1863. First Series, complete in 20 Vols. 8vo., with many Plates. Price £10; or, in Single Numbers, as follows:—Nos. 1 to 14, 6s. each; No. 15, 2 Parts, 4s. each; No. 16, 2 Parts, 4s. each; No. 17, 2 Parts, 4s. each; No. 18, 6s. These 18 Numbers form Vols. I. to IX.—Vol. X., Part 1, op.; Part 2, 5s.; Part 3, 5s.—Vol. XI., Part 1, 6s.; Part 2 not published.—Vol. XII., 2 Parts, 6s. each.—Vol. XIII., 2 Parts, 6s. each.—Vol. XIV., Part 1, 5s.; Part 2 not published.—Vol. XV., Part 1, 6s.; Part 2, with Maps, 10s.—Vol. XVI., 2 Parts, 6s. each.—Vol. XVII., 2 Parts, 6s. each.—Vol. XVIII., 2 Parts, 6s. each.—Vol. XIX., Parts 1 to 4, 16s.—Vol. XX., 3 Parts, 4s. each.

Asiatic Society.—Journal of the Royal Asiatic Society of Great

Britain and Ireland. *New Series.* Vol. I. In Two Parts. pp. iv. and 490, sewed. 16s.

CONTENTS—I. Vajra-chhedikâ, the "Kin Kong King," or Diamond Sûtra. Translated from the Chinese by the Rev. S. Beal, Chaplain, R.N.—II. The Páramitá-hridaya Sûtra, or, in Chinese, "Mo-ho-pó-ye-po-lo-mih-to-sin-king," *i.e.* "The Great Páramitá Heart Sûtra." Translated from the Chinese by the Rev. S. Beal, Chaplain, R.N.—III. On the Preservation of National Literature in the East. By Colonel F. J. Goldsmid.—IV. On the Agricultural, Commercial, Financial, and Military Statistics of Ceylon. By E. R. Power, Esq.—V. Contributions to a Knowledge of the Vedic Theogony and Mythology. By J. Muir, D.C.L., LL.D.—VI. A Tabular List of Original Works and Translations, published by the late Dutch Government of Ceylon at their Printing Press at Colombo. Compiled by Mr. Mat. P. J. Ondaatje, of Colombo.—VII. Assyrian and Hebrew Chronology compared, with a view of showing the extent to which the Hebrew Chronology of Ussher must be modified, in conformity with the Assyrian Canon. By J. W. Bosanquet, Esq.—VIII. On the existing Dictionaries of the Malay Language. By Dr. H. N. van der Tuuk.—IX. Bilingual Readings: Cuneiform and Phœnician. Notes on some Tablets in the British Museum, containing Bilingual Legends (Assyrian and Phœnician). By Major-General Sir H. Rawlinson, K.C.B., Director R.A.S.—X. Translations of Three Copper-plate Inscriptions of the Fourth Century A.D., and Notices of the Chálukya and Gurjjara Dynasties By Professor J. Dowson, Staff College, Sandhurst.—XI. Yama and the Doctrine of a Future Life, according to the Rig-Yajur-, and Atharva-Vedas. By J. Muir, Esq., D.C.L., LL.D.—XII. On the Jyotisha Observation of the Place of the Colures, and the Date derivable from it. By William D. Whitney, Esq., Professor of Sanskrit in Yale College, New Haven, U.S.—Note on the preceding Article. By Sir Edward Colebrooke, Bart., M.P., President R.A.S.—XIII. Progress of the Vedic Religion towards Abstract Conceptions of the Deity. By J. Muir, Esq., D.C.L., LL.D.—XIV. Brief Notes on the Age and Authenticity of the Work of Aryabhata, Varáhamihira, Brahmagupta, Bhattotpala, and Bháskaráchárya. By Dr. Bháu Dáji, Honorary Member R.A.S.—XV. Outlines of a Grammar of the Malagasy Language. By H. N. Van der Tuuk.—XVI. On the Identity of Xandrames and Krananda. By Edward Thomas, Esq.

Vol. II. In Two Parts. pp. 522, sewed. 16*s.*

CONTENTS.—I. Contributions to a Knowledge of Vedic Theogony and Mythology. No. 2. By J. Muir, Esq. —II. Miscellaneous Hymns from the Rig- and Atharva-Vedas. By J. Muir, Esq.—III. Five hundred questions on the Social Condition of the Natives of Bengal. By the Rev. J. Long.—IV. Short account of the Malay Manuscripts belonging to the Royal Asiatic Society. By Dr. H. N. van der Tuuk.—V. Translation of the Amitábha Sútra from the Chinese. By the Rev. S. Beal, Chaplain Royal Navy.—VI. The initial coinage of Bengal. By Edward Thomas, Esq.—VII. Specimens of an Assyrian Dictionary. By Edwin Norris, Esq.—VIII. On the Relations of the Priests to the other classes of Indian Society in the Vedic age. By J. Muir, Esq.—IX. On the Interpretation of the Veda. By the same.—X. An attempt to Translate from the Chinese a work known as the Confessional Services of the great compassionate Kwan Yin, possessing 1000 hands and 1000 eyes. By the Rev. S. Beal, Chaplain Royal Navy. —XI. The Hymns of the Gaupáyanas and the Legend of King Asamáti. By Professor Max Müller, M.A., Honorary Member Royal Asiatic Society.—XII. Specimen Chapters of an Assyrian Grammar. By the Rev. E. Hincks, D. D., Honorary Member Royal Asiatic Society.

Vol. III. In Two Parts. pp. 516, sewed. With Photograph. 22*s.*

CONTENTS.—I. Contributions towards a Glossary of the Assyrian Language. By H. F. Talbot. —II. Remarks on the Indo-Chinese Alphabets. By Dr. A. Bastian.—III. The poetry of Mohamed Rabadan, Arragonese. By the Hon. H. E. J. Stanley.—IV. Catalogue of the Oriental Manuscripts in the Library of King's College, Cambridge. By Edward Henry Palmer, B.A., Scholar of St. John's College, Cambridge ; Member of the Royal Asiatic Society ; Membre de la Société Asiatique de Paris.—V. Description of the Amravati Tope in Guntur. By J. Fergusson, Esq., F.R.S.—VI. Remarks on Prof. Brockhaus' edition of the Kathásarit-ságara, Lambaka IX. XVIII. By Dr. H. Kern, Professor of Sanskrit in the University of Leyden.—VII. The source of Colebrooke's Essay "On the Duties of a Faithful Hindu Widow." By Fitzedward Hall, Esq., M.A., D.C.L. Oxon. Supplement : Further detail of proofs that Colebrooke's Essay, "On the Duties of a Faithful Hindu Widow," was not indebted to the Vivádabhangárnava. By Fitzedward Hall, Esq.—VIII. The Sixth Hymn of the First Book of the Rig Veda. By Professor Max Müller, M.A., Hon. M.R.A.S.—IX. Sassanian Inscriptions. By E. Thomas, Esq.—X. Account of an Embassy from Morocco to Spain in 1690 and 1691. By the Hon. H. E. J. Stanley.— XI. The Poetry of Mohamed Rabadan, of Arragon. By the Hon. H. E. J. Stanley.—XII. Materials for the History of India for the Six Hundred Years of Mohammedan rule, previous to the Foundation of the British Indian Empire. By Major W. Nassau Lees, LL.D., Ph.D.—XIII. A Few Words concerning the Hill people inhabiting the Forests of the Cochin State. By Captain G. E. Fryer, Madras Staff Corps, M.R.A.S.—XIV. Notes on the Bhojpuri Dialect of Hindí, spoken in Western Behar. By John Beames, Esq., B.C.S., Magistrate of Chumparun.

Vol. IV. In Two Parts. pp. 521, sewed. 16*s.*

CONTENTS.—I. Contribution towards a Glossary of the Assyrian Language. By H. F. Talbot. Part II.—II. On Indian Chronology. By J. Fergusson, Esq., F.R.S.— III. The Poetry of Mohamed Rabadan of Arragon. By the Hon. E. J. Stanley.—IV. On the Magar Language of Nepal. By John Beames, Esq., B.C.S.—V. Contributions to the Knowledge of Parsee Literature. By Edward Sachau, Ph.D.—VI. Illustrations of the Lamaist System in Tibet, drawn from Chinese Sources. By Wm. Frederick Mayers, Esq., of H.B.M. Consular Service, China.— VII. Khuddaka Pátha, a Páli Text, with a Translation and Notes. By R. C. Childers, late of the Ceylon Civil Service.—VIII. An Endeavour to elucidate Rashiduddin's Geographical Notices of India. By Col. H. Yule, C.B.— IX. Sassanian Inscriptions explained by the Pahlavi of the Pársis. By E. W. West, Esq.—X. Some Account of the Senbyú Pagoda at Mengún, near the Burmese Capital, in a Memorandum by Capt. E. H. Sladan, Political Agent at Mandalé ; with Remarks on the Subject by Col. Henry Yule, C.B.— XI. The Brhat-Sanhitá ; or, Complete System of Natural Astrology of Varáha-Mihira. Translated from Sanskrit into English by Dr. H. Kern.—XII. The Mohammedan Law of Evidence, and its influence on the Administration of Justice in India. By N. B. E. Baillie, Esq.—XIII. The Mohammedan Law of Evidence in connection with the Administration of Justice to Foreigners. By N. B. E. Baillie, Esq.—XIV. A Translation of a Bactrian Páli Inscription. By Prof. J. Dowson.—XV. Indo-Parthian Coins. By E. Thomas, Esq.

Vol. V. Part I. pp. 197, sewed. 8*s.*

CONTENTS.—I. Two Játakas. The original Páli Text, with an English Translation. By V. Fausböll.—II. On an Ancient Buddhist Inscription at Keu-yung kwan, in North China. By A. Wylie.—III. The Brhat Sanhitá ; or, Complete System of Natural Astrology of Varáha-Mihira. Translated from Sanskrit into English by Dr. H. Kern.—IV. The Pongol Festival in Southern India. By Charles E. Gover.—V. The Poetry of Mohamed Rabadan, of Arragon. By the Right Hon. Lord Stanley of Alderley.—VI. Essay on the Creed and Customs of the Jangams. By Charles P. Brown.—VII. On Malabar, Coromandel, Quilon, etc. By C. P. Brown.—VIII. On the Treatment of the Nexus in the Neo-Aryan Languages of India. By John Beames, B.C.S.— IX. Some Remarks on the Great Tope at Sánchi. By the Rev. S. Beal.—X. Ancient Inscriptions from Mathura. Translated by Professor J. Dowson.—Note to the Mathura Inscriptions. By Major-General A. Cunningham.

Asiatic Society.—TRANSACTIONS OF THE ROYAL ASIATIC SOCIETY OF GREAT BRITAIN AND IRELAND. Complete in 3 vols. 4to., 80 Plates of Facsimiles, etc., cloth. London, 1827 to 1835. Published at £9 5*s.* ; reduced to £3 3*s.*

The above contains contributions by Professor Wilson, G. C. Haughton, Davis, Morrison, Colebrooke, Humboldt, Dorn, Grotefend, and other eminent Oriental scholars.

Atharva Veda Prátiçákhya.—See under WHITNEY.

Auctores Sanscriti. Edited for the Sanskrit Text Society; under the supervision of THEODOR GOLDSTÜCKER. Vol. I., containing the Jaiminîya-Nyáya-Málá-Vistara. Parts I. to V., pp. 1 to 400, large 4to. sewed. 10s. each part.

Axon.—THE LITERATURE OF THE LANCASHIRE DIALECT. A Bibliographical Essay. By WILLIAM E. A. AXON, F.R.S.L. Fcap. 8vo. sewed. 1870. 1s.

Bachmaier.—PASIGRAPHICAL DICTIONARY AND GRAMMAR. By ANTON BACHMAIER, President of the Central Pasigraphical Society at Munich. 18mo. cloth, pp. viii.; 26; 160. 1870. 3s. 6d.

Bachmaier.—PASIGRAPHISCHES WÖRTERBUCH ZUM GEBRAUCHE FÜR DIE DEUTSCHE SPRACHE. Verfasst von ANTON BACHMAIER, Vorsitzendem des Central-Vereins für Pasigraphie in München. 18mo. cloth, pp. viii.; 32; 128; 120. 1870. 2s. 6d.

Bachmaier.— DICTIONNAIRE PASIGRAPHIQUE, PRÉCEDÉ DE LA GRAMMAIRE. Redigé par ANTOINE BACHMAIER, Président de la Société Centrale de Pasigraphie à Munich. 18mo. cloth, pp. vi. 26; 168; 150. 1870. 2s. 6d.

Bálávatáro (A Translation of the). A Native Grammar of the Pali Language. See under LEE.

Ballad Society's Publications. — Subscriptions—Small paper, one guinea, and large paper, three guineas, per annum.

1868.

1. BALLADS FROM MANUSCRIPTS. Vol. I. Ballads on the condition of England in Henry VIII.'s and Edward VI.'s Reigns (including the state of the Clergy, Monks, and Friars), on Wolsey and Anne Boleyn. Part I. Edited by F. J. FURNIVALL, M.A. 8vo.

2. BALLADS FROM MANUSCRIPTS. Vol. II. Part 1. The Poore Mans Pittance. By Richard Williams. Edited by F. J. FURNIVALL, M.A. 8vo.

1869.

3. THE ROXBURGHE BALLADS. Part 1. With short Notes by W. CHAPPELL, Esq., F.S.A., author of "Popular Music of the Olden Time," etc., etc., and with copies of the Original Woodcuts, drawn by Mr. RUDOLPH BLIND and Mr. W. H. HOOPER, and engraved by Mr. J. H. RIMBAULT and Mr. HOOPER. 8vo.

1870.

4. THE ROXBURGHE BALLADS. Vol. I. Part II. With short Notes by W. CHAPPELL, Esq., F.S.A., and with copies of the Original Woodcuts, drawn by Mr. RUDOLPH BLIND and Mr. W. H. HOOPER, and engraved by Mr. J. H. RIMBAULT and Mr. HOOPER. 1871.

5. THE ROXBURGHE BALLADS. Vol. I. Part III. With an Introduction and short Notes by W. CHAPPELL, Esq., F.S.A., Author of "Popular Music of the Olden Times," etc., etc., and with Copies of the Original Woodcuts drawn by Mr. RUDOLPH BLIND and Mr. W. H. HOOPER, and engraved by Mr. J. H. RIMBAULT and Mr. HOOPER.

6. CAPTAIN COX, HIS BALLADS AND BOOKS; or, ROBERT LANEHAM'S Letter: Whearin part of the entertainment untoo the Queen's Majesty at Kellingworth Castl, in Warwik Sheer in this Soomer Progress, 1575, is signified; from a freend Officer attendant in the Court, unto his freend, a Citizen and Merchant of London. Re-edited, with Forewords describing all the accessible Books, Tales, and Ballads in Captain Cox's List, and the COMPLAYNT OF SCOTLAND, 1548–9 A.D. By F. J. FURNIVVLL, M.A., Cambs.

Ballantyne.—Elements of Hindí and Braj Bháká Grammar. By the late James R. Ballantyne, LL.D. Second edition, revised and corrected Crown 8vo., pp. 44, cloth. 5s.

Ballantyne.—First Lessons in Sanskrit Grammar; together with an Introduction to the Hitopadésa. Second edition. By James R. Ballantyne. LL.D., Librarian of the India Office. 8vo. pp. viii. and 110, cloth. 1869. 5s.

Bartlett.—Dictionary of Americanisms: a Glossary of Words and Phrases colloquially used in the United States. By John R. Bartlett. Second Edition, considerably enlarged and improved. 1 vol. 8vo., pp. xxxii. and 524, cloth. 16s.

Beal.—Travels of Fah Hian and Sung-Yun, Buddhist Pilgrims from China to India (400 A.D. and 518 A.D.) Translated from the Chinese, by S. Beal (B.A. Trinity College, Cambridge), a Chaplain in Her Majesty's Fleet, a Member of the Royal Asiatic Society, and Author of a Translation of the Pratimóksha and the Amithûba Sûtra from the Chinese. Crown 8vo. pp. lxxlii. and 210, cloth, ornamental, with a coloured map. 10s. 6d.

Beal.—A Catena of Buddhist Scriptures from the Chinese. By S. Beal, B.A., Trinity College, Cambridge; a Chaplain in Her Majesty's Fleet, etc. 8vo. cloth, pp. xiv. and 436. 1871. 15s.

Beames.—Outlines of Indian Philology. With a Map, showing the Distribution of the Indian Languages. By John Beames. Second enlarged and revised edition. Crown 8vo. cloth, pp. viii. and 96. 5s.

Beames.—Notes on the Bhojpuri Dialect of Hindí, spoken in Western Behar. By John Beames, Esq., B.C.S., Magistrate of Chumparun. 8vo. pp. 26, sewed. 1868. 1s. 6d.

Beames.—A Comparative Grammar of the Modern Aryan Languages of India (to wit), Hindi, Panjabi, Sindhi, Gujarati, Marathi, Uriya, and Bengali. By John Beames, Bengal C.S., M.R.A.S., &c. [*In preparation.*]

Bell.—English Visible Speech for the Million, for communicating the Exact Pronunciation of the Language to Native or Foreign Learners, and for Teaching Children and illiterate Adults to Read in few Days. By Alexander Melville Bell, F.E.I.S., F.R.S.S.A., Lecturer on Elocution in University College, London. 4to. sewed, pp. 16. 1s.

Bell.—Visible Speech; the Science of Universal Alphabetics, or Self-Interpreting Physiological Letters, for the Writing of all Languages in one Alphabet. Illustrated by Tables, Diagrams, and Examples. By Alexander Melville Bell, F.E.I.S., F.R.S.A., Professor of Vocal Physiology, etc. 4to., pp. 156, cloth. 15s.

Bellew.—A Dictionary of the Pukkhto, or Pukshto Language, on a New and Improved System. With a reversed Part, or English and Pukkhto. By H. W. Bellew, Assistant Surgeon, Bengal Army. Super Royal 8vo., pp. xii. and 356, cloth. 42s.

Bellew.—A Grammar of the Pukkhto or Pukshto Language, on a New and Improved System. Combining Brevity with Utility, and Illustrated by Exercises and Dialogues. By H. W. Bellew, Assistant Surgeon, Bengal Army. Super-royal 8vo., pp. xii. and 156. cloth. 21s.

Bellows.—English Outline Vocabulary, for the use of Students of the Chinese, Japanese, and other Languages. Arranged by John Bellows. With Notes on the writing of Chinese with Roman Letters. By Professor Summers, King's College, London. Crown 8vo., pp. 6 and 368, cloth. 6s.

Bellows.—Outline Dictionary, for the use of Missionaries, Explorers, and Students of Language. By Max Müller, M.A., Taylorian Professor in the University of Oxford. With an Introduction on the proper use of the ordinary English Alphabet in transcribing Foreign Languages. The Vocabulary compiled by John Bellows. Crown 8vo. Limp morocco, pp. xxxi. and 368. 7s. 6d.

Benfey.—A GRAMMAR OF THE LANGUAGE OF THE VEDAS. By Dr. THEODOR BENFEY. In 1 vol. 8vo., of about 650 pages. [*In preparation.*]

Benfey.—A PRACTICAL GRAMMAR OF THE SANSKRIT LANGUAGE, for the use of Early Students. By THEODOR BENFEY, Professor of Sanskrit in the University of Göttingen. Second, revised and enlarged, edition. Royal 8vo. pp. viii. and 296, cloth. 10s. 6d.

Beurmann.—VOCABULARY OF THE TIGRÉ LANGUAGE. Written down by MORITZ VON BEURMANN. Published with a Grammatical Sketch. By Dr. A. MERX, of the University of Jena. pp. viii. and 78, cloth. 3s. 6d.

Bhagavat-Geeta.—See under WILKINS.

Bholanauth Chunder.—THE TRAVELS OF A HINDOO TO VARIOUS PARTS OF BENGAL and Upper India. By BHOLANAUTH CHUNDER, Member of the Asiatic Society of Bengal. With an Introduction by J. Talboys Wheeler, Esq., Author of "The History of India." Dedicated, by permission, to His Excellency Sir John Laird Mair Lawrence, G.C.B., G.C.S.I., Viceroy and Governor-General of India, tc. In 2 volumes, crown 8vo., cloth, pp. xxv. and 440, viii. and 410. 21s.

Bibliotheca Hispano-Americana. A Catalogue of SPANISH BOOKS printed in Mexico, Guatemala, Honduras, The Antilles, Venezuela, Columbia, Ecuador, Peru, Chili, Uraguay, and the Argentine Republic; and of Portuguese Books printed in Brazil. Followed by a Collection of WORKS ON THE ABORIGINAL LANGUAGES OF AMERICA. On sale at the affixed prices, by Trübner & Co., 8 and 60, Paternoster Row. Fcap. 8vo. pp. 184, sewed. 1870. 1s. 6d.

Bigandet.—THE LIFE OR LEGEND OF GAUDAMA, the Buddha of the Burmese, with Annotations. The ways to Neibban, and Notice on the Phongyies, or Burmese Monks. By the Right Reverend P. BIGANDET, Bishop of Ramatha, Vicar Apostolic of Ava and Pegu. 8vo. sewed, pp. xi., 538, and v. 18s.

Bleek.—A COMPARATIVE GRAMMAR OF SOUTH AFRICAN LANGUAGES. By W. H. I. BLEEK, Ph.D. Volume I. I. Phonology. II. The Concord. Section I. The Noun. 8vo. pp. xxxvi. and 322, cloth. 16s.

Bleek.—REYNARD IN SOUTH AFRICA; or, Hottentot Fables. Translated from the Original Manuscript in Sir George Grey's Library. By Dr. W. H. I. BLEEK, Librarian to the Grey Library, Cape Town, Cape of Good Hope. In one volume, small 8vo., pp. xxxi. and 94, cloth. 3s. 6d.

Bombay Sanskrit Series. Edited under the superintendence of G. BÜHLER, Ph.D., Professor of Oriental Languages, Elphinstone College, and F. KIELHORN, Ph.D., Superintendent of Sanskrit Studies, Deccan College.

Already published.

1. PANCHATANTRA IV. AND V. Edited, with Notes, by G. BÜHLER, Ph.D. Pp. 84, 16. 4s. 6d.
2. NÁGOJÍBHAṬṬA'S PARIBHÁSHENDUŚEKHARA. Edited and explained by F. KIELHORN, Ph.D. Part I., the Sanskrit Text and various readings. pp. 116. 8s. 6d.
3. PANCHATANTRA II. AND III. Edited, with Notes, by G. BÜHLER, Ph.D. Pp. 86, 14, 2. 5s. 6d.
4. PANCHATANTRA I. Edited, with Notes, by F. KIELHORN, Ph.D. Pp. 114, 53. 6s. 6d.
5. KÁLIDÁSA'S RAGHUVAŚA. With the Commentary of Mallinátha. Edited, with Notes, by SHANKAR P. PANDIT, M.A. Part I. Cantos I.-VI. 9s.
6. KÁLIDÁSA'S MÁLAVIKÁGNIMITRA. Edited, with Notes, by SHANKAR P. PANDIT, M.A. 8s.
7. NÁGOJÍBHAṬṬA'S PARIBHÁSHENDUŚEKHARA Edited and explained by F. KIELHORN, Ph.D. Part II. Translation and Notes. (Paribháshás, i.-xxxvii.) pp. 184. 8s.

Bottrell.—TRADITIONS AND HEARTHSIDE STORIES OF WEST CORNWALL. By WILLIAM BOTTRELL (an old Celt). Demy 12mo. pp. vi. 292, cloth. 1870. 6*s.*

Boyce.—A GRAMMAR OF THE KAFFIR LANGUAGE.— By WILLIAM B. BOYES, Wesleyan Missionary. Third Edition, augmented and improved, with Exercises, by WILLIAM J. DAVIS, Wesleyan Missionary. 12mo. pp. xii. and 164, cloth. 8*s.*

Bowditch.—SUFFOLK SURNAMES. By N. I. BOWDITCH. Third Edition, 8vo. pp. xxvi. and 758, cloth. 7*s.* 6*d.*

Bretschneider.—ON THE KNOWLEDGE POSSESSED BY THE ANCIENT CHINESE OF THE ARABS AND ARABIAN COLONIES, and other Western Countries mentioned in Chinese Books. By E. BRETSCHNEIDER, M.D., Physician of the Russian Legation at Peking. 8vo. pp. 28, sewed. 1871. 1*s.*

Brhat-Sanhita (The).—See under Kern.

Brice.—A ROMANIZED HINDUSTANI AND ENGLISH DICTIONARY. Designed for the use of Schools and for Vernacular Students of the Language. Compiled by NATHANIEL BRICE. New Edition, Revised and Enlarged. Post 8vo. cloth, pp. vi. and 357. 8*s.*

Brinton.—THE MYTHS OF THE NEW WORLD. A Treatise on the Symbolism and Mythology of the Red Races of America. By DANIEL G. BRINTON, A.M., M.D. Crown 8vo. cloth, pp. viii. and 308. 10*s.* 6*d.*

Brown.—THE DERVISHES; or, ORIENTAL SPIRITUALISM. By JOHN P. BROWN, Secretary and Dragoman of the Legation of the United States of America at Constantinople. With twenty-four Illustrations. 8vo. cloth, pp. viii. and 415. 14*s.*

Brown.—CARNATIC CHRONOLOGY. The Hindu and Mahomedan Methods of Reckoning Time explained : with Essays on the Systems ; Symbols used for Numerals, a new Titular Method of Memory, Historical Records, and other subjects. By CHARLES PHILIP BROWN, Member of the Royal Asiatic Society ; late of the Madras Civil Service ; Telugu Translator to Government ; Senior Member of the College Board, etc. ; Author of the Telugu Dictionaries and Grammar, etc. 4to. sewed, pp. xii. and 90. 10*s.* 6*d.*

Brown.—SANSKRIT PROSODY AND NUMERICAL SYMBOLS EXPLAINED. By CHARLES PHILIP BROWN, Author of the Telugu Dictionary, Grammar, etc., Professor of Telugu in the University of London. Demy 8vo. pp. 64, cloth. 3*s.* 6*d.*

Buddhaghosha's Parables: translated from Burmese by Captain H. T. ROGERS, R.E. With an Introduction containing Buddha's Dhammapadam, or, Path of Virtue ; translated from Pali by F. MAX MÜLLER. 8vo. pp. 378, cloth. 12*s.* 6*d.*

Burgess.—SURYA-SIDDHANTA (Translation of the): A Text-book of Hindu Astronomy, with Notes and an Appendix, containing additional Notes and Tables, Calculations of Eclipses, a Stellar Map, and Indexes. By Rev. EBENEZER BURGESS, formerly Missionary of the American Board of Commissioners of Foreign Missions in India ; assisted by the Committee of Publication of the American Oriental Society. 8vo. pp. iv. and 354, boards. 15*s.*

Burnell.—CATALOGUE OF A COLLECTION OF SANSKRIT MANUSCRIPTS. By A. C. BURNELL, M.R.A.S., Madras Civil Service. PART 1. *Vedic Manuscripts.* Fcap. 8vo. pp. 64, sewed. 1870. 2*s.*

Byington.—GRAMMAR OF THE CHOCTAW LANGUAGE. By the Rev. CYRUS BYINGTON. Edited from the Original MSS. in the Library of the American Philosophical Society, by D. G. BRINTON, A.M., M.D., Member of the American Philosophical Society, the Pennsylvania Historical Society, Corresponding Member of the American Ethnological Society, etc. 8vo. sewed, pp. 56. 12*s.*

Calcutta Review.—THE CALCUTTA REVIEW. Published Quarterly. Price 8*s.* 6*d.*

Callaway.—IZINGANEKWANE, NENSUMANSUMANE, NEZINDABA, ZABANTU (Nursery Tales, Traditions, and Histories of the Zulus). In their own words, with a Translation into English, and Notes. By the Rev. HENRY CALLAWAY, M.D. Volume I., 8vo. pp. xiv. and 378, cloth. Natal, 1866 and 1867. 16*s.*

Callaway. — THE RELIGIOUS SYSTEM OF THE AMAZULU.

Part I.—Unkulunkulu; or, the Tradition of Creation as existing among the Amazulu and other Tribes of South Africa, in their own words, with a translation into English, and Notes. By the Rev. Canon CALLAWAY, M.D. 8vo. pp. 128, sewed. 1868. 4*s.*

Part II.—Amatongo; or, Ancestor Worship, as existing among the Amazulu, in their own words, with a translation into English, and Notes. By the Rev. CANON CALLAWAY, M.D. 1869. 8vo. pp. 127. sewed. 1869. 4*s.*

Part III.—Izinyanga Zokubula; or, Divination, as existing among the Amazulu, in their own words. With a Translation into English, and Notes. By the Rev. Canon CALLAWAY, M.D. 8vo. pp. 150, sewed. 1870. 4*s.*

Part IV.—On Medical Magic and Witchcraft. [*In preparation.*

Calligaris.—LE COMPAGNON DE TOUS, OU DICTIONNAIRE POLYGLOTTE. Par le Colonel LOUIS CALLIGARIS, Grand Officier, etc. (French—Latin—Italian—Spanish—Portuguese—German—English—Modern Greek—Arabic—Turkish.) 2 vols. 4to., pp. 1157 and 746. Turin. £4 4*s.*

Canones Lexicographici; or, Rules to be observed in Editing the New English Dictionary of the Philological Society, prepared by a Committee of the Society. 8vo., pp. 12, sewed. 6*d.*

Carpenter.—THE LAST DAYS IN ENGLAND OF THE RAJAH RAMMOHUN ROY. By MARY CARPENTER, of Bristol. With Five Illustrations. 8vo. pp. 272, cloth. 7*s.* 6*d.*

Carr.—ఆంధ్రలోకోక్తి చంద్రిక. A COLLECTION OF TELUGU PROVERBS, Translated, Illustrated, and Explained; together with some Sanscrit Proverbs printed in the Devnâgarî and Telugu Characters. By Captain M. W. CARR, Madras Staff Corps. One Vol. and Supplemnt, royal 8vo. pp. 488 and 148. 31*s.* 6*d*

Catlin.—O-KEE-PA. A Religious Ceremony of the Mandans. By GEORGE CATLIN. With 13 Coloured Illustrations. 4to. pp. 60, bound in cloth, gilt edges. 14*s.*

Chalmers.—THE ORIGIN OF THE CHINESE; an Attempt to Trace the connection of the Chinese with Western Nations in their Religion, Superstitions, Arts, Language, and Traditions. By JOHN CHALMERS, A.M. Foolscap 8vo. cloth, pp. 78. 2*s.* 6*d.*

Chalmers.—THE SPECULATIONS ON METAPHYSICS, POLITY, AND MORALITY OF "THE OLD PHILOSOPHER" LAU TSZE. Translated from the Chinese, with an Introduction by John Chalmers, M.A. Fcap. 8vo. cloth, xx. and 62. 4*s.* 6*d.*

Chalmers.—AN ENGLISH AND CANTONESE POCKET-DICTIONARY, for the use of those who wish to learn the spoken language of Canton Province. By JOHN CHALMERS, M.A. Third edition. Crown 8vo., pp. iv. and 146. Hong Kong, 1871. 15*s.*

Charnock.—LUDUS PATRONYMICUS; or, the Etymology of Curious Surnames. By RICHARD STEPHEN CHARNOCK, Ph.D., F.S.A., F.R.G.S. Crown 8vo., pp. 182, cloth. 7*s.* 6*d.*

Charnock.—VERBA NOMINALIA; or Words derived from Proper Names. By RICHARD STEPHEN CHARNOCK, Ph. Dr. F.S.A., etc. 8vo. pp. 326, cloth. 14*s.*

Charnock.—THE PEOPLES OF TRANSYLVANIA. Founded on a Paper read before THE ANTHROPOLOGICAL SOCIETY OF LONDON, on the 4th of May, 1869. By RICHARD STEPHEN CHARNOCK, Ph.D., F.S.A., F.R.G.S. Demy 8vo. pp. 36, sewed. 1870. 2*s.* 6*d.*

Chaucer Society's Publications. Subscription, two guineas per annum.

1868. *First Series.*

CANTERBURY TALES. Part I.

I. The Prologue and Knight's Tale, in 6 parallel Texts (from the 6 MSS. named below), together with Tables, showing the Groups of the Tales, and their varying order in 38 MSS. of the Tales, and in the old printed editions, and also Specimens from several MSS. of the " Moveable Prologues" of the Canterbury Tales,—The Shipman's Prologue, and Franklin's Prologue,—when moved from their right places, and of the substitutes for them.

II. The Prologue and Knight's Tale from the Ellesmere MS.

III.	,,	,,	·,	,,	,,	,,	,,	Hengwrt	,,	154.
IV.	,,	,,	,,	,,	,,	,,	,,	Cambridge	,,	Gg. 4. 27.
V.	,,	,,	,,	.	,,	,,	,,	Corpus	,,	Oxford.
VI.	,,	,,	,,	,,	,,	,,	,,	Petworth	,,	
VII.	,,	,,	,,	,,	,,	,,	,,	Lansdowne	,,	851.

Nos. II. to VII. are separate Texts of the 6-Text edition of the Canterbury Tales, Part I.

1868. *Second Series.*

ON EARLY ENGLISH PRONUNCIATION, with especial reference to Shakspere and Chaucer, containing an investigation of the Correspondence of Writing with Speech in England, from the Anglo-Saxon period to the present day, preceded by a systematic notation of all spoken sounds, by means of the ordinary printing types. Including a re-arrangement of Prof. F. J. Child's Memoirs on the Language of Chaucer and Gower, and Reprints of the Rare Tracts by Salesbury on English, 1547, and Welsh, 1567, and by Barcley on French, 1521. By ALEXANDER J. ELLIS, F.R.S., etc., etc. Part I. On the Pronunciation of the XIVth, XVIth, XVIIth, and XVIIIth centuries.

ESSAYS ON CHAUCER; His Words and Works. Part I. 1. Ebert's Review of Sandras's *Etude sur Chaucer, considéré comme Imitateur des Trouvères,* translated by J. W. Van Rees Hoets, M.A., Trinity Hall, Cambridge, and revised by the Author.—II. A Thirteenth Century Latin Treatise on the *Chilindre:* "For by my *chilindre* it is prime of day " (*Shipmannes Tale*). Edited, with a Translation, by Mr. EDMUND BROCK, and illustrated by a Woodcut of the Instrument from the Ashmole MS. 1522.

A TEMPORARY PREFACE to the Six-Text Edition of Chaucer's Canterbury Tales. Part I. Attempting to show the true order of the Tales, and the Days and Stages of the Pilgrimage, etc., etc. By F. J. FURNIVALL, Esq., M.A., Trinity Hall, Cambridge.

1869. *First Series.*

VIII.	The Miller's, Reeve's, Cook's, and Gamelyn's Tales :	Ellesmere MS.
IX.	,, ,, ,, ,, ,, ,, ,,	Hengwrt ,,
X.	,, ,, ,, ,, ,, ,, ,,	Cambridge ,,
XI.	,, ,, ,, ,, ,, ,, ,,	Corpus ,,
XII.	,, ,, ,· ,, ,, ,, ,,	Petworth ,,
XIII.	,, ,, ,, ,, ,, ,, ,,	Lansdowne ,,

These are separate issues of the 6-Text Chaucer's Canterbury Tales, Part II.

1869. *Second Series.*

ENGLISH PRONUNCIATION, with especial reference to Shakspere and Chaucer. By ALEXANDER J. ELLIS, F.R.S. Part II.

1870. *First Series.*

XIV. CANTERBURY TALES. Part II. The Miller's, Reeve's, and Cook's Tales, with an Appendix of the Spurious Tale of Gamelyn, in Six parallel Texts.

Chaucer Society's Publications—*continued.*

1870. *Second Series.*

ON EARLY ENGLISH PRONUNCIATION, with especial reference to Shakspere and Chaucer. By A. J. ELLIS, F.R.S., F.S.A. Part III. Illustrations
on the Pronunciation of xivth and xvith Centuries. Chaucer, Gower, Wycliffe,
Spenser, Shakespere, Salesbury, Barclay, Hart, Bullokar, Gill. Pronouncing
Vocabulary.

1871. *First Series.*

XV. CANTERBURY TALES. Part III. In Six Parallel Texts. The Man of
Law's Tale.—The Shipman's Tale.—The Prioress's Tale.—The Tale
of Sir Thopas.

XVI. The Man of Law's Tale, &c., &c. : Ellesmere MS.
XVII. „   „   „   „   Cambridge „
XVIII. „   „   „   „   Corpus „
XIX. „   „   „   „   Petworth „
XX. „   „   „   „   Lansdowne „

Childers.—KHUDDAKA PATHA. A Páli Text, with a Translation and
Notes. By R. C. CHILDERS, late of the Ceylon Civil Service. 8vo. pp. 32,
stitched. 1s. 6d.

Childers.—A PÁLI-ENGLISH DICTIONARY, with Sanskrit Equivalents,
and with numerous Quotations, Extracts, and References. Compiled by R. C.
CHILDERS, late of the Ceylon Civil Service.   [*In preparation.*

Childers.—A PÁLI GRAMMAR FOR BEGINNERS. By ROBERT C. CHILDERS.
In 1 vol. 8vo. cloth.   [*In preparation.*

Childers. — NOTES ON DHAMMAPADA, with special reference to the
question of Nirvâna. By R. C. CHILDERS, late of the Ceylon Civil Service.
8vo. pp. 12, sewed. Price 1s.

Childers. — ON THE ORIGIN OF THE BUDDHIST ARTHAKATHÁS. By
the Mudliar L. COMRILLA VIJASINHA, Government Interpreter to the
Ratnapura Court, Ceylon. With an Introduction by R. C. CHILDERS, late of
the Ceylon Civil Service. 8vo. sewed. 1871. 1s.

Clarke.—TEN GREAT RELIGIONS : an Essay in Comparative Theology.
By JAMES FREEMAN CLARKE. 8vo. cloth, pp. x. and 528. 1871. 14s.

Colebrooke.—THE LIFE AND MISCELLANEOUS ESSAYS OF HENRY THOMAS
COLEBROOKE. The Biography by his Son, Sir T. E. COLEBROOKE, Bart., M.P.,
The Essays edited by Professor Cowell. In 3 vols.   [*In the press.*

Colenso.—FIRST STEPS IN ZULU-KAFIR : An Abridgement of the Elementary Grammar of the Zulu-Kafir Language. By the Right Rev. JOHN W.
COLENSO, Bishop of Natal. 8vo. pp. 86, cloth. Ekukanyeni, 1859. 4s. 6d.

Colenso.—ZULU-ENGLISH DICTIONARY. By the Right Rev. JOHN W. Co-
LENSO, Bishop of Natal. 8vo. pp. viii. and 552, sewed. Pietermaritzburg, 1861.
£1 1s.

Colenso.—FIRST ZULU-KAFIR READING BOOK, two parts in one. By the
Right Rev. JOHN W. COLENSO, Bishop of Natal. 16mo. pp. 44, sewed. Natal. 1s.

Colenso.—SECOND ZULU-KAFIR READING BOOK. By the same. 16mo.
pp. 108, sewed. Natal. 3s.

Colenso.—FOURTH ZULU-KAFIR READING BOOK. By the same. 8vo.
pp. 160, cloth. Natal, 1859. 7s.

Colenso.—Three Native Accounts of the Visits of the Bishop of Natal
in September and October, 1859, to Upmande, King of the Zulus ; with Explanatory Notes and a Literal Translation, and a Glossary of all the Zulu Words
employed in the same : designed for the use of Students of the Zulu Language.
By the Right Rev. JOHN W. COLENSO, Bishop of Natal. 16mo. pp. 160, stiff
cover. Natal, Maritzburg, 1860. 4s. 6d.

Coleridge.—A GLOSSARIAL INDEX to the Printed English Literature of
the Thirteenth Century. By HERBERT COLERIDGE, Esq. 8vo. cloth. pp. 104,
2s. 6d.

Colleccao de Vocabulos e Frases usados na Provincia de S. Pedro, do Rio Grande do Sul, no Brasil. 12mo. pp. 32, sewed. 1s.

Contopoulos.—A LEXICON OF MODERN GREEK-ENGLISH AND ENGLISH MODERN GREEK. By N. CONTOPOULOS.
Part I. Modern Greek-English. 8vo. cloth, pp. 460. 12s.
Part II. English-Modern Greek. 8vo. cloth, pp. 582. 15s.

Cunningham.—THE ANCIENT GEOGRAPHY OF INDIA. I. The Buddhist Period, including the Campaigns of Alexander, and the Travels of Hwen-Thsang. By ALEXANDER CUNNINGHAM, Major-General, Royal Engineers (Bengal Retired). With thirteen Maps. 8vo. pp. xx. 590, cloth. 1870. 28s.

Cunningham.—AN ESSAY ON THE ARIAN ORDER OF ARCHITECTURE, as exhibited in the Temples of Kashmere. By Captain (now Major-General) ALEXANDER CUNNINGHAM. 8vo. pp. 86, cloth. With seventeen large folding Plates. 18s.

Cunningham.—THE BHILSA TOPES; or, Buddhist Monuments of Central India: comprising a brief Historical Sketch of the Rise, Progress, and Decline of Buddhism; with an Account of the Opening and Examination of the various Groups of Topes around Bhilsa. By Brev.-Major Alexander Cunningham, Bengal Engineers. Illustrated with thirty-three Plates. 8vo. pp. xxxvi. 370, cloth. 1854. 21s.

D'Alwis.—A DESCRIPTIVE CATALOGUE OF SANSKRIT, PALI, AND SINHALESE LITERARY WORKS OF CEYLON. By JAMES D'ALWIS, M.R.A.S., Advocate of the Supreme Court, &c., &c. In Three Volumes. Vol. I., pp. xxxii. and 244, sewed. 1870. 8s. 6d.   [*Vols. II. and III. in preparation.*

De Gubernatis.—MYTHICAL ZOOLOGY; or, the Legends of Animals. By ANGELO DE GUBERNATIS, Professor of Sanskrit and Comparative Literature at Florence.   [*In the press.*

Delepierre.—REVUE ANALYTIQUE DES OUVRAGES ÉCRITS EN CENTONS, depuis les Temps Anciens, jusqu'au xixième Siècle. Par un Bibliophile Belge. Small 4to. pp. 508, stiff covers. 1868. 30s.

Delepierre.—ESSAI HISTORIQUE ET BIBLIOGRAPHIQUE SUR LES RÉBUS. Par Octave Delepierre. 8vo. pp. 24, sewed. With 15 pages of Woodcuts. 1870. 3s. 6d.

Dennys.—CHINA AND JAPAN. A complete Guide to the Open Ports of those countries, together with Pekin, Yeddo, Hong Kong, and Macao; forming a Guide Book and Vade Mecum for Travellers, Merchants, and Residents in general; with 56 Maps and Plans. By WM. FREDERICK MAYERS, F.R.G.S. H.M.'s Consular Service; N. B. DENNYS, late H.M.'s Consular Service; and CHARLES KING, Lieut. Royal Marine Artillery. Edited by N. B. DENNYS. In one volume. 8vo. pp. 600, cloth. £2 2s.

Döhne.—A ZULU-KAFIR DICTIONARY, etymologically explained, with copious Illustrations and examples, preceded by an introduction on the Zulu-Kafir Language. By the Rev. J. L. DÖHNE. Royal 8vo. pp. xlii. and 418, sewed. Cape Town, 1857. 21s.

Döhne.—THE FOUR GOSPELS IN ZULU. By the Rev. J. L. DÖHNE, Missionary to the American Board, C.F.M. 8vo. pp. 208, cloth. Pietermaritzburg, 1866. 5s.

Doolittle.—AN ENGLISH AND CHINESE DICTIONARY. By the Rev. JUSTUS DOOLITTLE, China.   [*In the Press.*

Dowson.—A GRAMMAR OF THE HINDUSTANI LANGUAGE. By JOHN DOWSON, M.R.A.S., Staff College, Sandhurst. Cr. 8vo.   [*In the press.*

12   *Linguistic Publications of Trübner & Co.*

Early English Text Society's Publications. Subscription, one guinea per annum.

1. EARLY ENGLISH ALLITERATIVE POEMS. In the West-Midland Dialect of the Fourteenth Century. Edited by R. MORRIS, Esq., from an unique Cottonian MS. 16*s.*
2. ARTHUR (about 1440 A.D.). Edited by F. J. FURNIVALL, Esq., from the Marquis of Bath's unique MS. 4*s.*
3. ANE COMPENDIOUS AND BREUE TRACTATE CONCERNYNG YE OFFICE AND DEWTIE OF KYNGIS, etc. By WILLIAM LAUDER. (1556 A.D.) Edited by F. HALL, Esq., D.C.L. 4*s.*
4. SIR GAWAYNE AND THE GREEN KNIGHT (about 1320-30 A.D.). Edited by R. MORRIS, Esq., from an unique Cottonian MS. 10*s.*
5. OF THE ORTHOGRAPHIE AND CONGRUITIE OF THE BRITAN TONGUE; a treates, noe shorter than necessarie, for the Schooles, be ALEXANDER HUME. Edited for the first time from the unique MS. in the British Museum (about 1617 A.D.), by HENRY B. WHEATLEY, Esq. 4*s.*
6. LANCELOT OF THE LAIK. Edited from the unique MS. in the Cambridge University Library (ab. 1500), by the Rev. WALTER W. SKEAT, M.A. 8*s.*
7. THE STORY OF GENESIS AND EXODUS, an Early English Song, of about 1250 A.D. Edited for the first time from the unique MS. in the Library of Corpus Christi College, Cambridge, by R. MORRIS, Esq. 8*s.*
8. MORTE ARTHURE; the Alliterative Version. Edited from ROBERT THORNTON's unique MS. (about 1440 A.D.) at Lincoln, by the Rev. GEORGE PERRY, M.A., Prebendary of Lincoln. 7*s.*
9. ANIMADVERSIONS UPPON THE ANNOTACIONS AND CORRECTIONS OF SOME IMPERFECTIONS OF IMPRESSIONES OF CHAUCER'S WORKES, reprinted in 1598; by FRANCIS THYNNE. Edited from the unique MS. in the Bridgewater Library. By G. H. KINGSLEY, Esq., M.D. 4*s.*
10. MERLIN, OR THE EARLY HISTORY OF KING ARTHUR. Edited for the first time from the unique MS. in the Cambridge University Library (about 1450 A.D.), by HENRY B. WHEATLEY, Esq. Part I. 2*s.* 6*d.*
11. THE MONARCHE, and other Poems of Sir David Lyndesay. Edited from the first edition by JOHNE SKOTT, in 1552, by FITZEDWARD HALL, Esq., D.C.L. Part I. 3*s.*
12. THE WRIGHT'S CHASTE WIFE, a Merry Tale, by Adam of Cobsam (about 1462 A.D.), from the unique Lambeth MS. 306. Edited for the first time by F. J. FURNIVALL, Esq., M.A. 1*s.*
13. SEINTE MARHERETE, þE MEIDEN ANT MARTYR. Three Texts of ab. 1200, 1310, 1330 A.D. First edited in 1862, by the Rev. OSWALD COCKAYNE, M.A., and now re-issued. 2*s.*
14. KYNG HORN, with fragments of Floriz and Blauncheflur, and the Assumption of the Blessed Virgin. Edited from the MSS. in the Library of the University of Cambridge and the British Museum, by the Rev. J. RAWSON LUMBY. 3*s.* 6*d.*
15. POLITICAL, RELIGIOUS, AND LOVE POEMS, from the Lambeth MS. No. 306, and other sources. Edited by F. J. FURNIVALL, Esq., M.A. 7*s.* 6*d.*
16. A TRETICE IN ENGLISH breuely drawe out of þ book of Quintis essencijs in Latyn, þ Hermys þ prophete and king of Egipt after þ flood of Noe, fader of Philosophris, hadde by reuelacioun of an aungil of God to him sente. Edited from the Sloane MS. 73, by F. J. FURNIVALL, Esq., M.A. 1*s.*
17. PARALLEL EXTRACTS from 29 Manuscripts of PIERS PLOWMAN, with Comments, and a Proposal for the Society's Three-text edition of this Poem. By the Rev. W. SKEAT, M.A. 1*s.*
18. HALI MEIDENHEAD, about 1200 A.D. Edited for the first time from the MS. (with a translation) by the Rev. OSWALD COCKAYNE, M.A. 1*s.*

Early English Text Society's Publications—*continued.*

19. THE MONARCHE, and other Poems of Sir David Lyndesay. Part II., the Complaynt of the King's Papingo, and other minor Poems. Edited from the First Edition by F. HALL, Esq., D.C.L. 3s. 6d.

20. SOME TREATISES BY RICHARD ROLLE DE HAMPOLE. Edited from Robert of Thornton's MS. (ab. 1440 A.D.), by Rev. GEORGE G. PERRY, M.A. 1s.

21. MERLIN, OR THE EARLY HISTORY OF KING ARTHUR. Part II. Edited by HENRY B. WHEATLEY, Esq. 4s.

22. THE ROMANS OF PARTENAY, OR LUSIGNEN. Edited for the first time from the unique MS. in the Library of Trinity College, Cambridge, by the Rev. W. W. SKEAT. M.A. 6s.

23. DAN MICHEL'S AYENBITE OF INWYT, or Remorse of Conscience, in the Kentish dialect, 1340 A.D. Edited from the unique MS. in the British Museum, by RICHARD MORRIS, Esq. 10s. 6d.

24. HYMNS OF THE VIRGIN AND CHRIST; THE PARLIAMENT OF DEVILS, and Other Religious Poems. Edited from the Lambeth MS. 853, by F. J. FURNIVALL, M.A. 3s.

25. THE STACIONS OF ROME, and the Pilgrim's Sea-Voyage and Sea-Sickness, with Clene Maydenhod. Edited from the Vernon and Porkington MSS., etc., by F. J. FURNIVALL, Esq., M.A. 1s.

26. RELIGIOUS PIECES IN PROSE AND VERSE. Containing Dan Jon Gaytrigg's Sermon; The Abbaye of S. Spirit; Sayne Jon, and other pieces in the Northern Dialect. Edited from Robert of Thorntone's MS. (ab. 1460 A.D.), by the Rev. G. PERRY, M.A. 2s.

27. MANIPULUS VOCABULORUM : a Rhyming Dictionary of the English Language, by PETER LEVINS (1570). Edited, with an Alphabetical Index, by HENRY B. WHEATLEY. 12s.

28. THE VISION OF WILLIAM CONCERNING PIERS PLOWMAN, together with Vita de Dowel, Dobet et Dobest. 1362 A.D., by WILLIAM LANGLAND. The earliest or Vernon Text; Text A. Edited from the Vernon MS., with full Collations, by Rev. W. W. SKEAT, M.A. 7s.

29. OLD ENGLISH HOMILIES AND HOMILETIC TREATISES. (Sawles Warde and the Wohunge of Ure Lauerd : Ureisuns of Ure Louerd and of Ure Lefdi, etc.) of the Twelfth and Thirteenth Centuries. Edited from MSS. in the British Museum, Lambeth, and Bodleian Libraries; with Introduction, Translation, and Notes. By RICHARD MORRIS. *First Series.* Part I. 7s.

30. PIERS, THE PLOUGHMAN'S CREDE (about 1394). Edited from the MSS. by the Rev. W. W. SKEAT, M.A. 2s.

31. INSTRUCTIONS FOR PARISH PRIESTS. By JOHN MYRC. Edited from Cotton MS. Claudius A. II., by EDWARD PEACOCK, Esq., F.S.A., etc., etc. 4s.

32. THE BABEES BOOK, Aristotle's A B C, Urbanitatis, Stans Puer ad Mensam, The Lytille Childreues Lytil Boke. THE BOKES OF NURTURE of Hugh Rhodes and John Russell, Wynkyn de Worde's Boke of Kervynge, The Booke of Demeanor, The Boke of Curtasye, Seager's Schoole of Vertue, etc., etc. With some French and Latin Poems on like subjects, and some Forewords on Education in Early England. Edited by F. J. FURNIVALL, M.A., Trin. Hall, Cambridge. 15s.

33. THE BOOK OF THE KNIGHT DE LA TOUR LANDRY, 1372. A Father's Book for his Daughters, Edited from the Harleian MS. 1764, by THOMAS WRIGHT, Esq., M.A., and Mr. WILLIAM ROSSITER. 8s.

34. OLD ENGLISH HOMILIES AND HOMILETIC TREATISES. (Sawles Warde, and the Wohunge of Ure Lauerd: Ureisuns of Ure Louerd and of Ure Lefdi, etc.) of the Twelfth and Thirteenth Centuries. Edited from MSS. in the British Museum, Lambeth, and Bodleian Libraries; with Introduction, Translation, and Notes, by RICHARD MORRIS. *First Series.* Part 2. 8s.

14   *Linguistic Publications of Trübner & Co.*

Early English English Text Society's Publications—*continued.*

35. SIR DAVID LYNDESAY'S WORKS. PART 3. The Historie of ane
    Nobil and Wailzeand Sqvyer, WILLIAM MELDRUM, umqvhyle Laird of
    Cleische and Bynnis, compylit be Sir DAUID LYNDESAY of the Mont *alias*
    Lyoun King of Armes. With the Testament of the said Williame Mel-
    drum, Squyer, compylit alswa be Sir Dauid Lyndesay, etc. Edited by F.
    HALL, D.C.L. 2*s.*

36. MERLIN, OR THE EARLY HISTORY OF KING ARTHUR. A Prose
    Romance (about 1450–1460 A.D.), edited from the unique MS. in the
    University Library, Cambridge, by HENRY B. WHEATLEY. With an Essay
    on Arthurian Localities, by J. S. STUART GLENNIE, Esq. Part III. 1869. 12*s.*

37. SIR DAVID LYNDESAY'S WORKS. Part IV. Ane Satyre of the
    thrie estaits, in commendation of vertew and vitvperation of vyce. Maid
    be Sir DAVID LINDESAY, of the Mont, *alias* Lyon King of Armes. At
    Edinbvrgh. Printed be Robert Charteris, 1602. Cvm privilegio regis.
    Edited by F. HALL, Esq., D.C.L. 4*s.*

38. THE VISION OF WILLIAM CONCERNING PIERS THE PLOWMAN,
    together with Vita de Dowel, Dobet, et Dobest, Secundum Wit et Resoun,
    by WILLIAM LANGLAND (1377 A.D.). The "Crowley" Text; or Text B.
    Edited from MS. Laud Misc. 581, collated with MS. Rawl. Poet. 38, MS.
    B. 15. 17. in the Library of Trinity College, Cambridge, MS. Dd. 1. 17. in
    the Cambridge University Library, the MS. in Oriel College, Oxford, MS.
    Bodley 814, etc. By the Rev. WALTER W. SKEAT, M.A., late Fellow of
    Christ's College, Cambridge. 10*s.* 6*d.*

39. THE "GEST HYSTORIALE" OF THE DESTRUCTION OF TROY. An
    Alliterative Romance, translated from Guido De Colonna's "Hystoria
    Troiana." Now first edited from the unique MS. in the Hunterian Museum,
    University of Glasgow, by the Rev. GEO. A. PANTON and DAVID DONALDSON.
    Part I. 10*s.* 6*d.*

40. ENGLISH GILDS. The Original Ordinances of more than One
    Hundred Early English Gilds : Together with the olde usages of the cite of
    Wynchestre; The Ordinances of Worcester; The Office of the Mayor of
    Bristol ; and the Customary of the Manor of Tettenhall-Regis. From
    Original MSS. of the Fourteenth and Fifteenth Centuries. Edited with
    Notes by the late TOULMIN SMITH, Esq., F.R.S. of Northern Antiquaries
    (Copenhagen). With an Introduction and Glossary, etc., by his daughter,
    LUCY TOULMIN SMITH. And a Preliminary Essay, in Five Parts, ON THE
    HISTORY AND DEVELOPMENT OF GILDS, by LUJO BRENTANO, Doctor Juris
    Utriusque et Philosophiæ. 21*s.*

41. THE MINOR POEMS OF WILLIAM LAUDER, Playwright, Poet, and
    Minister of the Word of God (mainly on the State of Scotland in and about
    1568 A.D., that year of Famine and Plague). Edited from the Unique
    Originals belonging to S. CHRISTIE-MILLER, Esq., of Britwell, by F. J.
    FURNIVALL, M.A., Trin. Hall, Camb. 3*s.*

42. BERNARDUS DE CURA REI FAMULIARIS, with some Early Scotch
    Prophecies, etc. From a MS., KK 1. 5, in the Cambridge University
    Library. Edited by J. RAWSON LUMBY, M.A., late Fellow of Magdalen
    College, Cambridge. 2*s.*

43. RATIS RAVING, and other Moral and Religious Pieces, in Prose and
    Verse. Edited from the Cambridge University Library MS. KK 1. 5, by J.
    RAWSON LUMBY, M.A., late Fellow of Magdalen College, Cambridge. 3*s.*

44. JOSEPH OF ARIMATHIE : otherwise called the Romance of the
    Seint Graal, or Holy Grail: an alliterative poem, written about A.D. 1350,
    and now first printed from the unique copy in the Vernon MS. at Oxford.
    With an appendix, containing "The Lyfe of Joseph of Armathy," reprinted
    from the black-letter copy of Wynkyn de Worde ; "De sancto Joseph ab
    Arimathia," first printed by Pynson, A.D. 1516; and "The Lyfe of Joseph of
    Arimathia," first printed by Pynson, A.D. 1520. Edited, with Notes and
    Glossarial Indices, by the Rev. WALTER W. SKEAT, M.A. 5*s.*

Early English Text Society's Publications—*continued.*

45. KING ALFRED'S WEST-SAXON VERSION OF GREGORY'S PASTORAL CARE.
With an English translation, the Latin Text, Notes, and an Introduction
Edited by HENRY SWEET, Esq., of Balliol College, Oxford. Part I. 10*s.*

46. LEGENDS OF THE HOLY ROOD; SYMBOLS OF THE PASSION AND CROSS-
POEMS. In Old English of the Eleventh, Fourteenth, and Fifteenth Centuries. Edited from MSS. in the British Museum and Bodleian Libraries;
with Introduction, Translations, and Glossarial Index. By RICHARD
MORRIS, LL.D. 10*s.*

47. SIR DAVID LYNDESAY'S WORKS. PART V. The Minor Poems of
Lyndesay. Edited by J. A. H. MURRAY, Esq. 3*s.*

48. THE TIMES' WHISTLE : or, A Nowe Daunce of Seven Satires, and
other Poems: Compiled by R. C., Gent. Now first Edited from MS. Y. 8. 3.
in the Library of Canterbury Cathedral; with Introduction, Notes, and
Glossary, by J. M. COWPER. 6*s.*

Extra Series.   Subscriptions—Small paper, one guinea; large paper
two guineas, per annum.

1. THE ROMANCE OF WILLIAM OF PALERNE (otherwise known as the
Romance of William and the Werwolf). Translated from the French at the
command of Sir Humphrey de Bohun, about A.D. 1350, to which is added a
fragment of the Alliterative Romance of Alisaunder, translated from the
Latin by the same author, about A.D. 1340 ; the former re-edited from the
unique MS. in the Library of King's College, Cambridge, the latter now
first edited from the unique MS. in the Bodleian Library, Oxford. By the
Rev. WALTER W. SKEAT, M.A. 8vo. sewed, pp. xliv. and 328. £1 6*s.*

2. ON EARLY ENGLISH PRONUNCIATION, with especial reference to
Shakspere and Chaucer ; containing an investigation of the Correspondence
of Writing with Speech in England, from the Anglo-Saxon period to the
present day, preceded by a systematic Notation of all Spoken Sounds by
means of the ordinary Printing Types; including a re-arrangement of Prof.
F. J. Child's Memoirs on the Language of Chaucer and Gower, and reprints
of the rare Tracts by Salesbury on English, 1547, and Welsh, 1567, and by
Barcley on French, 1521. By ALEXANDER J. ELLIS, F.R.S. Part I. On
the Pronunciation of the XIVth, XVIth, XVIIth, and XVIIIth centuries. 8vo.
sewed, pp. viii. and 416. 10*s.*

3. CAXTON'S BOOK OF CURTESYE, printed at Westminster about 1477-8,
A.D., and now reprinted, with two MS. copies of the same treatise, from the
Oriel MS. 79, and the Balliol MS. 354. Edited by FREDERICK J. FURNI-
VALL, M.A. 8vo. sewed, pp. xii. and 58. 5*s.*

4. THE LAY OF HAVELOK THE DANE ; composed in the reign of
Edward I., about A.D. 1280. Formerly edited by Sir F. MADDEN for the
Roxburghe Club, and now re-edited from the unique MS. Laud Misc. 108, in
the Bodleian Library, Oxford, by the Rev. WALTER W. SKEAT, M.A. 8vo.
sewed, pp. lv. and 160. 10*s.*

5. CHAUCER'S TRANSLATION OF BOETHIUS'S "DE CONSOLATIONE
PHILOSOPHIE." Edited from the Additional MS. 10,340 in the British
Museum. Collated with the Cambridge Univ. Libr. MS. Ii. 3. 21. By
RICHARD MORRIS. 8vo. 12*s.*

6 THE ROMANCE OF THE CHEVELERE ASSIGNE. Re-edited from the
unique manuscript in the British Museum, with a Preface, Notes, and
Glossarial Index, by HENRY H. GIBBS, Esq., M.A. 8vo. sewed, pp.
xviii. and 38. 3*s.*

Early English Text Society's Publications—*continued.*

7. ON EARLY ENGLISH PRONUNCIATION, with especial reference to Shakspere and Chaucer. By ALEXANDER J. ELLIS, F.R.S., etc., etc. Part II. On the Pronunciation of the XIIIth and previous centuries, of Anglo-Saxon, Icelandic, Old Norse and Gothic, with Chronological Tables of the Value of Letters and Expression of Sounds in English Writing.   10s.

8. QUEENE ELIZABETHES ACHADEMY, by Sir HUMPHREY GILBERT. A Booke of Precedence, The Ordering of a Funerall, etc.   Varying Versions of the Good Wife, The Wise Man, etc., Maxims, Lydgate's Order of Fools, A Poem on Heraldry, Occleve on Lords' Men, etc., Edited by F. J. FURNIVALL, M.A., Trin. Hall, Camb.   With Essays on Early Italian and German Books of Courtesy, by W. M. ROSSETTI, Esq., and E. OSWALD, Esq.   8vo.   13s.

9. THE FRATERNITYE OF VACABONDES, by JOHN AWDELEY (licensed in 1560-1, imprinted then, and in 1575), from the edition of 1575 in the Bodleian Library.   A Caueat or Warening for Commen Cursetors vulgarely called Vagabones, by THOMAS HARMAN, ESQUIERE.   From the 3rd edition of 1567, belonging to Henry Huth, Esq., collated with the 2nd edition of 1567, in the Bodleian Library, Oxford, and with the reprint of the 4th edition of 1573.   A Sermon in Praise of Thieves and Thievery, by PARSON HABEN OR HYBERDYNE, from the Lansdowne MS. 98, and Cotton Vesp. A. 25.   Those parts of the Groundworke of Conny-catching (ed. 1592), that differ from *Harman's Caueat.*   Edited by EDWARD VILES & F. J. FURNIVALL.   8vo.   7s. 6d.

10. THE FYRST BOKE OF THE INTRODUCTION OF KNOWLEDGE, made by Andrew Borde, of Physycke Doctor.   A COMPENDYOUS REGYMENT OF A DYETARY OF HELTH made in Mountpyllier, compiled by Andrewe Boorde, of Physycke Doctor.   BARNES IN THE DEFENCE OF THE BERDE: a treatyse made, answerynge the treatyse of Doctor Borde upon Berdes.   Edited, with a life of Andrew Boorde, and large extracts from his Breuyary, by F. J. FURNIVALL, M.A., Trinity Hall, Camb.   8vo.   18s.

11. THE BRUCE; or, the Book of the most excellent and noble Prince, Robert de Broyss, King of Scots: compiled by Master John Barbour, Arch-deacon of Aberdeen. A.D. 1375.   Edited from MS. G 23 in the Library of St. John's College, Cambridge, written A.D. 1487; collated with the MS. in the Advocates' Library at Edinburgh, written A.D. 1489, and with Hart's Edition, printed A.D. 1616; with a Preface, Notes, and Glossarial Index, by the Rev. WALTER W. SKEAT, M.A.   Part I.   8vo.   12s.

12. ENGLAND IN THE REIGN OF KING HENRY THE EIGHTH.   A Dialogue between Cardinal Pole and Thomas Lupset, Lecturer in Rhetoric at Oxford.   By THOM s STARKEY, Chaplain to the King.   Edited, with Preface, Notes, and Glossary, by J. M. COWPER.   And with an Introduction containing the Life and Letters of Thomas Starkey, by the Rev. J. S. BREWER, M.A.   Part II.   12s.

(Part I., Starkey's Life and Letters, is in preparation.

13. A SUPPLICACYON FOR THE BEGGARS.   Written about the year 1529, by SIMON FISH.   Now re-edited by FREDERICK J. FURNIVALL.   With a Supplycacion to our moste Soueraigne Lorde Kynge Henry the Eyght (1544 A.D.), A Supplication of the Poore Commons (1546 A.D.), The Decaye of England by the great multitude of Shepe (1550-3 A.D.).   Edited by J. MEADOWS COWPER.   6s.

14. ON EARLY ENGLISH PRONUNCIATION, with especial reference to Shakspere and Chaucer.   By A. J. ELLIS, F.R.S., F.S.A.   Part III. Illustrations of the Pronunciation of the XIVth and XVIth Centuries. Chaucer, Gower, Wycliffe, Spenser, Shakspere, Salesbury, Barclay, Hart, Bullokar, Gill.   Pronouncing Vocabulary.   10s.

Edda Saemundar Hinns Froda—The Edda of Saemund the Learned. From the Old Norse or Icelandic.   Part I. with a Mythological Index. 12mo. pp. 152, cloth, 3s. 6d.   Part II. with Index of Persons and Places.   By BENJAMIN THORPE.   12mo. pp. viii. and 172, cloth. 1866. 4s.; or in 1 Vol. complete, 7s. 6d.

Edkins.—CHINA'S PLACE IN PHILOLOGY. An attempt to show that the Languages of Europe and Asia have a common origin. By the Rev. JOSEPH EDKINS. Crown 8vo., pp. xxiii.—403, cloth. 10s. 6d.

Edkins.—A VOCABULARY OF THE SHANGHAI DIALECT. By J. EDKINS. 8vo. half-calf, pp. vi. and 151. Shanghai, 1869. 21s.

Edkins.—A GRAMMAR OF COLLOQUIAL CHINESE, as exhibited in the Shanghai Dialect. By J. EDKINS, B.A. Second edition, corrected. 8vo. half-calf, pp. viii. and 225. Shanghai, 1868. 21s.

Edkins.—A GRAMMAR OF THE CHINESE COLLOQUIAL LANGUAGE, commonly called the Mandarin Dialect. By JOSEPH EDKINS. Second edition. 8vo. half-calf, pp. viii. and 279. Shanghai, 1864. £1 10s.

Eger and Grime; an Early English Romance. Edited from Bishop Percy's Folio Manuscript, about 1650 A.D. By JOHN W. HALES, M.A., Fellow and late Assistant Tutor of Christ's College, Cambridge, and FREDERICK J. FURNIVALL, M.A., of Trinity Hall, Cambridge. 1 vol. 4to., pp. 64, (only 100 copies printed), bound in the Roxburghe style. 10s. 6d.

Eitel.—HANDBOOK FOR THE STUDENT OF CHINESE BUDDHISM. By the Rev. E. J. EITEL, of the London Missionary Society. Crown 8vo. pp. viii., 224,cl., 18s.

Eitel.—THREE LECTURES ON BUDDHISM. By Rev. ERNEST J. EITEL. Medium 8vo., pp. 42, sewed. 3s. 6d.

Eitel.—SKETCHES FROM LIFE AMONG THE HAKKAS OF SOUTHERN CHINA. By the Rev. E. J. EITEL, Hong-Kong. [*In preparation.*]

Elliot.—THE HISTORY OF INDIA, as told by its own Historians. The Muhammadan Period. Edited from the Posthumous Papers of the late Sir H. M. ELLIOT, K.C.B., East India Company's Bengal Civil Service, by Prof. JOHN DOWSON, M.R.A.S., Staff College, Sandhurst.
Vols. I. and II. With a Portrait of Sir H. M. Elliot. 8vo. pp xxxii. and 542, x. and 580, cloth. 18s. each.
Vol. III. 8vo. pp. xii. and 627, cloth. 24s.

Elliot.—MEMOIRS ON THE HISTORY, FOLKLORE, AND DISTRIBUTION OF THE RACES OF THE NORTH WESTERN PROVINCES OF INDIA; being an amplified Edition of the original Supplementary Glossary of Indian Terms. By the late Sir HENRY M. ELLIOT, K.C.B., of the Hon. East India Company's Bengal Civil Service. Edited, revised, and re-arranged, by JOHN BEAMES, M.R.A.S., Bengal Civil Service; Member of the German Oriental Society, of the Asiatic Societies of Paris and Bengal, and of the Philological Society of London. In 2 vols. demy 8vo., pp. xx., 370, and 396, cloth. With two Lithographic Plates, one full-page coloured Map, and three large coloured folding Maps. 36s.

Ellis.—THE ASIATIC AFFINITIES OF THE OLD ITALIANS. By ROBERT ELLIS, B.D., Fellow of St. John's College, Cambridge, and author of "Ancient Routes between Italy and Gaul." Crown 8vo. pp. iv. 156, cloth. 1870. 5s.

English and Welsh Languages.—THE INFLUENCE OF THE ENGLISH AND Welsh Languages upon each other, exhibited in the Vocabularies of the two Tongues. Intended to suggest the importance to Philologers, Antiquaries, Ethnographers, and others, of giving due attention to the Celtic Branch of the Indo-Germanic Family of Languages. Square, pp. 30, sewed. 1869. 1s.

Etherington.—THE STUDENT'S GRAMMAR OF THE HINDÍ LANGUAGE. By the Rev. W. ETHERINGTON, Missionary, Benares. Crown 8vo. pp. xii. 220. xlviii. cloth. 1870. 10s. 6d.

Ethnological Society of London (The Journal of the). Edited by Professor HUXLEY, F.R.S., President of the Society; GEORGE BUSK, Esq., F.R.S.; Sir JOHN LUBBOCK, Bart., F.R.S.; Colonel A. LANE FOX, Hon. Sec.; THOMAS WRIGHT, Esq., Hon. Sec.; HYDE CLARKE, Esq.; Sub-Editor; and Assistant Secretary, J. H. LAMPREY, Esq. Published Quarterly.
Vol. I., No. 1. April, 1869. 8vo. pp. 88, sewed. 3s.
CONTENTS.—Flint Instruments from Oxfordshire and the Isle of Thanet. (Illustrated.) By Colonel A. Lane Fox.—The Westerly Drifting of Nomads. By H. H. Howorth.—On the Lion Shilling. By Hyde Clarke.—Letter on a Marble Armlet. By H. W. Edwards.—On a Bronze

18 Linguistic Publications of Trübner & Co.

Spear from Lough Gur, Limerick. (Illustrated.) By Col. A. Lane Fox.—On Chinese Charms. By W. H. Black.—Proto-ethnic Condition of Asia Minor. By Hyde Clarke.—On Stone Implements from the Cape. (Illustrated.) By Sir J. Lubbock.—Cromlechs and Megalithic Structures. By H. M. Westropp.—Remarks on Mr. Westropp's Paper. By Colonel A. Lane Fox.—Stone Implements from San José. By A. Steffens.—On Child-bearing in Australia and New Zealand. By J. Hooker, M.D.—On a Pseudo-cromlech on Mount Alexander, Australia. By Acheson.—The Cave Cannibals of South Africa. By Layland.—Reviews: Wallace's Malay Archipelago (with illustrations); Pryer's Hill Tribes of India (with an illustration); Reliquiæ Aquitanicæ, etc.—Method of Photographic Measurement of the Human Frame (with an illustration). By J. H. Lamprey.—Notes and Queries.

Vol. I., No. 2. July, 1869. 8vo. pp. 117, sewed. 3s.

CONTENTS.—Ordinary Meeting, March 9, 1869 (held at the Museum of Practical Geology), Professor Huxley, F.R.S., President, in the Chair. Opening Address of the President.—On the Characteristics of the population of Central and South India (Illustrated). By Sir Walter Elliot.—On the Races of India as traced in existing Tribes and Castes (With a Map). By G. Campbell, Esq.—Remarks by Mr. James Fergusson.—Remarks by Mr. Walter Dendy. —Ordinary Meeting, January 23rd, 1869. Professor Huxley, F.R.S., President, in the Chair. On the Lepchas. By Dr. A. Campbell, late Superintendent of Darjeeling.—On Prehistoric Archæology of India (Illustrated). By Colonel Meadows Taylor, C.S.I., M.R.A.S., M.R.I.A., etc.—Appendix I. Extract from description of the Pandoo Coolies in Malabar. By J. Babington, Esq. (Read before the Literary Society of Bombay, December 20th, 1820. Published in Volume III. of the Society's Transactions).—Appendix II. Extract from a letter from Captain, now Colonel, A. Doria, dated Camp Katangrieh, April 12th, 1852.—On some of the Mountain Tribes of the North Western frontier of India. By Major Fosbery, V.C.—On Permanence of type in the Human Race. By Sir William Denison.—Notes and Reviews.—Ethnological Notes and Queries.—Notices of Ethnology.

Vol. I., No. 3. October, 1869. pp. 137, sewed. 3s.

CONTENTS.—On the Excavation of a large raised Stone Circle or Barrow, near the Village of Wurreegaon, one mile from the military station of Kamptee, Central Provinces of India (Illustrated). By Major George Godfrey Pearse, Royal Artillery.—Remarks by Dr. Hooker on Dr. Campbell's paper.—North-American Ethnology: Address of the President.—On the Native Races of New Mexico (Illustrated). By Dr. A. W. Bell.—On the Arapahoes, Kiowas, and Comanches. By Morton C. Fisher.—The North-American Indians: a Sketch of some of the hostile Tribes; together with a brief account of General Sheridan's Campaign of 1868 against the Sioux, Cheyenne, Arapahoe, Kiowa, and Comanche Indians. By William Blackmore.—Notes and Reviews: The Ethnological Essays of William Ewart Gladstone. Juventus Mundi, the Gods and Men of the Homeric Age. By the Right Hon. William Ewart Gladstone. (The Review by Hyde Clarke, Esq.)—Notes and Queries.—Classification Committee.

Vol. I., No. 4. January, 1870. 8vo. pp. 98, sewed. 3s.

CONTENTS.—On New Zealand and Polynesian Ethnology: On the Social Life of the ancient Inhabitants of New Zealand, and on the national character it was likely to form. By Sir George Grey, K.C.B.—Notes on the Maories of New Zealand and some Melanesians of the south-west Pacific. By the Bishop of Wellington.—Observations on the Inhabitants and Antiquities of Easter Island. By J. L. Palmer.—On the westerly drifting of Nomades from the fifth to the nineteenth century. Part II. The Seljuks, Ghazdevides, etc. By H. H. Howorth, Esq.—Settle Cave Exploration.—Index.—Contents.—Report of the Council.—List of Fellows.

Vol. II., No. 1. April, 1870. 8vo. pp. 96, sewed. 3s.

CONTENTS:—On the Proposed Exploration of Stonehenge by a Committee of the British Association. By Col. A. Lane Fox.—On the Chinese Race, their Language, Government, Social Institutions, and Religion. By C. T. Gardner. Appendix I.: On Chinese Mythological and Legendary History II.: On Chinese Time.—Discussion.—On the Races and Languages of Dardistan. By Dr. G. W. Leitner.—Discussion.—Extract from a Communication by Munphool, Pundit to the Political Department, India Office, on the Relations between Gilgit, Chitral, and Kashmir.— On Quartzite Implements from the Cape of Good Hope. By Sir G. Grey.—Discussion.—Note on a supposed Stone Implement from County Wicklow, Ireland. By F. Atcheson.—Note on the Stature of American Indians of the Chipewyan Tribe. By Major-General Lefroy.— Report on the Present State and Condition of Pre-historic Remains in the Channel Islands. By Lieut. S. P. Oliver.—Appendix: The Opening and Restoration of the Cromlech of Le Conceron.— Discussion.—Description and Remarks upon an Ancient Calcaria from China, which has been supposed to be that of Confucius. By George Busk.—Discussion.—On the Westerly Drifting of Nomades, from the 5th to the 19th Century. Part III. The Comans and Petchenegs. By H. H. Howorth.—Review.—Notes and Queries.—Illustrated.

Vol. II., No. 2. July, 1870. 8vo. pp. 95, sewed. 3s.

CONTENTS:—On the Kitai and Kara-Kitai. By Dr. G. Oppert.—Discussion.—Note on the Use of the New Zealand Mere. By Colonel A. Lane Fox.—On Certain Pre-historic Remains discovered in New Zealand, and on the Nature of the Deposits in which they occurred. By Dr. Julius Haast.—Discussion.—On the Origin of the Tasmanians, geologically considered. By James Bonwick.—Discussion.—On a Frontier Line of Ethnology and Geology. By H. H. Howorth.—Notes on the Nicobar Islanders. By G. M. Atkinson.—On the Discovery of Flint and Chert under a Submerged Forest in West Somerset. By W. Boyd Dawkins.—Discussion.— Remarks by Dr. A. Campbell, introductory to the Rev. R. J. Mapleton's Report.—Report on Pre-historic Remains in the Neighbourhood of the Crinan Canal, Argyllshire. By the Rev. R. J. Mapleton.—Discussion—Supplementary Remarks to a Note on an Ancient Chinese Calva. By George Busk.—On Discoveries in Recent Deposits in Yorkshire. By C. Monkman.—Discussion. —On the Natives of Naga, in Luzon, Philippine Islands.—By Dr. Jagor.—On the Koords. By Major F. Millinger.—On the Westerly Drifting of Nomades, from the 5th to the 19th Century. Part IV. The Circassians and White Kazars. By H. H. Howorth.—Notes and Queries.— Illustrated.

Vol. II., No. 3.   October, 1870.   8vo. pp. 176, sewed.   3*s*.

CONTENTS:—On the Aymara Indians of Bolivia and Peru. By David Forbes. Appendix: A. Table of Detailed Measurements of Aymara Indians. B. Substances used as Medicines by the Aymara Indians, and their Names for Diseases. C. Vocabulary of Aymara Words—Discussion.—On the Opening of Two Cairns near Bangor, North Wales. By Colonel A. Lane Fox.—Discussion.—On the Earliest Phases of Civilization. By Hodder M. Westropp.—On Current British Mythology and Oral Traditions. By J. F. Campbell.—Note on a Cist with Engraved Stones on the Poltalloch Estate, Argyllshire. By the Rev. R. J. Mapleton.—Discussion—On the Tribal System and Land Tenure in Ireland under the Brehon Laws. By Hodder M. Westropp. —Discussion.—On the Danish Element in the Population of Cleveland, Yorkshire. By the Rev. J. C. Atkinson.—Discussion.—Notes and Queries.—Illustrated.

Vol. II., No. 4.   January, 1871.   8vo. pp. 524, sewed.   With a Coloured folded Map, and Seven full-page Illustrations.   3*s*.

CONTENTS.—On the Brain in the Study of Ethnology. By Dr. C. Donovan. (Abstract.)—The Philosophy of Religion among the Lower Races of Mankind. By E. B. Tylor, Esq., Vice-President (Discussion).—Address on the Ethnology of Britain. By Prof. T. H. Huxley, LL.D., F.R.S., President.—The Influence of the Norman Conquest on the Ethnology of Britain. By Dr. T. Nicholas, M.A., F.G.S. Discussion.—Note on a Supposed Ogham Inscription from Rus-Glass, Co. Cork. By R. Caulfield, Esq., LL.D., F.S.A. (with plate.) Discussion.—Notes on the Discovery of Copper Celts at Buttivant, Co. Cork. By J. P. Phair, Esq.—On the Geographical Distribution of the Chief Modifications of Mankind. By Prof. T. H. Huxley, LL.D., F.R.S., President (with chromo-lithograph map). Discussion.—On the threatened Destruction of the British Earthworks near Dorchester, Oxfordshire. By Col. A. Lane Fox, F.S.A., Hon. Sec. (with plate.)—Description of the Park Cwm Tumulus. By Sir John Lubbock, Bart., M.P., F.R.S., Vice-President (with plate).—On the Opening of Grimes' Graves in Norfolk. By the Rev. W. Greenwell, M.A., F.S.A. (with plates). Discussion.—On the Discovery of Platycnemic Men in Denbighshire. By W. Boyd Dawkins, Esq., M.A., F.R.S. With Notes on the Human Remains, by Prof. Busk, F.R.S. (with plate and 16 woodcuts.)—On the Westerly Drifting of Nomades, from the Fifth to the Nineteenth Century. Part V. The Hungarians. By H. H. Howorth, Esq.—Notes and Queries.—Index, &c., &c.

Facsimiles of Two Papyri found in a Tomb at Thebes. With a Translation by SAMUEL BIRCH, LL.D., F.S.A., Corresponding Member of the Institute of France, Academies of Berlin, Herculaneum, etc., and an Account of their Discovery. By A. HENRY RHIND, Esq., F.S.A., etc. In large folio, pp. 30 of text, and 16 plates coloured, bound in cloth. 21*s*.

Foss.—NORWEGIAN GRAMMAR, with Exercises in the Norwegian and and English Languages, and a List of Irregular Verbs. By FRITHJOF Foss, Graduate of the University of Norway. Crown 8vo., pp. 50, cloth limp. 2*s*.

Furnivall.—EDUCATION IN EARLY ENGLAND. Some Notes used as Forewords to a Collection of Treatises on "Manners and Meals in the Olden Time," for the Early English Text Society. By FREDERICK J. FURNIVALL, M.A., Trinity Hall, Cambridge, Member of Council of the Philological and Early English Text Societies. 8vo. sewed, pp. 74. 1*s*.

Gesenius' Hebrew Grammar. Translated from the 17th Edition. By Dr. T. J. CONANT. With grammatical Exercises and a Chrestomathy by the Translator. 8vo. pp. xvi. and 364, cloth. 20*s*.

Gesenius' Hebrew and English Lexicon of the Old Testament, including the Biblical Chaldee, from the Latin. By EDWARD ROBINSON. Fifth Edition. 8vo. pp. xii. and 1160, cloth. 36*s*.

God.—BOOK OF GOD. By ⊙. 8vo. cloth. Vol. I.: The Apocalypse. pp. 647. 12*s*. 6*d*.—Vol. II. An Introduction to the Apocalypse, pp. 752. 14*s*.—Vol. III. A Commentary on the Apocalypse, pp. 854. 16*s*.

God.—THE NAME OF GOD IN 405 LANGUAGES. Ἀγνώστῳ Θεῷ. 32mo. pp. 64, sewed. 2*d*.

Goldstücker.—A DICTIONARY, SANSKRIT AND ENGLISH, extended and improved from the Second Edition of the Dictionary of Professor H. H. WILSON, with his sanction and concurrence. Together with a Supplement, Grammatical Appendices, and an Index, serving as a Sanskrit-English Vocabulary. By THEODOR GOLDSTÜCKER. Parts I. to VI. 4to. pp. 400. 1856-1863. 6*s*. each.

Goldstücker.—A COMPENDIOUS SANSKRIT-ENGLISH DICTIONARY, for the Use of those who intend to read the easier Works of Classical Sanskrit Literature. By THEODOR GOLDSTÜCKER. Small 4to. pp. 900, cloth. [*In preparation.*

Goldstücker.—PANINI : His Place in Sanskrit Literature. An Investigation of some Literary and Chronological Questions which may be settled by
a study of his Work. A separate impression of the Preface to the Facsimile of
MS. No. 17 in the Library of Her Majesty's Home Government for India,
which contains a portion of the MANAVA-KALPA-SUTRA, with the Commentary
of KUMARILA-SWAMIN. By THEODOR GOLDSTÜCKER. Imperial 8vo. pp.
268, cloth. 12s.

Goldstücker.—ON THE DEFICIENCIES IN THE PRESENT ADMINISTRATION
OF HINDU LAW; being a paper read at the Meeting of the East India Association on the 8th June, 1870. By THEODOR GOLDSTÜCKER, Professor of
Sanskrit in University College, London, &c. Demy 8vo. pp. 56, sewed.
1s. 6d.

Grammatography.—A MANUAL OF REFERENCE to the Alphabets of
Ancient and Modern Languages. Based on the German Compilation of F.
BALLHORN. Royal 8vo. pp. 80, cloth. 7s. 6d.

The "Grammatography" is offered to the public as a compendious introduction to the reading
of the most important ancient and modern languages. Simple in its design, it will be consulted
with advantage by the philological student, the amateur linguist, the bookseller, the corrector of
the press, and the diligent compositor.

ALPHABETICAL INDEX.

Afghan (or Pushto).	Czechian (or Bohemian).	Hebrew (current hand).	Polish.
Amharic.	Danish.	Hebrew (Judæo-Ger-	Pushto (or Afghan).
Anglo-Saxon.	Demotic.	Hungarian. [man].	Romaic (Modern Greek)
Arabic.	Katrangelo.	Illyrian.	Russian.
Arabic Ligatures.	Ethiopic.	Irish.	Runes.
Aramaic.	Etruscan.	Italian (Old).	Samaritan.
Archaic Characters.	Georgian.	Japanese.	Sanscrit.
Armenian.	German.	Javanese.	Servian.
Assyrian Cuneiform.	Glagolitic.	Lettish.	Slavonic (Old).
Bengali.	Gothic.	Mantchu.	Sorbian (or Wendish).
Bohemian (Czechian).	Greek.	Median Cuneiform.	Swedish.
Bâgis.	Greek Ligatures.	Modern Greek (Romaic)	Syriac.
Burmese.	Greek (Archaic).	Mongolian.	Tamil.
Canarese (or Carnátaca).	Gujerati (or Guzzeratte).	Numidian	Telugu.
Chinese.	Hieratic.	OldSlavonic (or Cyrillic).	Tibetan.
Coptic.	Hieroglyphics.	Palmyrenian.	Turkish.
Croato-Glagolitic.	Hebrew.	Persian.	Wallachian.
Cufic.	Hebrew (Archaic).	Persian Cuneiform.	Wendish (or Sorbian).
Cyrillic (or Old Slavonic).	Hebrew (Rabbinical).	Phœnician.	Zend.

Green.—SHAKESPEARE AND THE EMBLEM-WRITERS : an Exposition of
their Similarities of Thought and Expression. Preceded by a View of the
Emblem-Book Literature down to A.D. 1616. By HENRY GREEN, M.A. In
one volume, pp. xvi. 572, profusely illustrated with Woodcuts and Photolith.
Plates, elegantly bound in cloth gilt, large medium 8vo. £1 11s. 6d ; large
imperial 8vo. 1870. £2 12s. 6d.

Grey.—HANDBOOK OF AFRICAN, AUSTRALIAN, AND POLYNESIAN PHI-
LOLOGY, as represented in the Library of His Excellency Sir George Grey,
K.C.B., Her Majesty's High Commissioner of the Cape Colony. Classed,
Annotated, and Edited by Sir GEORGE GREY and Dr. H. L BLEEK.

    Vol. I.   Part 1.—South Africa. 8vo. pp. 186. 7s. 6d.
    Vol. I.   Part 2.—Africa (North of the Tropic of Capricorn). 8vo. pp. 70. 2s.
    Vol. I.   Part 3.—Madagascar. 8vo. pp. 24. 1s.
    Vol. II. Part 1.—Australia. 8vo. pp. iv. and 44. 1s. 6d.
    Vol. II. Part 2.—Papuan Languages of the Loyalty Islands and New Hebrides, compris-
               ing those of the Islands of Nengone, Lifu, Aneitum, Tana, and
               others. 8vo. p. 12. 6d.
    Vol. II. Part 3.—Fiji Islands and Rotuma (with Supplement to Part II., Papuan Lan-
               guages, and Part I., Australia). 8vo. pp. 34. 1s.
    Vol. II. Part 4.—New Zealand, the Chatham Islands, and Auckland Islands. 8vo. pp.
               76. 3s. 6d.
    Vol. II. Part 4 (continuation).—Polynesia and Borneo. 8vo. pp. 77-154. 3s. 6d.
    Vol. III. Part 1.—Manuscripts and Incunables. 8vo. pp. viii. and 24. 2s.
    Vol. IV. Part 1.—Early Printed Books. England. 8vo. pp. vi. and 266.

Grey.—MAORI MEMENTOS : being a Series of Addresses presented by
the Native People to His Excellency Sir George Grey, K.C.B., F.R.S. With
Introductory Remarks and Explanatory Notes ; to which is added a small Collection of Laments, etc. By CH. OLIVER B. DAVIS. 8vo. pp. iv. and 228, cloth. 12s.

Griffith.—Scenes from the Ramayana, Meghaduta, etc. Translated by Ralph T. H. Griffith, M.A., Principal of the Benares College. Second Edition. Crown 8vo. pp. xviii., 244, cloth. 6s.

Contents.—Preface—Ayodhya—Ravan Doomed—The Birth of Rama—The Heir apparent—Manthara's Guile—Dasaratha's Oath—The Step-mother—Mother and Son—The Triumph of Love—Farewell!—The Hermit's Son—The Trial of Truth—The Forest—The Rape of Sita—Rama's Despair—The Messenger Cloud—Khumbakarna—The Suppliant Dove—True Glory—Feed the Poor—The Wise Scholar.

Griffith.—The Rámáyan of Válmíki. Translated into English verse. By Ralph T. H. Griffith, M.A., Principal of the Benares College. Vol. I., containing Books I. and II. 8vo. pp. xxxii. 440, cloth. 1870. 18s.

—— Vol. II., containing Book II., with additional Notes and Index of Names. 8vo. cloth, pp. 504. 18s.

Grout.—The Isizulu : a Grammar of the Zulu Language ; accompanied with an Historical Introduction, also with an Appendix. By Rev. Lewis Grout. 8vo. pp. lii. and 432, cloth. 21s.

Gubernatis.—Mythical Zoology ; or the Legends of Animals. By Angelo de Gubernatis, Professor of Sanskrit and Comparative Literature at Florence. [*In the press.*

Gundert.—A Malayalam and English Dictionary. By Rev. H. Gundert, D.Ph. Part I : The Vowels. Royal 8vo. pp. 192, sewed. 1871. 10s.

Haldeman.—A Grammar of the Pennsylvanian Dutch Language. By S. S. Haldeman. 8vo. [*In the Press.*

Hans Breitmann Ballads.—See under Leland.

Haug.—Essays on the Sacred Language, Writings, and Religion of the Parsees. By Martin Haug, Dr. Phil. Superintendent of Sanskrit Studies in the Poona College. 8vo. pp. 278, cloth. [*Out of print.*

Haug.—A Lecture on an Original Speech of Zoroaster (Yasna 45), with remarks on his age. By Martin Haug, Ph.D. 8vo. pp. 28, sewed. Bombay, 1865. 2s.

Haug.—Outline of a Grammar of the Zend Language. By Martin Haug, Dr. Phil. 8vo. pp. 82, sewed. 14s.

Haug.—The Aitareya Brahmanam of the Rig Veda : containing the Earliest Speculations of the Brahmans on the meaning of the Sacrificial Prayers, and on the Origin, Performance, and Sense of the Rites of the Vedic Religion. Edited, Translated, and Explained by Martin Haug, Ph.D., Superintendent of Sanskrit Studies in the Poona College, etc., etc. In 2 Vols. Crown 8vo. Vol. I. Contents, Sanskrit Text, with Preface, Introductory Essay, and a Map of the Sacrificial Compound at the Soma Sacrifice, pp. 312. Vol. II. Translation with Notes, pp. 544. £3 3s.

Haug.—An Old Zand-Pahlavi Glossary. Edited in the Original Characters, with a Transliteration in Roman Letters, an English Translation, and an Alphabetical Index. By Destur Hoshengji Jamaspji, High-priest of the Parsis in Malwa, India. Revised with Notes and Introduction by Martin Haug, Ph.D., late Superintendent of Sanscrit Studies in the Poona College, Foreign Member of the Royal Bavarian Academy. Published by order of the Government of Bombay. 8vo. sewed, pp. lvi. and 132. 15s.

Haug.—An Old Pahlavi-Pazand Glossary. Edited, with an Alphabetical Index, by Destur Hoshangji Jamaspji Asa, High Priest of the Parsis in Malwa, India. Revised and Enlarged, with an Introductory Essay on the Pahlavi Language, by Martin Haug, Ph.D. Published by order of the Government of Bombay. 8vo. pp. xvi. 152, 268, sewed. 1870. 28s.

Haug.—Essay on the Pahlavi Language. By Martin Haug, Ph. D., Professor of Sanscrit and Comparative Philology at the University of Munich, Member of the Royal Bavarian Academy of Sciences, etc. (From the Pahlavi-Pazand Glossary, edited by Destur Hoshangji and M. Haug.) 8vo. pp. 152, sewed. 1870. 3s. 6d.

Haug.—The Religion of the Zoroastrians, as contained in their Sacred Writings. With a History of the Zend and Pehlevi Literature, and a Grammar of the Zend and Pehlevi Languages. By Martin Haug, Ph.D., late Superintendent of Sanscrit Studies in the Poona College. 2 vols. 8vo. [*In preparation.*

Heaviside.—American Antiquities; or, the New World the Old, and the Old World the New. By John T. C. Heaviside. 8vo. pp. 46, sewed. 1s. 6d.

Hepburn.—A Japanese and English Dictionary. With an English and Japanese Index. By J. C. Hepburn, A.M., M.D. Imperial 8vo. cloth, pp. xii., 560 and 132. 5l. 5s.

Hernisz.—A Guide to Conversation in the English and Chinese Languages, for the use of Americans and Chinese in California and elsewhere. By Stanislas Hernisz. Square 8vo. pp. 274, sewed. 10s. 6d.
The Chinese characters contained in this work are from the collections of Chinese groups, engraved on steel, and cast into moveable types, by Mr. Marcellin Legrand, engraver of the Imperial Printing Office at Paris. They are used by most of the missions to China.

Hincks.—Specimen Chapters of an Assyrian Grammar. By the late Rev. E. Hincks, D.D., Hon. M.R.A.S. 8vo., pp. 44, sewed. 1s.

History of the Sect of Maharajahs; or, Vallabhacharyas in Western India. With a Steel Plate. 8vo. pp. 384, cloth. 12s.

Hoffmann.—Shopping Dialogues, in Japanese, Dutch, and English. By Professor J. Hoffmann. Oblong 8vo. pp. xiii. and 44, sewed. 3s.

Hoffmann.—A Japanese Grammar. By J. J. Hoffmann, Ph. Doc., Member of the Royal Academy of Sciences, etc., etc. Published by command of His Majesty's Minister for Colonial Affairs. Imp. 8vo. pp. viii. 352, sewed. 12s. 6d.

Historia y fundacion de la Ciudad de Tlaxcala, y sus cuatro caveceras. Sacada por Francisco de Loaiza de lengua Castellana à esta Mexicana. Año de 1718. Con una Traduccion Castellana, publicado por S. Leon Reinisch. In one volume folio, with 25 Photographic Plates. [*In preparation.*

Howse.—A Grammar of the Cree Language. With which is combined an analysis of the Chippeway Dialect. By Joseph Howse, Esq., F.R.G.S. 8vo. pp. xx. and 324, cloth. 7s. 6d.

Hunter.—A Comparative Dictionary of the Languages of India and High Asia, with a Dissertation, based on The Hodgson Lists, Official Records, and Manuscripts. By W. W. Hunter, B.A., M.R.A.S., Honorary Fellow, Ethnological Society, of Her Majesty's Bengal Civil Service. Folio, pp. vi. and 224, cloth. £2 2s.

Ikhwánu-s Safá.—Ikhwánu-s Safá; or, Brothers of Purity. Describing the Contention between Men and Beasts as to the Superiority of the Human Race. Translated from the Hindustáni by Professor J. Dowson, Staff College, Sandhurst. Crown 8vo. pp. viii. and 156, cloth. 7s.

Inman.—Ancient Faiths Embodied in Ancient Times; or, an attempt to trace the Religious Belief, Sacred Rites, and Holy Emblems of certain Nations, by an interpretation of the names given to children by Priestly authority, or assumed by prophets, kings and hierarchs. By Thomas Inman, M.D., Liverpool. 2 vols. 8vo. pp. l. and 1028, cloth, illustrated with numerous plates and woodcuts. £3.

Inman.—Ancient Pagan and Modern Christian Symbolism Exposed and Explained. By Thomas Inman, M.D. (London), Physician to the Royal Infirmary, Liverpool. 8vo. pp. xvi. 68, stiff covers, with numerous Illustrations. 1870. 5s.

Jaeschke.—A Short Practical Grammar of the Tibetan Language, with special Reference to the Spoken Dialects. By H. A. Jaeschke, Moravian Missionary. 8vo sewed. pp. ii. and 56. 2s. 6d.

Jaeschke.—Romanized Tibetan and English Dictionary, each word being re-produced in the Tibetan as well as in the Roman character. By H. A. Jaeschke, Moravian Missionary. 8vo. pp. ii. and 158, sewed. 5s.

Jaiminiya-Nyâya-Mâlâ-Vistara.—See under Auctores Sanscriti.

Jenkins's Vest-Pocket Lexicon.—An English Dictionary of all except Familiar Words ; including the principal Scientific and Technical Terms, and Foreign Moneys, Weights and Measures. By JABEZ JENKINS. 64mo., pp. 564. cloth. 1s. 6d.

Julien.—SYNTAXE NOUVELLE DE LA LANGUE CHINOISE.

Vol. I.—Fondée sur la position des mots, suivie de deux traités sur les particules et les principaux termes de grammaire, d'une table des idiotismes, de fables, de légendes et d'apologues traduits mot à mot. 8vo. sewed. 1869. 20s.

Vol. II.—Fondée sur la position des mots confirmée par l'analyse d'un texte ancien, suivie d'un petit Dictionnaire du Roman des DEUX COUSINES, et de Dialogues dramatiques traduits mot à mot, par M. STANISLAS JULIEN, de l'Institut. 8vo. pp. 436, sewed. 1870. 20s.

Justi.—HANDBUCH DER ZENDSPRACHE, VON FERDINAND JUSTI. Altbactrisches Woerterbuch. Grammatik Chrestomathie. Four parts, 4to. sewed, pp. xxii. and 424. Leipzig, 1864. 24s.

Kachchayano's Grammar (The Pali Text of), with ENGLISH GRAMMAR. See under MASON.

Kafir Essays, and other Pieces; with an English Translation. Edited by the Right Rev. the BISHOP OF GRAHAMSTOWN. 32mo. pp. 84, sewed. 2s 6d.

Kalidasa.—RAGHUVANSA. By KALIDASA. No. 1. (Cantos 1-3.) With Notes and Grammatical Explanations, by Rev. K. M. BANERJEA, Second Professor of Bishop's College, Calcutta; Member of the Board of Examiners, Fort-William ; Honorary Member of the Royal Asiatic Society, London. 8vo. sewed, pp. 70. 4s. 6d.

Kern.—THE BRHAT-SANHITÁ ; or, Complete System of Natural Astrology of Varáha-Mihira. Translated from Sanskrit into English by Dr. H. KERN, Professor of Sanskrit at the University of Leyden. 8vo. pp. 50, stitched, Part I. 2s. [*Will be completed in Nine Parts.*

Khirad-Afroz (The Illuminator of the Understanding). By Maulaví Hafízu'd-dín. A new edition of the Hindústání Text, carefully revised, with Notes, Critical and Explanatory. By EDWARD B. EASTWICK, M.P., F.R.S., F.S.A., M.R.A.S., Professor of Hindústání at the late East India Company's College at Haileybury. 8vo. cloth, pp. xiv. and 321. 18s.

Khuddaka Patha.—See under CHILDERS.

Kidd.—CATALOGUE OF THE CHINESE LIBRARY OF THE ROYAL ASIATIC SOCIETY. By the Rev. S. KIDD. 8vo. pp. 58, sewed. 1s.

Kielhorn.—A GRAMMAR OF THE SANSKRIT LANGUAGE. By F. KIELHORN, Ph.D., Superintendent of Sanskrit Studies in Deccan College. Registered under Act xxv. of 1867. Demy 8vo. pp. xvi. 260. cloth. 1870. 10s. 6d.

Kistner.—BUDDHA AND HIS DOCTRINES. A Bibliographical Essay. By OTTO KISTNER. Imperial 8vo., pp. iv. and 32, sewed. 2s. 6d.

Koran (The). Arabic text, lithographed in Oudh, A.H. 1284 (1867). 16mo. pp. 942, bound in red goatskin, Oriental style, silver tooling. 7s. 6d.

The printing, as well as the outer appearance of the book, is extremely tasteful, and the characters, although small, read very easily. As a cheap edition for reference this is preferable to any other, and its price puts it within the reach of every Oriental scholar. It is now first imported from India.

Laghu Kaumudí. A Sanskrit Grammar. By Varadarája. With an English Version, Commentary, and References. By JAMES R. BALLANTYNE, LL.D., Principal of the Snskrit College, Benares. 8vo. pp. xxxvi. and 424, cloth. £1 11s. 6d.

Lee.—A TRANSLATION OF THE BÁLÁVATÁRO : a Native Grammar of the Pali Language. With the Romanized Text, the Nagari Text, and Copious Explanatory Notes. By LIONEL F. LEE. In one vol. 8vo. (*In preparation*).

Legge.—THE CHINESE CLASSICS. With a Translation, Critical and Exegetical Notes, Prolegomena, and Copious Indexes. By JAMES LEGGE, D.D., of the London Missionary Society. In seven vols.

Vol. I. containing Confucian Analects, the Great Learning, and the Doctrine of the Mean. 8vo. pp. 526, cloth. £2 2s.

Vol. II., containing the Works of Mencius. 8vo. pp. 634, cloth. £2 2s.

Vol. III. Part I. containing the First Part of the Shoo-King, or the Books of Tang, the Books of Yu, the Books of Hea, the Books of Shang, and the Prolegomena. Royal 8vo. pp. viii. and 280, cloth. £2 2s.

Vol. III. Part II. containing the Fifth Part of the Shoo-King, or the Books of Chow, and the Indexes. Royal 8vo. pp. 281—736, cloth. £2 2s.

Legge.—THE LIFE AND TEACHINGS OF CONFUCIUS, with Explanatory Notes. By JAMES LEGGE, D.D. Reproduced for General Readers from the Author's work, "The Chinese Classics," with the original Text. Second edition. Crown 8vo. cloth, pp. vi. and 338. 10s. 6d.

Leigh.—THE RELIGION OF THE WORLD. By H. STONE LEIGH. 12mo. pp. xii. 66, cloth. 1869. 2s. 6d.

Leitner.—THE RACES AND LANGUAGES OF DARDISTAN. By G. W. LEITNER, M.A., Ph.D., Honorary Fellow of King's College London, etc.; late on Special Duty in Kashmir. Parts 1 and 2.—5s. each.

Leland.—THE BREITMANN BALLADS. THE ONLY AUTHORIZED EDITION. Complete in 1 vol., including Nineteen Ballads illustrating his Travels in Europe (never before printed), with Comments by Fritz Schwackenhammer. By CHARLES G. LELAND. Crown 8vo. handsomely bound in cloth, pp. xxviii. and 292. 6s.

HANS BREITMANN'S PARTY. With other Ballads. By CHARLES G. LELAND. Tenth Edition. Square, pp. xvi. and 74, sewed. 1s.

HANS BREITMANN'S CHRISTMAS. With other Ballads. By CHARLES G. LELAND. Second edition. Square, pp. 80, sewed. 1s.

HANS BREITMANN AS A POLITICIAN. By CHARLES G. LELAND. Second edition. Square, pp. 72, sewed. 1s.

HANS BREITMANN IN CHURCH. With other Ballads. By CHARLES G. Leland. With an Introduction and Glossary. Second edition. Square, pp. 80, sewed. 1870. 1s.

HANS BREITMANN AS AN UHLAN. Six New Ballads, with a Glossary. Square, pp. 72, sewed. 1s.

The first four Parts may be had in one Volume :—

BREITMANN BALLADS. *Four Series complete.* CONTENTS : — Hans Breitmann's Party. Hans Breitmann's Christmas. Hans Breitmann as a Politician. Hans Breitmann in Church. With other Ballads. BY CHARLES G. LELAND. With Introductions and Glossaries. Square, pp. 300, cloth. 1870. 4s. 6d.

Lesley.—MAN'S ORIGIN AND DESTINY, Sketched from the Platform of the Sciences, in a Course of Lectures delivered before the Lowell Institute, in Boston, in the Winter of 1865-6. By J. P. LESLEY, Member of the National Academy of the United States, Secretary of the American Philosophical Society. Numerous Woodcuts. Crown 8vo. pp. 392, cloth. 10s. 6d.

Liherien hag Avielen; or, the Catholic Epistles and Gospels for the Day up to Ascension. Translated for the first time into the BREHONEC of Brittany. Also in three other parallel columns a New Version of the same into BREIZOUNEC (commonly called Breton and Armorican); a Version into WELSH, mostly new, and closely resembling the Breton; and a Version GAELIC or MANX or CERNAWEG; with Illustrative Articles by CHRISTOLL TERRIEN and CHARLES WARING SAXTON, D.D. Ch. Ch., Oxford. The Penitential Psalms are also added. Oblong 4to. pp. 156, sewed. 5s.

Lobscheid.—English and Chinese Dictionary, with the Punti and Mandarin Pronunciation. By the Rev. W. Lobscheid, Knight of Francis Joseph, C.M.I.R.G.S.A., N.Z.B.S.V., etc. Folio, pp. viii. and 2016. In Four Parts. £8 8s.

Lobscheid.—Chinese and English Dictionary, Arranged according to the Radicals. By the Rev. W. Lobscheid, Knight of Francis Joseph, C.M.I.R.G.S.A., N.Z.B.S.V., &c. 1 vol. imp. 8vo. double columns, pp. 600, bound. £2 8s.

Ludewig (Hermann E.)—The Literature of American Aboriginal Languages. With Additions and Corrections by Professor Wm. W. Turner. Edited by Nicolas Trübner. 8vo. fly and general Title, 2 leaves; Dr. Ludewig's Preface, pp. v.—viii.; Editor's Preface, pp. iv.—xii.; Biographical Memoir of Dr. Ludewig, pp. xiii.—xiv.; and Introductory Biographical Notices, pp. xiv.—xxiv., followed by List of Contents. Then follow Dr. Ludewig's Bibliotheca Glottica, alphabetically arranged, with Additions by the Editor, pp. 1—209; Professor Turner's Additions, with those of the Editor to the same, also alphabetically arranged, pp. 210—246; Index, pp. 247—256; and List of Errata, pp. 257, 258. Handsomely bound in cloth. 10s. 6d.

Macgowan.—A Manual of the Amoy Colloquial. By Rev. J. Macgowan, of the London Missionary Society. 8vo. sewed, pp. xvii. and 200. Amoy, 1871. £1 1s.

Maclay and Baldwin.—An Alphabetic Dictionary of the Chinese Language in the Foochow Dialect. By Rev. R. S. Maclay, D.D., of the Methodist Episcopal Mission, and Rev. C. C. Baldwin, A.M., of the American Board of Mission. 8vo. half-bound, pp. 1132. Foochow, 1871. £4 4s.

Maha-Vira-Charita; or, the Adventures of the Great Hero Rama. An Indian Drama in Seven Acts. Translated into English Prose from the Sanskrit of Bhavabhúti. By John Pickford, M.A. Crown 8vo. cloth. 5s.

Maino-i-Khard (The Book of the). — The Pazand and Sanskrit Texts (in Roman characters) as arranged by Neriosengh Dhaval, in the fifteenth century. With an English translation, a Glossary of the Pazand texts, containing the Sanskrit, Rosian, and Pahlavi equivalents, a sketch of Pazand Grammar, and an Introduction. By E. W. West. 8vo. sewed, pp. 484. 1871. 16s.

Manava-Kalpa-Sutra; being a portion of this ancient Work on Vaidik Rites, together with the Commentary of Kumarila-Swamin. A Facsimile of the MS. No. 17, in the Library of Her Majesty's Home Government for India. With a Preface by Theodor Goldstücker. Oblong folio, pp. 268 of letterpress and 121 leaves of facsimiles. Cloth. £4 4s.

Manipulus Vocabulorum; A Rhyming Dictionary of the English Language. By Peter Levins (1570) Edited, with an Alphabetical Index, by Henry B. Wheatley. 8vo. pp. xvi. and 370, cloth. 14s.

Manning.—An Inquiry into the Character and Origin of the Possessive Augment in English and in Cognate Dialects. By the late James Manning, Q.A.S., Recorder of Oxford. 8vo.pp. iv. and 90. 2s.

Markham.—Quichua Grammar and Dictionary. Contributions towards a Grammar and Dictionary of Quichua, the Language of the Yncas of Peru; collected by Clements R. Markham, F.S.A., Corr. Mem. of the University of Chile. Author of "Cuzco and Lima," and "Travels in Peru and India." In one vol. crown 8vo., pp. 223, cloth. £1. 1s.

Markham.—Ollanta: A Drama in the Quichua Language. Text, Translation, and Introduction. By Clements R. Markham, F.R.G.S. Crown 8vo., pp. 128, cloth. 7s. 6d.

Marsden.—Numismata Orientalia Illustrata. The Plates of the Oriental Coins, Ancient and Modern, of the Collection of the late William Marsden, F.R.S., etc., etc., engraved from drawings made under his direction. 4to. pp. iv. (explanatory advertisement). cloth, gilt top. £1 11s. 6d.

Mason.—BURMAH : its People and Natural Productions; or Notes on the Nations, Fauna, Flora, and Minerals of Tenasserim, Pegu, and Burmah. By Rev. F. MASON, D.D., M.R.A.S., Corresponding Member of the American Oriental Society, of the Boston Society of Natural History, and of the Lyceum of Natural History, New York. 8vo. pp. xviii. and 914, cloth. Rangoon, 1860. 30s.

Mason.—THE PALI TEXT OF KACHCHAYANO'S GRAMMAR, WITH ENGLISH ANNOTATIONS. By FRANCIS MASON, D.D. I. The Text Aphorisms, 1 to 673. II. The English Annotations, including the various Readings of six independent Burmese Manuscripts, the Singalese Text on Verbs, and the Cambodian Text on Syntax. To which is added a Concordance of the Aphorisms. In Two Parts. 8vo. sewed, pp. 208, 75, and 28. Toongoo, 1871. £1 11s. 6d.

Mathurápprasáda Misra.—A TRILINGUAL DICTIONARY, being a comprehensive Lexicon in English, Urdú, and Hindí, exhibiting the Syllabication, Pronunciation, and Etymology of English Words, with their Explanation in English, and in Urdú and Hindí in the Roman Character. By MATHURÁPRASÁDA MISRA, Second Master, Queen's College, Benares. 8vo. pp. xv. and 1330, cloth. Benares, 1865. £2 2s.

Mayers.—ILLUSTRATIONS OF THE LAMAIST SYSTEM IN TIBET, drawn from Chinese Sources. By WILLIAM FREDERICK MAYERS, Esq., of Her Britannic Majesty's Consular Service, China. 8vo. pp. 24, sewed. 1869. 1s. 6d.

Medhurst.—CHINESE DIALOGUES, QUESTIONS, and FAMILIAR SENTENCES, literally translated into English, with a view to promote commercial intercourse and assist beginners in the Language. By the late W. H. MEDHURST, D.D. A new and enlarged Edition. 8vo. pp. 226. 18s.

Megha-Duta (The). (Cloud-Messenger.) By Kálidása. Translated from the Sanskrit into English verse, with Notes and Illustrations. By the late H. H. WILSON, M.A., F.R.S., Boden Professor of Sanskrit in the University of Oxford, etc., etc. The Vocabulary by FRANCIS JOHNSON, sometime Professor of Oriental Languages at the College of the Honourable the East India Company, Haileybury. New Edition. 4to. cloth, pp. xi. and 180. 10s. 6d.

Memoirs read before the ANTHROPOLOGICAL SOCIETY OF LONDON, 1863 1864. 8vo., pp. 542, cloth. 21s.

Memoirs read before the ANTHROPOLOGICAL SOCIETY OF LONDON, 1865-6. Vol. II. 8vo., pp. x. 464, cloth. 21s.

Moffat.—THE STANDARD ALPHABET PROBLEM ; or the Preliminary Subject of a General Phonic System, considered on the basis of some important facts in the Sechwana Language of South Africa, and in reference to the views of Professors Lepsius, Max Müller, and others. A contribution to Phonetic Philology. By ROBERT MOFFAT, junr., Surveyor, Fellow of the Royal Geographical Society. 8vo. pp. xxviii. and 174, cloth. 7s. 6d.

Molesworth.—A DICTIONARY, MÁRATHI and ENGLISH. Compiled by J. T. MOLESWORTH, assisted by GEORGE and THOMAS CANDY. Second Edition, revised and enlarged. By J. T. MOLESWORTH. Royal 4to. pp. xxx. and 922, boards. Bombay, 1857. £3 3s.

Molesworth.—A COMPENDIUM OF MOLESWORTH'S MARATHI AND ENGLISH DICTIONARY. By BABA PADMANJI. Small 4to., pp. xii. and 482, cloth. 16s.

Morfill.—THE SLAVES : their Ethnology, early History, and popular Traditions, with some account of Slavonic Literature. Being the substance of a course of Lectures delivered at Oxford. By W. R. MORFILL, M.A. [*In preparation.*

Morley.—A DESCRIPTIVE CATALOGUE of the HISTORICAL MANUSCRIPTS in the ARABIC and PERSIAN LANGUAGES preserved in the Library of the Royal Asiatic Society of Great Britain and Ireland. By WILLIAM H. MORLEY, M.R.A.S. 8vo. pp. viii. and 160, sewed. London, 1854. 2s. 6d.

Morrison.—A DICTIONARY OF THE CHINESE LANGUAGE. By the Rev. R. MORRISON, D.D. Two vols. Vol. I. pp. x. and 762; Vol. II. pp. 828, cloth. Shanghae, 1865. £6 6s.

Muhammed.—THE LIFE OF MUHAMMED. Based on Muhammed Ibn Ishak. By Abd El Malik Ibn Hisham. Edited by Dr. FERDINAND WÜSTEN-FELD. One volume containing the Arabic Text. 8vo. pp. 1026, sewed. Price 21s. Another volume, containing Introduction, Notes, and Index in German. 8vo. pp. lxxii. and 266, sewed. 7s. 6d. Each part sold separately

The text based on the Manuscripts of the Berlin, Leipsic, Gotha and Leyden Libraries, has been carefully revised by the learned editor, and printed with the utmost exactness.

Muir.—ORIGINAL SANSKRIT TEXTS, on the Origin and History of the People of India, their Religion and Institutions. Collected, Translated, and Illustrated by JOHN MUIR, Esq., D.C.L., LL.D., Ph.D.

Vol. I. Mythical and Legendary Accounts of the Origin of Caste, with an Inquiry into its existence in the Vedic Age. Second Edition, re-written and greatly enlarged. 8vo. pp. xx. 532, cloth. 1868. 21s.

Vol. II. The Trans-Himalayan Origin of the Hindus, and their Affinity with the Western Branches of the Aryan Race. Second Edition, revised, with Additions. 8vo. pp. xxxii. and 512, cloth. 12s.

Second Edition. 8vo. pp. xxxii., 512. 1871. 21s.

Vol. III. The Vedas: Opinions of their Authors, and of later Indian Writers, on their Origin, Inspiration, and Authority. Second Edition, revised and enlarged. 8vo. pp. xxxii. 312, cloth. 1868. (16s.) Rs. 8.

Vol. IV. Comparison of the Vedic with the later representation of the principal Indian Deities. 8vo. pp. xii. 440, cloth. 1863. 15s. (Out of print. A second edition is preparing.)

Vol. V. Contributions to a Knowledge of the Cosmogony, Mythology, Religious Ideas, Life and Manners of the Indians in the Vedic Age. 8vo. pp. xvi. 492, cloth, 1870. 21s.

Müller.—THE SACRED HYMNS OF THE BRAHMINS, as preserved to us in the oldest collection of religious poetry, the Rig-Veda-Sanhita, translated and explained. By F. MAX MÜLLER, M.A., Fellow of All Souls' College; Professor of Comparative Phiiology at Oxford; Foreign Member of the Institute of France, etc., etc. In 8 vols. Volume I. 8vo. pp. clii. and 264. 12s. 6d.

Müller.—A NEW EDITION OF THE HYMNS OF THE RIG-VEDA IN THE SANHITÁ TEXT, without the Commentary of the Sâyana. Based upon the Editio princeps of Max Müller. Large 8vo. of about 800 pages. [*In preparation.*

"The above New Edition of the Sanhitá Text of the Rig-Veda, without the Commentary of Sâyana, will contain foot-notes of the names of the Authors, Deities, and Metres. It will be comprised in about fifty large 8vo. sheets, and will be carefully corrected and revised by Prof. F. Max Müller. The price to subscribers before publication will be 24s. per copy. After publication the price will be 36s. per copy.

Müller.—LECTURE ON BUDDHIST NIHILISM. By F. MAX MÜLLER, M.A., Professor of Comparative Philology in the University of Oxford; Member of the French Institute, etc. Delivered before the General Meeting of the Association of German Philologists, at Kiel, 28th September, 1869. (Translated from the German.) Sewed. 1869. 1s.

Nagananda.—A DRAMA TRANSLATED FROM THE ORIGINAL SANSKRIT; with Notes, by PALMER BOYD, B.A., Trinity Hall. With a Preface by Prof. E. B. COWELL, Cambridge. Crown 8vo. [*In the Press.*

Naphegyi.—THE ALBUM OF LANGUAGE, illustrated by the Lord's Prayer in one hundred languages, with historical descriptions of the principal languages, interlinear translation and pronunciation of each prayer, a dissertation on the languages of the world, and tables exhibiting all known languages, dead and living. By G. NAPHEGYI, M.D., A.M., Member of the " Sociedad Geográfica y Estadística" of Mexico, and " Mejoras Materiales" of Texoco, of the Numismatic and Antiquarian Society of Philadelphia, etc. In one splendid folio volume of 322 pages, illuminated frontispiece and title-page, elegantly bound in cloth, gilt top. £2 10s.

CONTENTS.—Preface (pp. 2).—Introduction.—Observations on the Origin of Language (pp. 12). —Authors of Collections of the Lord's Prayer (pp. 8).—Families of Language (pp. 13).—Alphabets (pp. 25). The Lord's Prayer in the following languages (each accompanied by a transliteration into Roman characters, a translation into English, and a Monograph of the language), printed in the original characters.

A. ARYAN FAMILY.—1. Sanskrit. 2. Bengalee. 3. Moltanee. 4. Hindoostanee. 5. Gipsy. 6. Greek. 7. Modern Greek. 8. Latin. 9. Italian. 10. French. 11. Spanish. 12. Portuguese. 13. Celtic. 14. Welsh. 15. Cornish. 16. Irish. 17. Gothic. 18. Anglo-Saxon. 19. Old Saxon and Dano-Saxon. 20. English (4 varieties). 21. German (4 varieties). 22. Dutch. 23. Runic. 24. Wallachian. 25. Icelandic. 26. Danish. 27. Norwegian. 28. Swedish. 29 Lithuanian. 30. Old Prussian. 31. Servian. 32. Sclavonic. 33. Polavian. 34. Bohemian. 35. Polish. 36. Russian. 37. Bulgaric. 38. Armenian. 39. Armenian-Turkish. 40. Albanian. 41. Persian.

B. SEMITIC FAMILY.—1. Hebrew. 2. Chaldee. 3. Samaritan. 4. Syriac. 5. Syro-Chaldæic. 6. Carshun. 7. Arabic. 8. Æthiopic. 8. Amharic.

C. TURANIAN FAMILY.—1. Turkish. 2. Hungarian. 3. Finnish. 4. Estonian. 5. Lapponian. 6. Laplandic (Dialect of Umä-Lappmark). 7. Basque. 8. Javanese. 9. Hawaiian. 10. Maori (New Zealandic). 11. Malay. 12. Ceylonese. 13. Moorish. 14. Coptic. 15. Berber. 16. Hottentot. 17. Susuio. 18. Burmese. 19. Siamese. 20. Mongolian. 21. Chinese. 22. Kalmuk. 23. Cashmere.

D. AMERICAN FAMILY.—1. Cherokee. 2. Delawar. 3. Micmac. 4. Totonac. 5. Othomi. 6. Cora. 7. Kolusic. 8. Greenland. 9. Mexican. 10. Mistekic. 11. Maya. 12. Brazilian. 13. Chiquitio. 14. Amaric.

Nayler.—COMMONSENSE OBSERVATIONS ON THE EXISTENCE OF RULES (not yet reduced to System in any work extant) regarding THE ENGLISH LANGUAGE ; on the pernicious effects of yielding blind obedience to so-called authorities, whether DICTIONARY-COMPILERS, GRAMMAR-MAKERS, or SPELLING-BOOK MANUFACTURERS, instead of examining and judging for ourselves on all questions that are open to investigation ; followed by a Treatise, entitled PRONUNCIATION MADE EASY ; also an ESSAY ON THE PRONUNCIATION OF PROPER NAMES. By B. S. NAYLER, accredited Elocutionist to the most celebrated Literary Societies in London. 8vo. pp. iv. 148, boards. 1869. 5s.

Newman.—A DICTIONARY OF MODERN ARABIC.—1. Anglo-Arabic Dictionary. 2. Anglo-Arabic Vocabulary. 3. Arabo-English Dictionary. By F. W. NEWMAN, Emeritus Professor of University College, London. In 2 vols. crown 8vo., pp. xvi. and 376—464, cloth. £1 1s.

Newman.—A HANDBOOK OF MODERN ARABIC, consisting of a Practical Grammar, with numerous Examples, Dialogues, and Newspaper Extracts, in a European Type. By F. W. NEWMAN, Emeritus Professor of University College, London ; formerly Fellow of Balliol College, Oxford. Post 8vo. pp. xx. and 192, cloth. London, 1866. 6s.

Newman.—THE TEXT OF THE IGUVINE INSCRIPTIONS, with interlinear Latin Translation and Notes. By FRANCIS W. NEWMAN, late Professor of Latin at University College, London. 8vo. pp. xvi. and 54, sewed. 2s.

Newman.—ORTHOËPY : or, a simple mode of Accenting English, for the advantage of Foreigners and of all Learners. By FRANCIS W. NEWMAN, Emeritus Professor of University College, London. 8vo. pp. 28, sewed. 1869. 1s.

Notley.—A COMPARATIVE GRAMMAR OF THE FRENCH, ITALIAN, SPANISH, AND PORTUGUESE LANGUAGES. By EDWIN A. NOTLEY. Crown oblong 8vo. cloth, pp. xv. and 396. 7s. 6d.

Ollanta: A DRAMA IN THE QUICHUA LANGUAGE. See under MARKHAM.

Oriental Text Society.—(*The Publications of the Oriental Text Society.*)

1. THEOPHANIA ; or, Divine Manifestations of our Lord and Saviour. By EUSEBIUS, Bishop of Cæsarea. Syriac. Edited by Prof. S. LEE. 8vo. 1842. 15s.

2. ATHANASIUS's FESTAL LETTERS, discovered in an ancient Syriac Version. Edited by the Rev. W. CURETON. 8vo. 1848. 15s.

3. SHAHRASTANI : Book of Religious and Philosophical Sects, in Arabic. Two Parts. 8vo. 1842. 30s.

4. UMDAT AKIDAT AHL AL SUNNAT WA AL TAMAAT ; Pillar of the Creed of the Sunnites. Edited in Arabic by the Rev. W. CURETON. 8vo. 1843. 5s.

5. HISTORY OF THE ALMOHADES. Edited in Arabic by Dr. R. P. A. DOZY. 8vo. 1847. 10s. 6d.

Oriental Text Society—*continued.*

6. SAMA VEDA. Edited in Sanskrit by Rev. G. STEVENSON. 8vo. 1843. 12s.

7. DASA KUMARA CHARITA. Edited in Sanskrit by Professor H. H. WILSON. 8vo. 1846. £1 4s.

8. MAHA VIRA CHARITA, or a History of Rama. A Sanskrit Play. Edited by F. H. TRITHEN. 8vo. 1848. 15s.

9. MAZHZAN UL ASRAR : The Treasury of Secrets. By NIZAMI. Edited in Persian by N. BLAND. 4to. 1844. 10s. 6d.

10. SALAMAN-U-UBSAL; A Romance of Jami (Dshami). Edited in Persian by F. FALCONER. 4to. 1843. 10s.

11. MIRKHOND'S HISTORY OF THE ATABEKS. Edited in Persian by W. H. MORLEY. 8vo. 1850. 12s.

12. TUHFAT-UL-AHRAR; the Gift of the Noble. A Poem. By Jami (Dshami). Edited in Persian by F. FALCONER. 4to. 1843. 10s.

Osburn.—THE MONUMENTAL HISTORY of EGYPT, as recorded on the Ruins of her Temples, Palaces, and Tombs. By WILLIAM OSBURN. Illustrated with Maps, Plates, etc. 2 vols. 8vo. pp. xii. and 461 ; vii. and 643, cloth. £2 2s.
Vol. I.—From the Colonization of the Valley to the Visit of the Patriarch Abram.
Vol. II.—From the Visit of Abram to the Exodus.

Palmer.—EGYPTIAN CHRONICLES, with a harmony of Sacred and Egyptian Chronology, and an Appendix on Babylonian and Assyrian Antiquities. By WILLIAM PALMER, M.A., and late Fellow of Magdalen College, Oxford. 2 vols., 8vo. cloth, pp. lxxiv. and 428, and viii. and 636. 1861. 12s.

Pand-Námah. — THE PAND-NÁMAH ; or, Books of Counsels. By ADARBÁD MÁRÁSPAND. Translated from Pehlevi into Gujerathi, by Harbad Sheriarjee Dadabhoy. And from Gujerathi into English by the Rev. Shapurji Edalji. Fcap. 8vo. sewed. 1870. 6d.

Pandit's (A) Remarks on Professor Max Müller's Translation of the " RIG-VEDA." Sanskrit and English. Fcap. 8vo. sewed. 1870. 6d.

Paspati.—ÉTUDES SUR LES TCHINGHIANÉS (GYPSIES) OU BOHÉMIENS DE L'EMPIRE OTTOMAN. Par ALEXANDRE G. PASPATI, M.D. Large 8vo. sewed, pp. xii. and 652. Constantinople, 1871. 28s.

Patell.—COWASJEE PATELL'S CHRONOLOGY, containing corresponding Dates of the different Eras used by Christians, Jews, Greeks, Hindús, Mohamedans, Parsees, Chinese, Japanese, etc. By COWASJEE SORABJEE PATELL. 4to. pp. viii. and 184, cloth. 50s.

Pauthier.—LE LIVRE DE MARCO POLO, Citoyen de Vénise, Conseiller Privé et Commissaire Impérial de Khoubilaï-Khaán. Rédigé en français sous sa dictée en 1298 par Rusticien de Pise ; Publié pour la première fois d'après trois manuscrits inédits de la Bibliothèque Impériale de Paris, présentant la rédaction primitive du Livre, revue par Marco Polo lui-même et donnée par lui, en 1307, à Thiébault de Cépoy, accompagnée des Variantes, de l'Explication des mots hors d'usage, et de commentaires géographiques et historiques, tirés des écrivains orientaux, principalement Chinois, avec une Carte générale de l'Asie par M. G. PAUTHIER. Two vols. roy. 8vo. pp. clvi. 832. With Map and View of Marco Polo's House at Venice. £1 8s.

Percy.—BISHOP PERCY'S FOLIO MANUSCRIPTS—BALLADS AND ROMANCES. Edited by John W. Hales, M.A., Fellow and late Assistant Tutor of Christ's College, Cambridge ; and Frederick J. Furnivall, M.A., of Trinity Hall, Cambridge ; assisted by Professor Child, of Harvard University, Cambridge, U.S.A., W. Chappell, Esq., etc. In 3 volumes. Vol. I., pp. 610; Vol. 2, pp. 681.; Vol. 3, pp. 640. Demy 8vo. half-bound, £4 4s. Extra demy 8vo. half-bound, on Whatman's ribbed paper, £6 6s. Extra royal 8vo., paper covers, on Whatman's best ribbed paper, £10 10s. Large 4to., paper covers, on Whatman's best ribbed paper, £12.

Perny.—Dictionnaire Français-Latin-Chinois de la Langue Mandarine Parlée. Par Paul Perny. M.A., de la Congrégation des Missions Etrangères. 4to. pp. viii. 459, sewed. £2 2s.

Perny.—Grammaire Pratique de la Langue Mandarine Parlée. Par Paul Perny, M.A., de la Congrégation des Missions Etrangères.
[*In the Press.*

Perny.—Proverbes Chinois, Recueillis et mis en ordre. Par Paul Perny, M.A., de la Congrégation des Missions Etrangères. 12mo. pp. iv. 135. 3s.

Perrin.—English-Zulu Dictionary. New Edition, revised by J. A. Brickhill, Interpreter to the Supreme Court of Natal. 12mo. pp. 226, cloth, Pietermaritzburg, 1865. 5s.

Philological Society.—Proposals for the Publication of a New English Dictionary. 8vo. pp. 32, sewed. 6d.

Pierce the Ploughman's Crede (about 1394 Anno Domini). Transcribed and Edited from the MS. of Trinity College, Cambridge, R. 3, 15. Collated with the MS. Bibl. Reg. 18. B. xvii. in the British Museum, and with the old Printed Text of 1553, to which is appended "God spede the Plough" (about 1500 Anno Domini), from the Lansdowne MS. 762. By the Rev. Walter W. Skeat, M.A., late Fellow of Christ's College, Cambridge. pp. xx. and 75, cloth. 1867. 2s. 6d.

Prakrita-Prakasa; or, The Prakrit Grammar of Vararuchi, with the Commentary (Manorama) of Bhamaha. The first complete edition of the Original Text with Various Readings from a Collation of Six Manuscripts in the Bodleian Library at Oxford, and the Libraries of the Royal Asiatic Society and the East India House; with copious Notes, an English Translation, and Index of Prakrit words, to which is prefixed an easy Introduction to Prakrit Grammar. By Edward Byles Cowell, of Magdalen Hall, Oxford, Professor of Sanskrit at Cambridge. Second issue, with new Preface, and corrections. 8vo. pp. xxxii. and 204. 14s.

Priaulx.—Quæstiones Mosaicæ; or, the first part of the Book of Genesis compared with the remains of ancient religions. By Osmond de Beauvoir Priaulx. 8vo. pp. viii. and 548, cloth. 12s.

Raghuvansa.—No. 1. (Cantos 1-3.) See under Kalidasa.

Raja-Niti.—A Collection of Hindu Apologues, in the Braj Bhāshá Language. Revised edition. With a Preface, Notes, and Supplementary Glossary. By Fitzedward Hall, Esq. 8vo. cloth, pp. 204. 21s.

Rámáyan of Válmiki.—Vols. I. and II. See under Griffith.

Ram Jasan.—A Sanskrit and English Dictionary. Being an Abridgment of Professor Wilson's Dictionary. With an Appendix explaining the use of Affixes in Sanskrit. By Pandit Ram Jasan, Queen's College. Benares. Published under the Patronage of the Government, N.W.P. Royal 8vo. cloth, pp. ii. and 707. 28s.

Ram Raz.—Essay on the Architecture of the Hindus. By Ram Raz, Native Judge and Magistrate of Bangalore, Corresponding Member of the R.A.S. of Great Britain and Ireland. With 48 plates. 4to. pp. xiv. and 64, sewed. London, 1834. Original selling price, £1 11s. 6d., reduced (for a short time) to 12s.

Rask.—A Grammar of the Anglo-Saxon Tongue. From the Danish of Erasmus Rask, Professor of Literary History in, and Librarian to, the University of Copenhagen, etc. By Benjamin Thorpe, Member of the Munich Royal Academy of Sciences, and of the Society of Netherlandish Literature, Leyden. Second edition, corrected and improved. 18mo. pp. 200, cloth. 5s. 6d.

Rawlinson.—A Commentary on the Cuneiform Inscriptions of Babylonia and Assyria, including Readings of the Inscription on the Nimrud Obelisk, and Brief Notice of the Ancient Kings of Nineveh and Babylon, Read before the Royal Asiatic Society, by Major H. C. Rawlinson. 8vo., pp. 84, sewed. London, 1850. 2s. 6d.

Rawlinson.—OUTLINES OF ASSYRIAN HISTORY, from the Inscriptions of Nineveh. By Lieut. Col. RAWLINSON, C.B., followed by some Remarks by A. H. LAYARD, Esq., D.C.L. 8vo., pp. xliv., sewed. London, 1852. 1s.

Renan.—AN ESSAY ON THE AGE AND ANTIQUITY OF THE BOOK OF NABATHÆAN AGRICULTURE. To which is added an Inaugural Lecture on the Position of the Shemitic Nations in the History of Civilization. By M. ERNEST RENAN, Membre de l'Institut. Crown 8vo., pp. xvi. and 148, cloth. 3s. 6d.

Revue Celtique.—THE REVUE CELTIQUE, a Quarterly Magazine for Celtic Philology, Literature, and History. Edited with the assistance of the Chief Celtic Scholars of the British Islands and of the Continent, and Conducted by H. GAIDOZ. 8vo. Subscription, £1 per Volume.

Ridley.—KAMILAROI, DIPPIL, AND TURRUBUL. Languages Spoken by Australian Aborigines. By Rev. WM. RIDLEY, M.A., of the University of Sydney; Minister of the Presbyterian Church of New South Wales. Printed by authority. Small 4to. cloth, pp. vi. and 90. 30s.

Rig-Veda.—A NEW EDITION OF THE HYMNS OF THE RIG-VEDA IN THE SANHITÁ TEXT, without the Commentary of the Sâyana. Based upon the Editio princeps of MAX MÜLLER. Large 8vo. of about 800 pages. *See also under Max Müller.* [*In preparation.*

Rig-Veda-Sanhita: THE SACRED HYMNS OF THE BRAHMANS. Translated and explained by F. MAX MÜLLER, M.A., LL.D., Fellow of All Soul's College, Professor of Comparative Philology at Oxford, Foreign Member of the Institute of France, etc., etc. Vol. I. HYMNS TO THE MARUTS, OR THE STORM-GODS. 8vo. pp. clii. and 264. cloth. 1869. 12s. 6d.

Rig-Veda Sanhita.—A COLLECTION OF ANCIENT HINDU HYMNS. Constituting the First Ashtaka, or Book of the Rig-veda; the oldest authority for the religious and social institutions of the Hindus. Translated from the Original Sanskrit. By the late H. H. WILSON, M.A., F.R.S., etc. etc. etc. Second Edition, with a Postscript by Dr. FITZEDWARD HALL. Vol. I. 8vo. cloth, pp. lii. and 348, price 21s.

Rig-veda Sanhita.—A Collection of Ancient Hindu Hymns, constituting the Fifth to Eighth Ashtakas, or books of the Rig-Veda, the oldest Authority for the Religious and Social Institutions of the Hindus. Translated from the Original Sanskrit by the late HORACE HAYMAN WILSON, M.A., F.R.S., etc. Edited by E. B. COWELL, M.A., Principal of the Calcutta Sanskrit College. Vol. IV., 8vo., pp. 214, cloth. 14s. *A few copies of Vols. II. and III. still left.* [*Vols. V. and VI. in the Press.*

Rudy.—THE CHINESE MANDARIN LANGUAGE, after Ollendorff's new method of learning languages. By CHARLES RUDY. [*In preparation.*

Sâma-Vidhâna-Brâhmana. With the Commentary of Sâyana. Edited, with Notes, Translation, and Index, by A. C. BURNELL, M.R.A.S., Madras Civil Service. In 1 vol. 8vo. [*In preparation.*

Sayce.—AN ASSYRIAN GRAMMAR. By the Rev. A. H. SAYCE, Queen's College, Oxford. Crown 8vo. [*In the Press.*

Schele de Vere.—STUDIES IN ENGLISH; or, Glimpses of the Inner Life of our Language. By M. SCHELE DE VERE, LL.D., Professor of Modern Languages in the University of Virginia. 8vo. cloth, pp. vi. and 365. 10s. 6d.

Schemeil.—EL MUBTAKER; or, First Born. (In Arabic, printed at Beyrout). Containing Five Comedies, called Comedies of Fiction, on Hopes and Judgments, in Twenty-six Poems of 1092 Verses, showing the Seven Stages of Life, from man's conception unto his death and burial. By EMIN IBRAHIM SCHEMEIL. In one volume, 4to. pp. 166, sewed. 1870. 5s.

Schlagintweit.—BUDDHISM IN TIBET. Illustrated by Literary Documents and Objects of Religious Worship. With an Account of the Buddhist Systems preceding it in India. By EMIL SCHLAGINTWEIT, LL.D. With a Folio Atlas of 20 Plates, and 20 Tables of Native Prints in the Text. Royal 8vo., pp. xxiv. and 404. £2 2s.

Schlagintweit.—GLOSSARY OF GEOGRAPHICAL TERMS FROM INDIA AND TIBET, with Native Transcription and Transliteration. By HERMANN DE SCHLAGINTWEIT. Forming, with a " Route Book of the Western Himalaya, Tibet, and Turkistan," the Third Volume of H., A., and R. DE SCHLAGINTWEIT'S "Results of a Scientific Mission to India and High Asia." With an Atlas in imperial folio, of Maps, Panoramas, and Views. Royal 4to., pp. xxiv. and 293. *£4.*

Schlottmann.—THE MONUMENT OF A VICTORY OF MESHA, King of the Moabites. A Contribution to Hebrew Archæology by Dr. KONSTANTIN SCHLOTTMANN, Professor of Theology at the University of Halle. Translated from the German.   [*In the Press.*

Shápurjí Edaljí.—A GRAMMAR OF THE GUJARÁTÍ LANGUAGE. By SHÁPURJÍ EDALJÍ. Cloth, pp. 127. 10s. 6d.

Shápurjí Edaljí.—A DICTIONARY, GUJRATI AND ENGLISH. By SHÁPURJÍ EDALJÍ. Second Edition. Crown 8vo. cloth, pp. xxiv. and 874. 21s.

Sherring—THE SACRED CITY OF THE HINDUS. An Account of Benares in Ancient and Modern Times. By the Rev. M. A. SHERRING, M.A., LL.D.; and Prefaced with an Introduction by FITZEDWARD HALL, Esq., D.C.L. 8vo. cloth, pp. xxxvi. and 388, with numerous full-page illustrations. 21s.

Smith.—A VOCABULARY OF PROPER NAMES IN CHINESE AND ENGLISH. of Places, Persons, Tribes, and Sects, in China, Japan, Corea, Assam, Siam, Burmah, The Straits, and adjacent Countries. By F. PORTER SMITH, M.B., China. 4to. half-bound, pp. vi., 72, and x. 1870. 10s. 6d.

Smith.—CONTRIBUTIONS TOWARDS THE MATERIA MEDICA AND NATURAL HISTORY OF CHINA. For the use of Medical Missionaries and Native Medical Students. By F. PORTER SMITH, M.B. London, Medical Missionary in Central China. Imp. 4to. cloth, pp. viii. and 240. 1870. *£1 1s.*

Sophocles.—A GLOSSARY OF LATER AND BYZANTINE GREEK. By E. A. SOPHOCLES. 4to., pp. iv. and 624, cloth. £2 2s.

Sophocles.—ROMAIC OR MODERN GREEK GRAMMAR. By E. A. SOPHOCLES. 8vo. pp. xxviii. and 196. 7s. 6d.

Sophocles.—GREEK LEXICON OF THE ROMAN AND BYZANTINE PERIODS (from B.C. 146 to A.D. 1100). By E. A. SOPHOCLES. Imp. 8vo. pp. xvi. 1188, cloth. 1870. *£2 8s.*

Steele.—AN EASTERN LOVE STORY. KUSA JÁTAKAYA: a Buddhistic Legendary Poem, with other Stories. By THOMAS STEELE, Ceylon Civil Service. Crown 8vo. cloth, pp. xii. and 260. 1871. 6s.

Stratmann.—A DICTIONARY OF THE ENGLISH LANGUAGE. Compiled from the writings of the XIIIth, XIVth, and XVth centuries. By FRANCIS HENRY STRATMANN. Second Edition. Part I. Small 4to., pp. 160, price 10s. 6d.

Stratmann.—AN OLD ENGLISH POEM OF THE OWL AND THE NIGHTINGALE. Edited by FRANCIS HENRY STRATMANN. 8vo. cloth, pp. 60. 3s.

Surya-Siddhanta (Translation of the).—A TEXT BOOK OF HINDU ASTRONOMY, with Notes and Appendix, &c. By Rev. EBENEZER BURGESS. 8vo. pp. iv. and 354, boards. 15s.

Syed Ahmed.—A SERIES OF ESSAYS ON THE LIFE OF MOHAMMED, and Subjects subsidiary thereto. By SYED AHMED KHAN BAHADOR, C.S.I., Author of the " Mohammedan Commentary on the Holy Bible," Honorary Member of the Royal Asiatic Society, and Life Honorary Secretary to the Allygurh Scientific Society. 8vo. pp. 532, with 4 Genealogical Tables, 2 Maps, and a Coloured Plate, handsomely bound in cloth. 30s.

Tabari.— CHRONIQUE DE ABOU-DJAFAR-MOHAMMED-BEN-DJARIR-BEN-YEZID. Traduite par Monsieur HERMANN ZOTENBERG. Vol. I. 8vo. pp. 608. Vol. II, 8vo. pp. ii. and 252, sewed. 7s. 6d. each. (*To be completed in Four Volumes.*)

Táittiríya-Pratiçakhya.—See under WHITNEY.

The Boke of Nurture. By JOHN RUSSELL, about 1460–1470 Anno
Domini. The Boke of Keruynge. By WYNKYN DE WORDE, Anno Domini
1513. The Boke of Nurture. By HUGH RHODES, Anno Domini 1577. Edited
from the Originals in the British Museum Library, by FREDERICK J. FURNI-
VALL, M.A., Trinity Hall, Cambridge, Member of Council of the Philological
and Early English Text Societies. 4to. half-morocco, gilt top, pp. xix. and 146,
28, xxviii. and 56. 1867. 1*l.* 11*s.* 6*d.*

The Vision of William concerning Piers Plowman, together with
Vita de Dowel, Dobet et Dobest, secundum wit et resoun. By WILLIAM
LANGLAND (about 1362–1380 anno domini). Edited from numerous Manu-
scripts, with Prefaces, Notes, and a Glossary. By the Rev. WALTER W. SKEAT
M.A. pp. xliv. and 158, cloth, 1867. Vernon A. Text; Text 7*s.* 6*d.*

Thomas.—EARLY SASSANIAN INSCRIPTIONS, SEALS AND COINS, illustrating
the Early History of the Sassanian Dynasty, containing Proclamations of Arde-
shir Babek, Sapor I., and his Successors. With a Critical Examination and
Explanation of the Celebrated Inscription in the Hâjiábad Cave, demonstrating
that Sapor, the Conqueror of Valerian, was a Professing Christian. By EDWARD
THOMAS, Esq. Illustrated. 8vo. cloth, pp. 148. 7*s.* 6*d.*

Thomas.—THE CHRONICLES OF THE PATHÁN KINGS OF DEHLI. Illustrated by Coins, Inscriptions, and other Antiquarian Remains. By EDWARD
THOMAS, F.R.A.S., late of the East India Company's Bengal Civil Service. With
numerous Copperplates and Woodcuts. Demy 8vo. cloth, pp. xxiv. and 467.'
1871. 28*s.*

Thomas.—THE REVENUE RESOURCES OF THE MUGHAL EMPIRE IN INDIA,
from A.D. 1593 to A.D. 1707. A Supplement to "The Chronicles of the Pathán
Kings of Delhi." By EDWARD THOMAS, F.R.S., late of the East India
Company's Bengal Civil Service. Demy 8vo., pp. 60, cloth. 3*s.* 6*d.*

Thomas.—ESSAYS ON INDIAN ANTIQUITIES : following up the Discoveries
of James Prinsep, with specimens of his Engravings, and selections from his
Useful Tables, and embodying the most recent investigations into the History,
Palæography, and Numismatics of Ancient India. By EDWARD THOMAS, late
of the East India Company's Bengal Civil Service. In 2 vols. 8vo., profusely
illustrated. [*In preparation.*

Thomas.—THE THEORY AND PRACTICE OF CREOLE GRAMMAR. By J. J.
THOMAS. Port of Spain (Trinidad), 1869. One vol. 8vo. boards, pp. viii. and
135. 12*s.*

Thonissen.—ÉTUDES SUR L'HISTOIRE DU DROIT CRIMINEL DES PEUPLES
Anciens (Inde Brahmanique, E'gypte, Judée), par J. J. THONISSEN, Professeur
à l'Université Catholique de Louvain, Membre de l'Academie Royale de Bel-
gique. 2 vols. 8vo. pp. xvi. 248, 320, sewed. 1869. 12*s.*

Thorpe.—DIPLOMATARIUM ANGLICUM ÆVI SAXONICI. A Collection of
English Charters, from the reign of King Æthelberht of Kent, A.D., DCV., to
that of William the Conqueror. Containing : I. Miscellaneous Charters. II.
Wills. III. Guilds. IV. Manumissions and Acquittances. With a Translation of the Anglo-Saxon. By the late BENJAMIN THORPE, Member of the Royal
Academy of Sciences at Munich, and of the Society of Netherlandish Literature
at Leyden. 8vo. pp. xlii. and 682, cloth. 1865. £1 1*s.*

Tindall.—A GRAMMAR AND VOCABULARY OF THE NAMAQUA-HOTTENTOT
LANGUAGE. By HENRY TINDALL, Wesleyan Missionary. 8vo. pp. 124, sewed. 6*s.*

Van der Tuuk.—OUTLINES OF A GRAMMAR OF THE MALAGASY LANGUAGE.
By H. N. VAN DER TUUK. 8vo., pp. 28, sewed. 1*s.*

Van der Tuuk.—SHORT ACCOUNT OF THE MALAY MANUSCRIPTS BELONGING
TO THE ROYAL ASIATIC SOCIETY. By H. N. VAN DER TUUK. 8vo., pp. 52. 2*s.* 6*d.*

Vishnu-Purana (The) ; a System of Hindu Mythology and Tradition.
Translated from the original Sanskrit, and Illustrated by Notes derived chiefly
from other Puránas. By the late H. H. WILSON, M.A., F.R.S., Boden Professor of Sanskrit in the University of Oxford, etc., etc. Edited by FITZEDWARD
HALL. In 6 vols. 8vo. Vol. I. pp. cxl and 200; Vol. II. pp. 343; Vol. III.
pp. 348; Vol. IV. pp. 346, cloth; Vol. V. pp. 392, cloth. 10*s.* 6*d.* each.

Vullers.—A GRAMMAR OF THE PERSIAN LANGUAGE. By J. A. VULLERS, Professor of Oriental Languages in the University of Giessen. 8vo.
[*In the Press.*

Wade.—YÜ-YEN TZÚ-ERH CHI. A progressive course designed to assist the Student of Colloquial Chinese, as spoken in the Capital and the Metropolitan Department. In eight parts, with Key, Syllabary, and Writing Exercises. By THOMAS FRANCIS WADE, C.B., Secretary to Her Britannic Majesty's Legation, Peking. 3 vols. 4to. Progressive Course, pp. xx. 296 and 16; Syllabary, pp. 126 and 36; Writing Exercises, pp. 48; Key, pp. 174 and 140, sewed. £4.

Wade.—WÊN-CHIEN TZÚ-ERH CHI. A series of papers selected as specimens of documentary Chinese, designed to assist Students of the language, as written by the officials of China. In sixteen parts, with Key. Vol. I. By THOMAS FRANCIS WADE, C.B., Secretary to Her Britannic Majesty's Legation at Peking. 4to., half-cloth, pp. xii. and 455; and iv, 72, and 52. £1 16s.

Wake.—CHAPTERS ON MAN. With the Outlines of a Science of comparative Psychology. By C. STANILAND WAKE, Fellow of the Anthropological Society of London. Crown 8vo. pp. viii. and 344, cloth. 7s. 6d.

Watson.—INDEX TO THE NATIVE AND SCIENTIFIC NAMES OF INDIAN AND OTHER EASTERN ECONOMIC PLANTS AND PRODUCTS, originally prepared under the authority of the Secretary of State for India in Council. By JOHN FORBES WATSON, M.A., M.D., F.L.S., F.R.A.S., etc., Reporter on the Products of India. Imperial 8vo., cloth, pp. 650. £1 11s. 6d.

Watts.—ESSAYS ON LANGUAGE AND LITERATURE. By THOMAS WATTS, late of the British Museum. Reprinted, with Alterations and Additions, from the Transactions of the Philological Society, and elsewhere. In 1 vol. 8vo.
[*In preparation.*

Webster.—AN INTRODUCTORY ESSAY TO THE SCIENCE OF COMPARATIVE THEOLOGY; with a Tabular Synopsis of Scientific Religion. By EDWARD WEBSTER, of Ealing, Middlesex. Read in an abbreviated form as a Lecture to a public audience at Ealing, on the 3rd of January, 1870, and to an evening congregation at South Place Chapel, Finsbury Square, London, on the 27th of February, 1870. 8vo. pp. 28, sewed. 1870. 1s.

Wedgwood.—A DICTIONARY OF THE ENGLISH LANGUAGE. By HENSLEIGH WEDGWOOD, M.A. late Fellow of Christ's College, Cambridge. Vol. I. (A to D) 8vo., pp. xxiv. 508, cloth, 14s.; Vol. II. (E to P) 8vo. pp. 578, cloth, 14s.; Vol. III., Part I. (Q to Sy), 8vo. pp. 366, 10s. 6d.; Vol. III. Part II. (T to W) 8vo. pp. 200, 5s. 6d. completing the Work. Price of the complete work, £2 4s.

" Dictionaries are a class of books not usually esteemed light reading; but no intelligent man were to be pitied who should find himself shut up on a rainy day in a lonely house in the dreariest part of Salisbury Plain, with no other means of recreation than that which Mr. Wedgwood's Dictionary of Etymology could afford him. He would read it through from cover to cover at a sitting, and only regret that he had not the second volume to begin upon forthwith. It is a very able book, of great research, full of delightful surprises, a repertory of the fairy tales of linguistic science."—*Spectator.*

Wedgwood.—A DICTIONARY OF ENGLISH ETYMOLOGY. By HENSLEIGH WEDGWOOD. Second Edition, thoroughly revised and corrected by the Author, and extended to the Classical Roots of the Language. With an Introduction on the Formation of Language. Imperial 8vo., about 800 pages, double column. In Five Monthly Parts, of 160 pages. Price 5s. each; or complete in one volume, cl., price 25s.

Wedgwood.—ON THE ORIGIN OF LANGUAGE. By HENSLEIGH WEDGWOOD, late Fellow of Christ's College, Cambridge. Fcap. 8vo. pp. 172, cloth. 3s. 6d.

Wékey.—A GRAMMAR OF THE HUNGARIAN LANGUAGE, with appropriate Exercises, a Copious Vocabulary, and Specimens of Hungarian Poetry. By SIGISMUND WÉKEY, late Aide-de-Camp to Kossuth. 12mo., pp. xii. and 150, sewed. 4s. 6d.

West and Bühler.—Digest of Hindu Law, from the Replies of the Shastris in the several Courts of the Bombay Presidency. With an Introduction, Notes, and Appendix. Edited by Raymond West and Johann Georg Bühler. Vol. I. 8vo. cloth. £3 3s. Vol. II. 8vo. pp. v. 118, cloth. 12s.

Wheeler.—The History of India from the Earliest Ages. By J. Talboys Wheeler, Assistant Secretary to the Government of India in the Foreign Department, Secretary to the Indian Record Commission, author of "The Geography of Herodotus," etc. etc.

Vol. I., The Vedic Period and the Maha Bharata. 8vo. cloth, pp. lxxv. and 576. 18s.

Vol. II., The Ramayana and the Brahmanic Period. 8vo. cloth, pp. lxxxviii. and 680, with 2 Maps. 21s.

Wheeler.—Journal of a Voyage up the Irrawaddy to Mandalay and Bhamo. By J. Talboys Wheeler. 8vo. pp. 104, sewed. 1871. 3s. 6d.

Whitney.—Atharva Veda Prátiçákhya; or, Çáunakíyá Caturádhyáyiká (The). Text, Translation, and Notes. By William D. Whitney, Professor of Sanskrit in Yale College. 8vo. pp. 286, boards. 12s.

Whitney.—Language and the Study of Language: Twelve Lectures on the Principles of Linguistic Science. By William Dwight Whitney, Professor of Sanskrit, etc., in Yale College. Third Edition, augmented by an Analysis. Crown 8vo. cloth, pp. xii. and 504. 10s. 6d.

Whitney.—Táittiríya-Prátiçákhya, with its Commentary, the Tribháshyaratna: Text, Translation, and Notes. By W. D. Whitney, Prof. of Sanskrit in Yale College, New Haven. 8vo. pp. 469. 1871. 25s.

Wilkins.—The Bhagavat-Geeta; or, Dialogues of Kreeshna and Arjoon. Translated by Chas. Wilkins. A faithful reprint of the now very scarce Original London Edition of 1785, made at the Bradsheet Press, New York. In one vol. 8vo. Beautifully printed with old face type on laid paper. 261 copies were produced of this edition, of which only a few now remain. 12s.

Williams.—First Lessons in the Maori Language, with a Short Vocabulary. By W. L. Williams, B.A. Square 8vo., pp. 80, cloth, London, 1862. 10s.

Williams.—Lexicon Cornu-Britannicum. A Dictionary of the Ancient Celtic Language of Cornwall, in which the words are elucidated by copious examples from the Cornish works now remaining, with translations in English. The synonyms are also given in the cognate dialects of Welsh, Armoric, Irish, Gaelic, and Manx, showing at one view the connexion between them. By the Rev. Robert Williams, M.A., Christ Church, Oxford, Parish Curate of Llangadwaladr and Rhydycroesan, Denbighshire. Sewed. 3 parts, pp. 400. £2 5s.

Williams.—A Dictionary, English and Sanscrit. By Monier Williams, M.A. Published under the Patronage of the Honourable East India Company. 4to. pp. xii. 862, cloth. London, 1855. £3 3s.

Wilson.—Works of the late Horace Hayman Wilson, M.A., F.R.S., Member of the Royal Asiatic Societies of Calcutta and Paris, and of the Oriental Society of Germany, etc., and Boden Professor of Sanskrit in the University of Oxford.

Vols I. and II. Essays and Lectures chiefly on the Religion of the Hindus, by the late H. H. Wilson, M.A., F.R.S., etc. Collected and edited by Dr. Reinhold Rost. 2 vols. cloth, pp. xiii. and 399, vi. and 416. 21s.

Vols. III, IV. and V. Essays Analytical, Critical, and Philological, on Subjects connected with Sanskrit Literature. Collected and Edited by Dr. Reinhold Rost. 3 vols. 8vo. pp. 408, 406, and 390, cloth. Price 36s

Vols. VI., VII., VIII, IX. and X. Vishnu Puráná, a System of Hindu My-thology and Tradition. Translated from the original Sanskrit, and Illus-trated by Notes derived chiefly from other Puránás. By the late H. H. Wilson, Boden Professor of Sanskrit in the University of Oxford, etc., etc. Edited by Fitzedward Hall, M.A., D.C.L., Oxon. Vols. I. to V. 8vo., pp. cxl. and 2C0 ; 344 ; 344 ; 346, cloth. *2l. 12s. 6d.*

Vols. XI. and XII. Select Specimens of the Theatre of the Hindus. Trans-lated from the Original Sanskrit. By the late Horace Hayman Wilson, M.A., F.R.S. Third corrected Edition. 2 vols. 8vo. pp. lxi. and 384 ; and iv. and 418, cloth. *21s.*

Wilson.—Select Specimens of the Theatre of the Hindus. Trans-lated from the Original Sanskrit. By the late Horace Hayman Wilson, M.A., F.R.S. Third corrected edition. 2 vols. 8vo., pp. lxxi. and 384; iv. and 418, cloth. *21s.*

CONTENTS.

Vol. I.—Preface—Treatise on the Dramatic System of the Hindus—Dramas translated from the Original Sanskrit—The Mrichchakati, or the Toy Cart—Vikram aand Urvasi, or the Hero and the Nymph—Uttara Ráma Charitra, or continuation of the History of Ráma.

Vol. II.—Dramas translated from the Original Sanskrit—Maláti and Mádhava, or the Stolen Marriage—Mudrá Rakshasa, or the Signet of the Minister—Ratnávali, or the Necklace—Appendix, containing short accounts of different Dramas.

Wilson.—The Present State of the Cultivation of Oriental Literature. A Lecture delivered at the Meeting of the Royal Asiatic Society. By the Director, Professor H. H. Wilson. 8vo., pp. 26, sewed. London, 1852. *6d.*

Wise.—Commentary on the Hindu System of Medicine. By T. A. Wise, M.D., Bengal Medical Service. 8vo., pp. xx. and 432, cloth. *7s. 6d.*

Wright.—The Homes of other Days. A History of Domestic Manners and Sentiments during the Middle Ages. By Thomas Wright, Esq., M.A., F.S.A. With Illustrations from the Illuminations in Contemporary Manu-scripts and other Sources. Drawn and Engraved by F. W. Fairholt, Esq., F.S.A. 1 vol. medium 8vo., 350 Woodcuts, pp. xv. and 512, handsomely bound in cloth. *21s.*

Wright.—A Volume of Vocabularies, illustrating the Condition and Manners of our Forefathers, as well as the History of the forms of Elementary Education, and of the Languages Spoken in this Island from the Tenth Century to the Fifteenth. Edited by Thomas Wright, Esq., M.A., F.S.A., &c., &c.

[*In the Press.*

Wright.—The Celt, the Roman, and the Saxon; a History of the Early Inhabitants of Britain down to the Conversion of the Anglo-Saxons to Christianity. Illustrated by the Ancient Remains brought to light by Recent Research. By Thomas Wright, Esq., M.A., F.S.A., etc., etc. Third Cor-rected and Enlarged Edition. [*In the Press.*

Wylie.—Notes on Chinese Literature; with introductory Remarks on the Progressive Advancement of the Art ; and a list of translations from the Chinese, into various European Languages. By A. Wylie, Agent of the British and Foreign Bible Society in China. 4to. pp. 296, cloth. Price, *1l. 16s.*

Yates.—A Bengálí Grammar. By the late Rev. W. Yates, D.D. Reprinted, with improvements, from his Introduction to the Bengáli Language, Edited by I.Wenger. Fcap. 8vo., pp. iv. and 150, bds. Calcutta, 1864. *3s. 6d.*

www.ingramcontent.com/pod-product-compliance
Lightning Source LLC
Chambersburg PA
CBHW030539270326
41927CB00008B/1440